AMERICAN PURGATORY

AMERICAN PURGATORY

PRISON IMPERIALISM
AND THE RISE OF
MASS INCARCERATION

BENJAMIN WEBER

NEW YORK
LONDON

Requests for permission to reproduce selections from this book should be made through our website: https://thenewpress.com/contact.

Published in the United States by The New Press, New York, 2023
Distributed by Two Rivers Distribution

ISBN 978-1-62097-590-9 (hc)
ISBN 978-1-62097-591-6 (ebook)
CIP data is available

The New Press publishes books that promote and enrich public discussion and understanding of the issues vital to our democracy and to a more equitable world. These books are made possible by the enthusiasm of our readers; the support of a committed group of donors, large and small; the collaboration of our many partners in the independent media and the not-for-profit sector; booksellers, who often hand-sell New Press books; librarians; and above all by our authors.

www.thenewpress.com

Book design and composition by Bookbright Media
This book was set in Adobe Garamond and DIN Condensed

Furthermore:
a program of the J.M. Kaplan Fund

Support for this book is, in part, from Furthermore grants in publishing, a program of the J.M. Kaplan Fund.

Printed in the United States of America

10 9 8 7 6 5 4 3 2 1

Contents

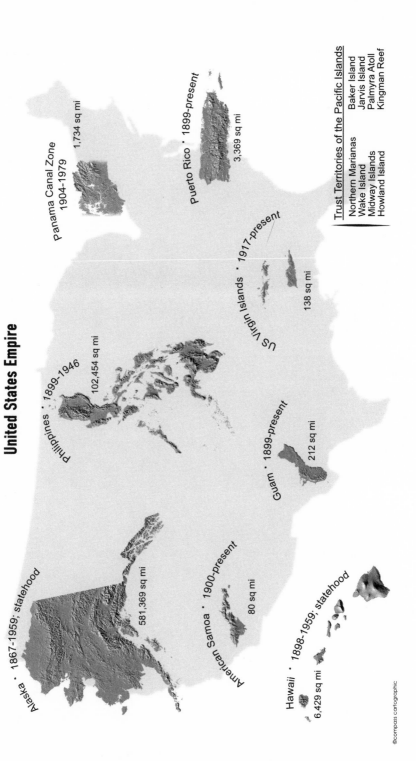

United States Empire

Alaska · 1867-1959; statehood
581,369 sq mi

Panama Canal Zone
1904-1979
1,734 sq mi

Puerto Rico · 1899-present
3,369 sq mi

Philippines · 1899-1946
102,454 sq mi

US Virgin Islands · 1917-present
138 sq mi

American Samoa · 1900-present
80 sq mi

Guam · 1899-present
212 sq mi

Hawaii · 1898-1959; statehood
6,429 sq mi

Trust Territories of the Pacific Islands

Northern Marianas
Wake Island
Midway Islands
Howland Island

Baker Island
Jarvis Island
Palmyra Atoll
Kingman Reef

©compass cartographic

Preface
Purgatory's Ghosts

Imperialism is the root cause of racism. It is the ideology which upholds colonial rule and exploitation. It is the ideology which breeds fascism.

—Claudia Jones[1]

I remember when I first sat down to sift through tawny old prison records inside New Bilibid Prison in Manila, a decade ago. Staring from the top of the stack was a young laborer named Fausto Balomer. Listed among his "peculiar marks and scars" was a "shaded star face" tattoo. Beneath his mug shot was another seventeen-year-old laborer, his tattoo described as "8 pt. star circl. face in center." The eight-pointed star face carries particular political significance: it was the symbol of the Katipunan brotherhood of revolutionaries who fought against first Spanish and then U.S. colonial rule. As I looked through the records, stacked on a glass-covered desk encasing a modern-day fingerprint chart, sadness set into my bones. It was as if the weight of the past was closing in on the present. I realized how the subjects of these records had been turned from anticolonial freedom fighters into outlaws by a series of sedition and bandolerismo laws.[2] The police index card and prison intake record were vital to that process, providing visual evidence of the subjects' supposed criminality.

U.S. officials spread this technology to the Philippines, and other sites of empire, at the dawn of the twentieth century. As colonial police and prison administrators amassed index cards on three-quarters of Manila's population in their search for "messianic" leaders capable of leading the Katipunan, this seemingly banal and bureaucratic form of record keeping became a linchpin of the rise of the American surveillance state.[3] For me, the stack of prison records raised ongoing questions about the stories of those who have been caught up and crushed by U.S. modes of imprisonment, within and beyond U.S. borders. I spent the next decade following the trace of U.S. prison imperialism across the United States, the Caribbean, and the Pacific.

Prison imperialism's documentary record is found not only in brick-and-mortar prisons and state archives but also in the halls of higher learning. In Harvard University's library sits the *Album of Philippine Types*, for instance, a collection of mug shots and measurements purporting to capture the characteristics of some three thousand people inside Bilibid Prison during the U.S. occupation of the Philippines (1899–1946). In the basement of the Peabody Museum nearby lie the bones of nineteen people of African descent believed to have been enslaved, whose families endured the Middle Passage aboard transatlantic slave ships, America's archetypal prisons. Next to them are the life casts of sixty-four people from the Kiowa, Comanche, Cheyenne, Arapaho, and Caddo nations, who were imprisoned at Fort Marion in St. Augustine, Florida, for their staunch resistance to

U.S. colonialism. They are among the 22,000 sets of human remains in Harvard's collections alone. Together with the millions who have been churned through American prisons and the bodies being exhumed from Indian boarding schools and Jim Crow reform schools, these human remains, life casts, and mug shots are part of a far-reaching counter-archive testifying to the entanglement of penology and foreign policy, silently indicting those who have sought to govern the prison, and the world.

This book, *American Purgatory*, explains how mass incarceration arose out of successive eras of empire building across North America, the Caribbean, and the Pacific and around the globe. It traces the unspoken doctrine of "prison imperialism"—how U.S. policy makers sought to govern the world through the codification and regulation of crime. Even as prison imperialism expanded outward, it always returned home, producing new forms of social control over the growing number of people ensnared in prison in the United States. Like other colonial practices, the prison system has produced racial hierarchy, in ever-adapting ways, for the past four hundred years.

Over successive eras of empire building, intersecting ideas about race, crime, and punishment, not only within the United States but around the globe, have been central to making mass incarceration and the modern American state. The Black chain gangs in the New South appear little different from the Black road gangs in the Panama Canal Zone during the same period. Prison labor at Parchman Farm in Mississippi was not unlike plantation work at the Iwahig Penal Colony in the Philippines, said to be the largest penal farm in the world by the 1920s. The forms of policing and record keeping that gave rise to the surveillance state between World War II and the Cold War were pioneered through overseas colonialism, covert operations, and military interventions.

As the migration to American cities of militarized police and torture techniques from overseas sites like Guantanamo and Abu Ghraib renew concern over the consequences of war making at home, the United States continues to train police forces and export its model of incarceration abroad. Grassroots groups like the Alliance for Global Justice have identified this new age of prison imperialism, beginning with the globalization of the supermax prison at the turn of the twenty-first century.[4] As we enter the newest age of empire, marked by the rise of "e-carceration," it is clear that prison imperialism is not just a creature of the past but continues to spread U.S.-style structural racism around the world. This process is deeply rooted in centuries-long practices of slavery and empire building that spawned federal policies of criminal transportation, family separation, excessive sentencing, and overreliance on imprisonment.

To reverse course requires reckoning with the deeply rooted legacies of racism and colonialism in penology and foreign policy. Usually treated as distinct areas, penology and foreign policy actually share a set of foundational theories and continue to employ common assumptions about preemption and deterrence, containment and incapacitation, retribution and rehabilitation. Examining how these were developed into federal policies and implemented on the ground in particular places, a set of historic and contemporary black sites, is essential to understanding prison imperialism's long career.

* * *

As it uncovers the root causes and continued workings of America's prison empire, this history also amplifies a long and powerful protest tradition. The entanglement of foreign policy and penal policy has long been condemned by those held in prisons, the epicenter of racial state violence. From leaders of rebellions aboard slave ships, fugitives, communists, conscientious objectors, Black and Native nationalists, and anticolonial fighters to contemporary prison abolitionists, imprisoned activists and their allies have established a strong tradition of anti-carceral critique. Members of the American Indian Movement, Black Panthers, Brown Berets, and Young Lords all argued that their communities were treated like internal colonies and that overseas colonies were administered like geographic prisons. These communities experienced firsthand how threadbare the tenets of preemption and deterrence, incapacitation and containment, retribution and rehabilitation have proved to be and the deadly blowback they have caused.[5] Out of this protest tradition, moreover, has emerged a powerful framework for addressing the consequences of prison imperialism based on the principle of reimagining justice, suggesting a path toward repairing historic and institutional harms.

From the nation's founding to the present, people in prison and their allies in the anti-prison movement have likened their condition to a kind of purgatory. They have described how it feels to be treated like a slave of the state, governed like a modern-day colonial subject. To be in purgatory is to be held in judgment, fighting perpetual damnation, seeking liberation. Purgatory also aptly names the existential condition of justice in America. Reckoning with the ongoing impacts of racism and colonialism in the U.S. prison system is not the work of Black, Indigenous, and people of color alone. Mass incarceration has become the defining social justice issue of our time, as the prison system continues to produce racial inequality, and it will take ever-greater numbers of people working in solidarity within and across communities to begin to undo the massive harm it has caused and to reimagine justice for the future we all deserve.

AMERICAN PURGATORY

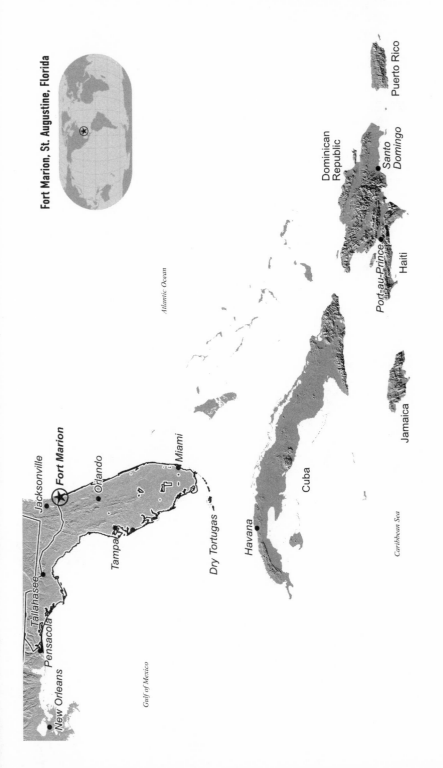

Fort Marion, St. Augustine, Florida

1

Prisons and Placemaking

Decolonization, as we know, is a historical process: that is to say it cannot be understood, it cannot become intelligible nor clear to itself except in the exact measure that we can discern the movements which give it historical form and content.

—Frantz Fanon[1]

"America begins here." Castillo de San Marcos in St. Augustine, Florida, was designated a national monument just two decades after the last people imprisoned there were finally released. The fort is said to symbolize the "clash between cultures which ultimately resulted in our uniquely unified nation."[2] As an infamous prison where Black and Indigenous people from the Seminole, Kiowa, Cheyenne, Arapaho, Comanche, Caddo, and Apache nations were held captive, it also represents something else entirely: one of the first cornerstones of U.S. prison imperialism, part of a network of historical and contemporary black sites that reveal the colonial roots and global dimensions of the U.S. carceral state.

In the swampy and forested Florida panhandle, the Muscogee-speaking Creeks and Seminoles were known to be the most powerful nations in the region.[3] Conflict between Spanish and

British empires intensified in the early seventeenth century, as English plantation colonies took hold in the Chesapeake Bay, the Carolinas, and the Bahamas. The French held the island of San Domingue (Haiti and the Dominican Republic) in the Caribbean and claimed a vast amount of land in the so-called Louisiana Territory through its slave-trading stronghold in New Orleans. To claim land in the New World, the European theory went, an empire had to plant a flag, erect military fortifications, and establish trading posts and colonial settlements. The dungeon was the terrifying underbelly of these forts, where captives were incapacitated, punished, worked, and traded. It represented the most militant aspects of imperial sovereignty: the use of racial violence in claims to power.[4]

The Black Fort

Across Florida's panhandle, at the mouth of the Apalachicola River, lies the obliterated and built-over remains of a less commemorated site, the Black Fort on Prospect Bluff. Since the time when Indigenous people and enslaved Africans first built outposts like the Castillo de San Marcos (1695), runaway refuges and maroon settlements dotted the thickly forested and swampy landscape. The fort itself was originally built under Spanish command. By the 1730s, it became home to a growing band of Black maroons, fugitives from slavery who integrated themselves with the Seminole peoples. It was taken over and occupied as an outpost for the British Colonial Marines in 1763 but returned to the maroons when the British evacuated during the War of 1812. The fort's Black founders allied themselves with the Seminole, Creek, and Choctaw people in the region and welcomed thousands of fugitives from slavery in Spanish and neighboring U.S.-claimed territories.[5] In these places, Black and Indigenous people evaded, refused, and renegotiated the terms of the European colonial slave system. These sites of Black and Indigenous placemaking existed below, across, and through the Spanish, French, British, and U.S. empires' claims to jurisdiction, an alternate universe colored over by the deceptively even shading of imperial maps. For a time, the Black Fort, or Negro Fort as it was called, blinked bright as a beacon of freedom.[6]

The Black Fort became an international gathering place. The thousands of people who passed through or settled there spoke West African, Muskogee, Spanish, French, English, and Creole languages. They brought a wide range of backgrounds, skills, and capacities, from soldiering and sailing to domestic and agricultural work, blacksmithing, and carpentry to cooping and masonry. They had growers, cooks, and washers handling the everyday social reproduction of the community, and shoemakers, seamstresses, and tailors ensuring they were the "best-dressed" fugitives in the history of American slavery. They had shipwrights to build a small fleet and veterans from the Spanish and British Colonial Marines to sail it. They had cultural-knowledge bearers, teachers, and healers who tended the artistic and ceremonial life of the community. While it is impossible to say precisely how many came through the Black Fort over the years, by the early nineteenth century there were 250 to 350 people living in the fort itself, and as many as 700 to 1,000 living and growing crops along the surrounding banks of the Apalachicola River. The Black Fort was led by three formerly enslaved men, a twenty-six-year-old cooper named Cyrus, a twenty-six-year-old master carpenter named Prince, and most of all, a thirty-six-year-old former lieutenant of the British Colonial Marines named Garçon. They had taken control of Isla de Perros (Dog Island), at the entrance to the Apalachicola Bay in the Gulf, and established extensive trading networks and alliances with coastal pirates. Garçon and twenty-five of his soldiers had been spotted stopping Spanish vessels and ordering the crew to remain aboard while they checked their passports.[7] By exercising this military aspect of sovereignty, they posed an explicit challenge both to the profits of slave traders and to rival state powers at the edges of Spanish, British, French, and emerging U.S. empires. Having fled from slavery or having won their freedom, they formed a defiantly antislavery community.[8]

The Black Fort represented a grave threat to the slave system, and news of its existence spread through the fugitive networks enslaved people developed to plan futures free of slavery's horrors.[9] Rather than treating the fort as the rival political force it represented, however, slaveholding presidents and policy makers joined prominent newspapers in condemning the Black Fort as a "hornets' nest" of bandits, outlaws, and pirates.[10] Their sensationalized stories attempted to turn fugitives from slavery into "dangerous criminals," raising the specter that armed Black militants were on the loose, ready to rampage at a moment's notice. This form of condemnation revolved around the unspoken assumption that since the fugitives had been brutalized under slavery, it was only a matter of time before they would take revenge. Reports that the Black Fort would syphon enslaved people across the border stoked slaveholders' fear that they were finding ways to interrupt the expansion of slavery, then carried on by the interregional slave trade, since the transatlantic slave trade had been outlawed, at least officially, in 1808. News that the maroons were "multiplying" further enraged white slaveholders, who were obsessed with racial theories of biological reproduction, with the idea that the fugitive slave community's free reproduction might outpace their own. To them, it symbolized their loss of control over Black life. Paranoia over Black criminality and race war revealed the moral precariousness of white settler slave society itself.

Federal officials knew firsthand how violence was required to police and maintain the racial inequality of slave society. Among the Black Fort maroons were eight enslaved people who had escaped from U.S. Indian agent Timothy Bernard, five fugitives claimed by U.S. military colonel Benjamin Hawkins, and an African-descended Spanish-speaking corporal who had fled St. Augustine with thirty or forty others. Federal agents like Bernard and Hawkins complained that their slaves had run away because of the existence of "Negro Fort," and State Department officials received word that slavery on the southern frontier was not secure. Secretary of state James Monroe blamed the British for creating a hub for the "massive force" of Indians and Black fugitive slaves. Military generals vowed to destroy it. "The destruction of the Fort, and the band of negroes who hold it, is of great and manifest importance to the United States," Colonel Robert Patterson exclaimed. General Andrew Jackson was obsessed with the settlement, believing he could have forced the Creeks to agree to the terms of the Treaty of Fort Jackson had it not been for Britain's Black and Indian allies. If they could not pressure the Spanish to destroy it, Jackson planned to take matters into his own hands.[11] Ultimately, slave-owning policy makers' and the U.S. military's response was predicated on a doctrine of preemption grounded in a geospatial imaginary that extended from the Deep South to places like revolutionary Haiti, to revolts aboard slave ships in the Caribbean, and across the Atlantic to Africa's west coast.[12]

In the sweltering summer heat of 1816, U.S. troops, on Andrew Jackson's orders, invaded Spanish (Seminole) Florida to destroy the Black Fort. When the gunboats opened fire, the fort's Black maroons and Seminoles stood firm in defense of their free settlement, reputedly shouting "Give me liberty, or give me death!" as they returned fire. U.S. troops shot a cannonball into the Black Fort's central powder magazine, instantly incinerating 270 people inside. "The scene was horrible beyond description," the attack's commander, Edmund P. Gaines, reflected. As the smoke cleared, U.S. troops hunted the survivors, seeking to kill, imprison, transport, or force them into slavery in neighboring Georgia, Mississippi, and Louisiana territories. Garçon, the Black Fort's leader, who had somehow survived the explosion, was summarily executed by a firing squad. Other fort inhabitants who had managed to escape joined forces with the Seminole and prepared for ensuing war.[13]

The invasion of Florida and the bombing of the Black Fort marked the beginning of what was called the First Seminole War. Better understood as a ferocious series of imperial military incursions, Jackson's Florida campaigns destroyed Black and Indigenous settlements, slaughtering and executing Seminole, Creek, and African-descended peoples. Monroe had officially instructed Jackson to enter Florida "only if pursuing the enemy," yet his private letters make clear he believed the invasion would increase pressure on Spain to relinquish its territorial claim. Monroe instructed Jackson to "punish" the Red Stick Creeks beyond U.S. borders if necessary. By April of 1818, Jackson's forces had burned hundreds of Black and Seminole homes in the maroon settlements along Lake Miccosukee and the Apalachicola and Suwannee Rivers. In justifying the Florida campaigns, Monroe, Jackson, and John C. Calhoun all maintained the attack was a matter of national security, to safeguard the "peace and security" of the southern frontier against the threat of "Indian and Negro war."

By invading Spanish-claimed, Seminole-controlled, and African-inhabited Florida, the United States asserted a new status in the world. These preemptive attacks carried out in a foreign territory had profound diplomatic consequences. Spanish envoy Luis de Onís y González-Vara argued that "civilized nations" did not enter foreign territory to seize people who had taken asylum there. When U.S. representatives refused to discuss the Spanish envoy's carefully prepared legal documents outlining Spanish territorial claims, González-Vara realized the United States aimed to seize Florida by force. This action was blatantly aimed at establishing U.S. dominion through violence and bloodshed. In fact, U.S. policy makers openly rejected the natural rights theory that all human beings were entitled to certain basic protections. Instead, they drew a sharp line between European-descended and non-European-descended peoples, between "old world" and "new," calling one "civilized" and the other "savage." In so doing, federal officials selectively applied international law to dealings with European empires but not with African-descended and Indigenous peoples.[14]

When the decimated remains of the Black Fort continued to attract maroons and fugitives from slavery, the U.S. military tried to cover the fort by building Fort Gadsden over the top of it. As travelers like William Cooper Nell wrote when visiting the site forty years later, "Its ramparts are now covered with a dense growth of underbrush. [. . .] The whole scene is one of gloomy solitude, associated, as it is, with one of the most cruel massacres which ever disgraced American Arms."[15] Still, Black and Indigenous people in the region would remember the Black Fort and others, like Fort Mose, as a kind of Caribbean-bound Underground Railroad. In turning it into a beacon of Black and Indigenous freedom, the Black Fort's maroons had managed for a time to invert its intended purpose.

The Battle of Negro Fort was a battle over placemaking. With a deadly preemptive strike in foreign territory, the federal government committed itself to an imperial policy path that would eventually spread forts, bases, and prisons throughout continental North America, across the Pacific, and all over the world. The invasion of Florida targeted the destruction of a powerful symbol of Black and Indigenous freedom. In its place, federal officials laid the groundwork for the Monroe Doctrine, the national Indian Removal policy, and the infamous *Dred Scott* Supreme Court ruling, demonstrating that the "allocation of rights, persecution of alleged criminals, and treatment of prisoners" would all be "racially differentiated."[16] The story of the Black Fort uncovers how understanding the root causes of the contemporary crisis of over-imprisonment is not only about what prisons purported to contain but also about what they covered over: the unrealized possibilities that were caged in, killed off, and otherwise foreclosed.

Wildcat's Escape

Jackson's Florida campaigns triggered what became known as the Second Seminole War. At the national level a succession of foreign policy doctrines, such as the Adams-Onís Treaty between the United States and Spain (1819), projected territorial claims from the southeast corner of Florida to the far northwest tip of Oregon Country. The Monroe Doctrine (1823) expanded the threat of military force across the Western Hemisphere, and the Indian Removal Act (1830) further authorized the violent expulsion of Indigenous peoples from their lands. In Florida, many Seminole people chose to stay and defend their homeland.

In winter of 1837, after a prolonged all-out U.S. military offensive, a group of 230 Seminoles were deceitfully captured at Fort Peyton under the internationally recognized truce flag and imprisoned at Castillo de San Marcos (Fort Marion), which had been taken over by the United States. Seminole chief Osceola and Coacoochee (Wildcat), the son of King Philip (Emathla), were among those captured. Fort Marion prison was a daunting place, surrounded by water on three sides and accessible only from the north, by drawbridge over the moat. The fort had a rectangular 30-by-20-foot dungeon and a long and narrow 5-by-20-foot torture chamber, which included a rack for suspending prisoners from the wall. According to a U.S. Army lieutenant's report shortly before the Seminole prisoners arrived, there was a secret dungeon with a small opening, just 36 by 30 inches, leading to a 13-by 20-foot cell.[17] Coacoochee (Wildcat) was imprisoned with medicine man Talmus Hadjo in a cell with only one tiny window, high in the 20-foot stone wall.

Still, they managed to escape. According to Coacoochee, to prepare they effectively went on a hunger strike, becoming sick until they were allowed to collect roots and store up five days' worth of medicine and starving themselves enough to fit their emaciated bodies through the narrow window high in the prison wall. Using a rope they made from forage bags, Coacoochee stood on Hadjo's shoulders to reach the window high in the wall. He squeezed through, scraping his chest and back, leaving some of his skin on the rock. Hadjo had even more trouble squeezing through and broke his leg when falling to the ground. They traveled five days by foot through the palmetto and hammock thickets to join Coacoochee's band at the headwaters of the Tomoka River, near the Atlantic coast. Hadjo was discovered on the road by armed and mounted militia, who killed and scalped him, but Coacoochee was able to slip quietly off his mule and disappear into the pine forest.

The U.S. Army's cowardly capture and imprisonment of the Seminoles renewed their anticolonial resolve. "When I was taken prisoner," Coacoochee said, "my band was included to leave the country, but upon my return, they said, let us all die in Florida."[18] Many Seminoles in Florida today trace their ancestry to the prisoners who escaped the old castillo (Fort Marion) in 1837, during the long war the United States waged against the Seminole. Active combat of the Second Seminole War subsided in 1842, but there was never an official treaty ending the conflict. Many Seminoles retreated into the Everglades and stayed in Florida, where they remain an "unconquered people" living in unceded territory. The prison tried to consign them to the past, but they refused to be forever frozen in purgatory. When U.S. Army officials again used Fort Marion as a prison, this time sending Western Plains Indian prisoners of war there, news media fanned white settlers' fears that another escape would lead to a "Third Seminole War."[19]

The "Florida Boys"

In winter of 1874, U.S. Army lieutenant Richard Henry Pratt received confidential orders to investigate alleged crimes committed by "Plains Indians" (Kiowa, Cheyenne, Arapaho, and Caddo) who were being held captive in Indian Agency jails and military posts around Fort Sill, at the base of the Washita Mountains, in present-day Oklahoma. His assignment was to single out those alleged to have committed serious crimes, like acts of theft or murder, and transport them to Fort Marion. Pratt collected testimony from fellow army officers, former captives, and rival prisoners, recording the accusations and rumors in his ledger books. Alongside his growing list of suspects, he noted pledges of immunity for those who incriminated others. By the end of his investigation, Pratt selected seventy-four of the "most truculent" Cheyenne, Kiowa, Arapaho, and Caddo prisoners, along with several children, Mexicans, and "negroes." He grouped his suspects into three categories: those charged with murder, stealing stock, and assaulting troopers; chiefs and warriors engaged in "criminal activities"; and those whom he generally considered "troublesome," "disobedient," and "agitators," but who had not actually been charged with any crime.[20]

Among the so-called Florida Boys was Cheyenne warrior Mochi and her husband, Medicine Water. Mochi had survived the Sand Creek massacre at Black Kettle's camp a decade before, where she witnessed her parents slaughtered in front of her. Colonel John Chivington, who led the assault, declared, "I have come to kill Indians. . . . Kill and scalp them, big and little, nits and lice." General Nelson A. Miles reflected that Sand Creek "was perhaps the foulest and most unjustified crime in the annals of America."[21] Mochi's grief must have been sharpened by the fear of being tracked and hunted as she fled, and it eventually hardened into resolve for revenge. She then survived the Washita River massacre, where more of her loved ones were murdered, captured, and imprisoned. Originally from the Tse-Tse Stus band of Southern Cheyenne, she joined Chief Medicine Water's Bowstring band and fought in a series of battles in what came to be called the Red River Wars. In the fall of 1874, their band found white settlers camping on Cheyenne land northwest of the Smoky Hill River, in present-day Kansas. They descended on them and killed former Confederate John German and his wife, Lydia, and took two of their daughters captive. In the spring of 1875, taking stock of the U.S. Army's tightening stranglehold on their means of survival through the systematic slaughter of the bison, they surrendered themselves. Mochi and Medicine Water, along with thirty others, were placed in leg irons and jailed in the guardhouse before being selected for deportation to "Fort San Marco" (Fort Marion).[22]

Mochi, Medicine Water, and seventy-one others made the six-week, one-thousand-mile journey from Fort Sill to Fort Marion, shackled and strung together by chains. They were loaded into ten army wagons, guarded by sixty Tenth Cavalry troopers patrolling the line, and transported 165 miles to the train station at Caddo. Forced into boxcars, their leg irons bolted to the floor, they were then transported to Fort Leavenworth, on to Kansas City, Louisville, and Nashville, before turning south through Chattanooga, Atlanta, and Macon and down to the Florida panhandle. On the train, Mochi, Medicine Water, and their daughter Tahnae were joined by Black Horse, his wife Pe-ah-in, and their daughter Ah-kah. As Pratt patrolled the rows of hunched and manacled captives, Cheyenne chief Gray Beard asked how *he* would like to be chained by the legs and taken away from his six-year-old girl and all that was familiar. Pratt admitted it was a good question, noting in his ledger that Gray Beard said he wanted to die ever since being taken from his home. The trip was torturous. Gray Beard attempted suicide en route but was revived. Then, when the train slowed, he escaped. But the troopers hunted him down and shot him from behind at close range. Kiowa warrior Zotom, who witnessed the execution firsthand, later drew the scene in a ledger book at Fort Marion. Other captives also attempted to end the misery by taking their own lives. Lean Bear stabbed himself twice in the neck with a pen knife. When he was revived, he went on a hunger strike.[23]

Journalists for popular newspapers, magazines, and penny press tabloids thronged to snap photographs and cover the story as frenzied crowds gathered at each of the stops the train made between Fort Sill and Fort Marion. The crowds grew as large as twenty thousand when the train passed through Kansas City, Missouri. At other stops the captives had to be hidden from excited and angry white mobs. In 1875, a reporter for the *St. Louis Republican* captured the larger message that U.S. officials were sending, writing that the Florida prisoners had "no rights that a white man should regard," echoing the phrase Justice Roger Taney used to strip Black people of rights in the Supreme Court's infamous *Dred Scott* decision (1857). The sensationalized news stories "put in print the fear that if they escaped into the everglades there would be a Third Seminole War."[24]

When the Florida prisoners crossed the moat into the foreboding old fort, troopers patrolled the central courtyard, ready to fire from the terreplein above. The entire fort had been refitted into a prison, complete with exercise yard, holding cells, and five dungeons. The Florida prisoners would spend the next three years there at hard labor, as the first test subjects in Pratt's blueprint for the federal Indian boarding schools. Despite harsh conditions, the captives, like people in prison everywhere, negotiated the terms of their imprisonment, documenting their experiences, writing petitions, and carefully carving out spaces for ritual, healing, and cultural celebration. Making Medicine and Mimimic crafted a powerful plea to Washington to reunite them with their families. Young Ah-kah wrote to the federal Indian Department directly: "Dear Washington, Me want to go home, see my little sister. Me and my people here all time three years. Me tired now. My mother's name Peonie; my father's name Black Horse, Comanche Chief; my name Ah-Kah."[25]

The local and national media was acutely aware of the Florida prisoners' peculiar status, being forcibly transported and indefinitely detained without trial in such spectacular fashion. As Sidney Lanier pointed out in an 1875 Florida tourist guide, there were those who constituted most of the "criminals," but then there were those against whom there was no particular charge but who were "confined on the principle that prevention is better than cure."[26] Fort Marion was being used as a kind of military prison, Lizzie Chapman wrote for *The Independent* in 1878, yet those imprisoned there were not prisoners of war. Rather, they were considered among "the most bloodthirsty criminals of their race." Classifying them as prisoners of war, however, created the same issue that acknowledging broken treaties did. "Think what a shameful thing it would be for the United States to break a treaty with a foreign nation, how quickly it would declare war against us, and how all other civilized nations would despise us," she pointed out.[27]

The Fort Marion incarceration orders caused debate with the Justice Department over precisely what kind of jurisdiction applied to these captives. Technically, according to the Supreme Court's decision in *Worcester v. Georgia* (1832), they could not be classified as "prisoners of war" because a state of war could not exist between the state and its "wards." While the federal government had made the claim that all Native Americans were to be treated as "domestic wards," making that claim real required a highly publicized procedure of shifting jurisdiction from the War and State Departments to the Interior Department, and eventually to the Indian Office (Bureau), in the wake of asymmetric warfare, vicious massacres, and forced relocations that characterized "Indian policy" at the time. This process relied on the prison as a mechanism to do more than incapacitate allegedly dangerous "criminals." The prison was used to produce wards of the state, forming a key pillar in the early architecture of prison imperialism. Pratt served as architect. At Fort Sill, he had turned war captives into criminals. At Fort Marion, he had turned criminals into prisoners. Next, he would turn their children into wards. The prototype he experimented with at Fort Marion became the blueprint for the first federal Indian boarding school, in Carlisle, Pennsylvania. With it, the federal government developed a multigenerational strategy that relied on family separation, forced assimilation, and imprisonment on reservations, in residential schools, and in Indian Country jails to exterminate Indigenous placemaking and lifeways.

When Mochi, Medicine Water, and the other Florida prisoners were finally released from indefinite detention in 1878, they were sent to Fort Leavenworth, Darlington, and other Indian agencies. The imprisonment had taken its toll on Mochi, and she died of tuberculosis at the age of forty-one, just three years after being released from Fort Marion. Their great-grandson, Cheyenne historian John L. Sipes, recalled that his great-grandfather Medicine Water would point to the scars on his ankles from the shackles and say, "This is what the government did to us to get control of our land, buffalo, ways of life as a people, and take away our freedom as Cheyennes."[28]

Wards of the State

The War Department ordered the Florida prisoners released from Fort Marion in order to transfer them to the custody of the Interior Department's Indian Office (Bureau of Indian Affairs).

Pratt took possession of seventeen of the imprisoned children, taking them first to the Hampton Normal and Agricultural Institute for "Negro industrial education" in Virginia while he awaited approval to build a residential school in the old Carlisle army barracks in Pennsylvania. After getting the approval eighteen months later, Pratt moved the children to Carlisle, where he founded the first federal Indian boarding school. By the end of the first year, he had transported 200 young people from 15 different Native American tribes to the former army barracks, now the Carlisle Indian Industrial School. By 1900, that number grew to 1,000 people from 80 different tribes. In total, over the lifetime of the school, federal officials sent over 10,000 children from 140 tribes there.[29]

Pratt found ideological justification for his model in the foreign policy and national security statements of presidents Thomas Jefferson, James Monroe, and Andrew Jackson, from whom he selected and reprinted his favorite quotes. Pratt followed Jefferson's theory that the "ultimate point of rest" for Indians was to "blend together, to intermix" rather than to be "exposed to the dangers of being a separate people." He saw himself as helping to fulfil Monroe's domestic sovereignty doctrine, namely that "control of the United States over them should be complete and undisputed." Pratt believed that "to civilize them and even prevent extinction it is indispensable that their independence as communities should cease." He selected Jackson's blunt opinion that "if they refuse to assimilate, they are doomed to decay."[30] In designing the Indian boarding school system, Pratt aimed, in his words, to "kill the Indian, save the man."[31]

The federal boarding school system did not develop in

isolation. It was backed by a series of federal legislation aimed at increasing jurisdiction over Native people. The Major Crimes Act (1885) and the Allotment Act (1887) made traditional Indigenous practices of holding land and of defining group membership illegal. This enabled a form of criminalization that already broke up families, sending many parents to jails in Indian Country and on the reservations.[32] Even for families who saw the boarding school as one of very few options for a better life for their children, federal officials used their "good behavior" on the reservation to coerce their children's "good behavior" at the school, and vice versa. Pratt's model for forced assimilation through family separation became copied across the country. By the turn of the twentieth century, there were already 25 off-reservation residential schools in fifteen states and territories. By the time the last facility shut its doors, hundreds of thousands of native children had been processed through 408 federal Indian boarding schools across thirty-seven states and territories.[33]

Freedom on Trial

Following the Civil War, federal officials wrestled with the status of free Black and Indigenous people. Pratt's ideas about race were forged in response to the upheaval of the war and to continued settler expansion and amid fierce debates over political integration, cultural assimilation, and racial segregation. Pratt was born in New York in 1840, resettled in Indiana as a child, and enlisted in the Union Army at twenty-one during the Civil War, fighting in Kentucky, Tennessee, and Georgia. After the war, he reenlisted and was deployed in Indian Territory and placed in command of a battalion of buffalo soldiers, the name for Black people conscripted into the army during the Civil War who were then deployed to fight Native Americans in the West.

By the time Pratt arrived at the Hampton Institute in 1878 with the children and teens he had taken from Fort Marion, he had come to the conclusion that Black and Indian peoples should be kept separate, believing it unwise to unite "the two race problems."[34] To Pratt, slavery had broken African-descended people down to bare material, had stripped them of their customs and culture, so that they might become civilized. "One race we found here, and another we brought from their homes on the other side of the earth," he wrote, and "forced them into the prison life of slavery of the most degrading sort." Place an eagle in prison, he analogized, and it loses all his grand powers. "His courage passes away and he becomes a contemptible thing, only to be looked at because of his size and peculiarities."[35] Still, "slavery uplifted the African," Pratt claimed. Slavery had taken "worthless people" and "compelled usefulness." Yet for Pratt, "under slavery the master only trained the hand." Under emancipation, the "whole man," he believed, could be retrained: "As bad as it was, it is not impossible for its evils to become minor in the presence of the greater evils of mismanaged and improperly used freedom."[36]

At Hampton and Carlisle, according to Pratt, Black and Indigenous freedom was on trial. "Will her life be in danger from her youngest children?" he asked rhetorically. "Will gratitude for freedom prove a better spur than the lash to inspire good conduct and higher usefulness?"[37] To transform Black and Indigenous people into desired subjects of white settler society, they first had to be separated from the land. The "Indian problem," according to Pratt, was that they existed independently on reservations and allotments of land, which continued group cohesion and cultural integrity. "Clannishness," he derided, rather than absorption into white society. Once, he wrote, "the blacks, a lower race than the Indians, were distributed among us," they "forgot their language and habits and acquired ours: not one of our ten millions of negroes can tell his tribal origins simply because all these have been forgotten through constant participation in American opportunities."[38] Through an intergenerational strategy of targeted confinement, white civilization would swallow up and ingest Indigenous civilization: "Feed the Indian to America, and America will do the assimilating, and annihilate the problem."[39]

In calculating the costs of the so-called Indian problem, Pratt argued that it was far more expensive to fight them than to eliminate them through forced assimilation. In his proposal to Interior secretary Henry M. Teller, he explained that if the federal government appropriated $200 per child per year over four years, he could grow the off-reservation residential schooling system from 10,000 to 25,000 children between 1884 and 1888 for a total expense of only $2 million to $5 million.[40] Military authorities estimated that the cost of "Indian hostilities" was nearly $224 million ($223,801,254.50) over the preceding decade alone (1872–82), or over $22 million ($22,369,126.45) per year plus an additional $5 million in rations for "subsistence." What enabled this kind of comparison to even be made was the growing awareness in Congress and the various divisions of the federal government that forced assimilation was an effective form of counterinsurgency. In fact, significant funding for

Carlisle came from the Civilization Fund created from the sale of Osage lands in Kansas, which had been set aside for general use by the Bureau of Indian Affairs for "civilizing the Indians."[41]

To populate the old Carlisle army barracks with pupils, Pratt traveled to the Pine Ridge and Rosebud Indian Agencies in 1879 to "recruit" first from among those people he had held captive at Fort Marion: the Cheyennes, Arapahos, Kiowas, Comanches, and Apaches. At Pine Ridge, several chiefs refused to send their children. Chief Red Cloud and others explained that the government had always cheated them, so why would they entrust their children to them? As Spotted Tail put it: "The white people are thieves and liars, and we refuse to send our children, because we do not want them to learn such things." In response, Pratt laid out his racial-biological theory of white supremacy. "The white people are multiplying," he told them, and "lacking in education and experience in our affairs you are not able to protect the interests of your own people." The ultimatum he presented was clear. Send your children to be assimilated or be annihilated either way. Pratt was able to take only eighteen children from Pine Ridge, so he "filled the shortage" by "selecting" an additional fifty-four from Rosebud. He somehow gathered another ten en route and boarded all eighty-two young people on the steamboat bound for Pennsylvania.[42]

Twelve-year-old Ota Kte (Plenty Kill), son of Chief Standing Bear, was among those taken from Rosebud. He remembered that he had seen his last great Sun Dance that summer, and that his father told him to be brave, that it was better to die young on the battlefield far away than to get sick and die old.[43] His sister, Zint-kaziwin, agreed to go with him at first, but then

had a change of heart. As he boarded the steamboat after riding fifty miles, it began to sink in. "So they pulled in the little
bridge, while the parents of the children stood up on the shore
and began crying. Then all the children on the boat started to
cry." He told himself to be brave. "I just stood in the corner of
the room we were in and watched the others all crying as if their
hearts would break." The journey was sleepless and frightening.
At times, like when the train turned behind the moon or frenzied crowds of white people whooped and clamored alongside
the train as they passed through urban stations, they believed
they were going to be killed.[44]

When they arrived in Carlisle, they were made to turn the
former army barracks into a "school," which quickly began to
more resemble a prison. After walking two miles to the barracks,
Plenty Kill felt bone tired. The rooms were empty. No beds, no
fire. "We went to sleep on the hard floor, and it was so cold!"[45]
Pratt had them build a seven-foot-tall fence around the entire
perimeter of the twenty-seven-acre barracks, which he claimed
was "to protect and keep the Indians in and the whites out." The
physical layout of the barracks structured a kind of panopticon
of surveillance, complete with an elevated platform from which
the prison warden turned superintendent could see into buildings and far fence corners. The "man on the bandstand" enlisted
a mysterious network of spooks to listen in, capture whispers,
and report to him. He even officially deputized eleven older boys
from Fort Marion prison to form part of the disciplinary apparatus of the Carlisle Indian School.

The first days at Carlisle, Plenty Kill remembered, were
marked by soul-destroying loneliness. "The big boys would sing

brave songs, and that would set the girls crying." Their hair was cut short, and the names of white people were sewn onto their backs. He was dunked under water, baptized as "Luther" in the Episcopal Church. His days were now filled with inspections and bell schedules. The big boys told them, "If the Indians go on the war-path now, we will all be killed at this school." They felt like hostages. Stuck in limbo, neither killed nor allowed fully to live. "No matter how humble your home is, it is yet home," Luther Standing Bear wrote.[46]

Like the apprenticeship system in the former British colonies in the Caribbean, which forced formerly enslaved people to continue working the plantations, the Indian residential schooling system relied on a set of degrees of freedom extending beyond the physical walls. Pratt called it his "outing system." By hiring out Native American children to farming families, he aimed to mold them through unpaid and low-wage child labor. When Luther Standing Bear was sent to work for a farmer, he remembered feeling the immense pressure of being told he was not only working for the school "but for your whole race."[47] The process of "bounding out" young people under the control of the state had been used by juvenile reformatories before. Indeed, Austin Reed, in the earliest known African American prison memoir, recalled how boys and girls from the nation's first juvenile reformatory, New York's House of Refuge, would be bound out to faraway farms or on long voyages at sea.[48]

Death and disease ran rampant at Carlisle. In detailing the genocidal impact of American Indian residential schools, historian Ward Churchill describes how the torture techniques used on children and young people resembled those from the harshest of prisons: namely sensory deprivation, solitary confinement, and forced obedience and submission. Likening what these children must have experienced to a form of posttraumatic stress, or concentration camp syndrome, he describes the "worlds of pain" that produced lowered self-esteem, conflicted self-concept, emotional numbing, chronic depression, anxiety, insomnia, nightmares, dissociation, paranoia, sexual dysfunction, heightened irritability, and tendencies toward alcoholism, drug addiction, and suicidality among survivors.[49]

Family Separation

Fort Marion continued to be used as a site of domination and deterrence after the federal Indian boarding school system was established. In fact, in the wake of the ongoing military conquest of western territories, family separation formed the fulcrum of the triangular system of control between the reservation, the prison, and the residential school. Native acts of frontier violence resisting ongoing settler warfare increasingly came under the jurisdiction of state and federal courts. Modes of theft and violence that had previously been understood as acts of warfare were now criminalized to bring Indigenous people under the territorial jurisdiction of local courts. This process of targeted criminalization was central to extending territorial jurisdiction and state control.[50]

During the Apache Wars, the federal government again decided Fort Marion would be the place to banish and imprison some five hundred Chiricahua Apache, including one hundred children, from the so-called Arizona Territory, a decade after

Pratt's initial experiment. As the Committee on Indian Affairs' *Removal of the Apache Indian Prisoners* report makes clear, Fort Marion prison was selected for its location on a peninsula just off the coast of Florida.[51] The Apaches have "a perfect knowledge of the country," General Nelson A. Miles told the Committee on Indian Affairs. It was impossible for troops to overtake or capture them if they knew they were being followed, he contended. The Chiricahua Apache are a "mountain race" he continued, and from a military perspective, they must be removed from the mountainous regions of the Arizona and New Mexico Territories.[52]

Herded into boxcars by cavalry from Fort Apache, the prisoners were shipped to Florida. Fort Marion was designed to hold no more than 150 people, but the military sent 502 there, where they would be confined for nearly three decades, from 1886 to 1913. Fort Marion's new jailer, Lieutenant Colonel Loomis L. Langdon, invited Pratt to come assess the children as potential candidates for family separation and forced assimilation in the Carlisle Indian School. The famous Apache leader Geronimo's own daughter, Ih-Tedda, was born in the prison, becoming the youngest of the five hundred Chiricahua Apache imprisoned there.[53] The guards named her Marion; she renamed herself Lenna. Pratt returned to Fort Marion in 1886 and left with 44 Chiricahua children, 32 boys and 12 girls, between the ages of twelve and twenty, who were called "wild, untrained, filthy savages." In all, 103 children would be transported to Carlisle.[54]

Geronimo and sixteen of his men, meanwhile, were separated from their wives and children and imprisoned at Fort Pickens, on Florida's west coast. The separation was a direct violation of

the terms on which Geronimo surrendered, complained the secretary of the Indian Rights Association, Herbert Welsh, which
supposedly guaranteed that the men would be united with their
families at Fort Marion. Not more than 30 of the nearly 500
who remained imprisoned, he added, "have been guilty of any
recent misdoing." Yet even white advocates for "Indian rights,"
like Welsh, believed in a softer form of carceral colonialism,
essentially suggesting that they be placed under the watch of
military officers on a reservation, where they could be trained
more completely in "civilized habits" and where they could
acquire permanent farms and homes. The children, he believed,
should be made to remain at Carlisle, "as there is no better place
for them."[55]

What Pratt engineered and oversaw was a multigenerational process of turning prisoners of war into wards of the state
through indefinite detention. Fort Marion became the birthplace of the federal Indian boarding school system, which held
hostage and eliminated thousands of Indigenous children.

*   *   *

Castillo de San Marcos, renamed Fort Marion, was originally constructed by the Spanish after the city of St. Augustine's
founding in 1565. When city officials began planning the
celebration for the four hundredth anniversary of "America's
oldest city," to take place in 1965, local Black activists saw an
opportunity to nationalize their own long-standing struggle
over placemaking in this segregationist stronghold. They began
by defying racist laws and policies and refusing to obey orders
barring them from protesting. Then, with growing support,
they began to clog the courts and fill the jail with more and

more protestors. As civil rights leaders and the national media poured in, the police and the Ku Klux Klan's increasingly desperate attempts to suppress the St. Augustine Movement with acts of intimidation, violence, and mass arrests were broadcast to millions of people across the country against Fort Marion's looming silhouette. "For 399 years, St. Augustine has trapped, preserved, and perpetuated all of the prejudice, Jim Crowism, bigotry and hate toward non-white Americans that have ever resided—even temporarily—within her boundaries," civil rights leader Hosea Williams proclaimed on the eve of the city's quadricentennial.[56] St. Augustine remained haunted. The dream of Black and Indigenous freedom had not dried up nor festered, as Langston Hughes wrote of dreams deferred, but was now ready to explode.[57] Although different accounts of St. Augustine's old fort have fallen under separate historical headings, weaving back together the stories of Native Americans, Black maroons, and Freedom Movement fighters who resisted colonial state violence helps to open the way for a still-needed reckoning.

The St. Augustine Four

When seven teenagers were arrested for a sit-in at St. Augustine's whites-only Woolworth's lunch counter during the summer of 1963, they were hauled off to a jail down the road from Fort Marion. When they appeared before the judge, the judge instructed their parents to sign an order barring the teenagers from participating in any demonstrations until the age of twenty-one. Audrey Nell Edwards, JoeAnn Anderson Ulmer, Samuel White, and Willie Carl Singleton begged their parents to refuse. Willie

Carl locked eyes with his mother, saying, "Mama, don't sign."
When they each said no to Judge Mathis, he turned beet red,
telling the sheriff, "'You take those communist niggers out of
here,'" Audrey Nell recalled. "'Lock them up and throw away
the key.'" While their parents were led to believe they would
spend only a few nights in the local jail, where they could check
on them, the judge had something else in store. Seemingly
channeling the spirit of Fort Marion's jailer, he compounded
confinement with family separation, banishing the teenagers to
the Florida School for Boys, in Marianna, and the School for
Girls, in Ocala. When Civil Rights Movement lawyers tried to
free them, the judge informed them the teens were beyond the
jurisdiction of his court. They had become wards of the state.[58]

Young people were the lifeblood of the St. Augustine Movement. Inspired by the St. Augustine Four, hundreds of high
school students staged a walkout to protest at the Ponce de
Leon Hotel. The news media's photographs of the resulting
mass arrests document scenes of horrific violence, replete with
police beating and herding people off to jail with dogs and cattle
prods. They also reveal young people defiantly raising their fists,
singing, and chanting, bravely asking to be arrested and taken
to jail and forming shoulder-to-shoulder lines of solidarity and
tight circles for protection. Together they staged sit-ins, pray-ins,
swim-ins, wade-ins, and night marches protesting racism in the
city. Over the ensuing tense and violent two years, these young
people and their allies inspired millions across the country with
their successful "flood the jails" direct action strategy. This form
of protest, as in other cities across the country, caused many people to shift their view of imprisonment from a brand of shame to

a badge of pride by showing how blatantly the prison system was being used as a tool of repression and control.[59]

Letter from St. Augustine Jail

After Audrey Nell Edwards was finally released, she went straight down to join the crowds gathering to hear Jackie Robinson and Martin Luther King Jr. speak. As Robinson pulled Edwards up on stage and hugged her, and as King praised the St. Augustine Four as "movement heroes," she must have been thinking of JoeAnn, Sam, and Willie Carl, who remained locked up. Three months later Edwards would find herself arrested again, this time alongside King at the Monson Motor Lodge.[60] The night of their arrest, King sent his *Letter from St. Augustine Jail*, via telegram, to Rabbi Israel Dresner, his friend in New Jersey. He called on Dresner "to come bear prophetic witness against the social evils of our time" and to send a delegation from the Central Conference of American Rabbis to support the St. Augustine Movement. The next week, sixteen rabbis who had come to support the movement were arrested outside the Monson. Inside jail, they wrote their own prison manifesto, called *Why We Went*. They went because they could not stand silently by. "We came as Jews who remember the millions of faceless people who stood quietly, watching the smoke rise from Hitler's crematoria. We came because we know that, second to silence, the greatest danger to man is loss of faith in man's capacity to act," they scrawled on the backs of pages of a mimeographed report on KKK violence in St. Augustine. "In the battle against racism, we have participated in only a skirmish. But the total effect of such demonstrations has created a Revolution," the rabbis predicted. "Blessed art Thou, o Lord, who freest the captives."[61] It was the largest mass arrest of rabbis in U.S. history.

While Edwards and King were locked in jail, hundreds of civil rights demonstrators continued to march, chanting, singing freedom songs, and carrying signs asking, "Are You Proud of Your 400-Year History of Slavery and Segregation?" The demonstrators were attacked by a mob of six hundred angry whites, led by Halstead "Hoss" Manucy, "Exalted Cyclops" of the St. Augustine Ku Klux Klan. Manucy held Klan rallies at the old St. Augustine slave market, with white crowds holding up confederate flags and posters with King's face on them reading: "Most Wanted Man" and "America's King Coon."[62] The Klan, accompanied by local police, proceeded to lead a march through St. Augustine's Black neighborhood. It was clear that police were determined to uphold segregation and back the Klan, and Sheriff L.O. Davis had even deputized Manucy into his volunteer "special deputies." King reflected that he had never been treated so badly: "I've been in fifteen jails, but this is the first time I've been treated like a hog."[63]

Allies in the youth movement against racism answered the calls for support, and college students from the northeast began to join the Florida Spring Project, organized by the Southern Christian Leadership Council (SCLC).[64] Black and white young people standing in solidarity, holding hands, and staging sit-ins at restaurants, swim-ins at hotel pools, and wade-ins at segregated beaches particularly enraged local white supremacists. A local white group calling themselves Irate Loyal True Americans claimed that an "interstate gang" of "nigger loving communists" and communist "fellow-travelers" was viciously defying God who "made the races separate and distinct." To their mind, these young people were "seeking to destroy white America." They warned of impending race war: "Don't for one moment forget, you are now promoting and inciting civil war and much bloodshed."[65] Local whites threatened the young movement allies, hurling rocks, bricks, and acid and attacking them with clubs and bats.

The St. Augustine sheriff and chief of police fanned the flames of the outside agitators trope, characterizing the Florida Spring Project as an "Easter Invasion." The fact that "young teenage white girls" began to show up dating and mixing socially with "negro male students," according to police reports, "created resentment."[66] By the summer, two hundred demonstrators defied the police order banning them from marching and were arrested. Fifteen "refused to post bond, electing to remain in jail," which was "devised to attract the greatest publicity to civil disobedience," police complained.[67] Police chief Virgil Stuart claimed to have uncovered a plot whereby integrated busloads carrying thousands of out-of-state youths were aiming to "break-down Law and Order" by "flooding the jails." Stuart had managed to "save the city" and claimed, "We uncovered this plot through informants and gave advance publicity of the plan, which we think resulted in only hundreds coming here instead of thousands."[68] Along with interstate "gangs," teaming full of racist dog whistles—"hoodlums," "mobsters," "communists," and "criminals"—police worried that "Black Muslims" were coming into town to "stir up trouble."[69] By the end of the summer, seven hundred cases were pending against protesters in local courts.[70]

Freedom's Tree

"Come, see, hear the one and only Mr. Hosea Williams at the Freedom Tree on the lawn of the Old Fort." Castillo de San Marcos, as Fort Marion had been rechristened, served as a stark symbol of imprisonment and ongoing racial oppression hanging over the city. "Historically, age and time designate wisdom. This is not true in St. Augustine, Florida," Williams explained. "The enslavement of nonwhite people had only become more sophisticated since the formal end of slavery," he continued. Here in this city the mayor publicly proclaimed he is a segregationist, the police chief deputized known Ku Klux Klan members, and white racists firebombed people's homes and cars. Black youth were imprisoned indefinitely for refusing to stop protesting, eighty people were jailed for demonstrating against discrimination, and the mother of a three-year-old sat locked away in the county jail. Still, Williams lamented, there is the illusion that the city's past and present should be celebrated.[71]

Black organizers chose the Freedom Tree site strategically, holding rallies on the grounds of Castillo de San Marcos because it was a major tourist destination and federal property, for which they were more likely to obtain permits than they were for city, county, or state properties controlled by segregationists. In a way, the tree itself was symbolic of how they might salvage some living, growing piece of the natural world to gather under and hold on to in direct contrast to the horrors of the Old Fort's dungeon. As a vital part of the nonhuman world, the Freedom Tree also represents the entwined Black and Indigenous genealogy of protest fighting against the racism and colonialism of the expanding carceral state. The juxtaposition of the Freedom Tree outside the Old Fort frames a series of confrontations in a long series of struggles over placemaking.

At the center of these ongoing struggles are competing under-standings of history itself. At the time, St. Augustine's Black community banded together to form the Ancient City Charity Club, a mutual aid society, in direct opposition to the racism represented by the Ku Klux Klan's Ancient City Hunting Club, white supremacist police officers, and St. Augustine jailers.[72] Similarly, the SCLC's report on the St. Augustine Movement— *St. Augustine: 400 Years of Bigotry and Hate*—stands in stark contrast to the far-right John Birch Society's story of events, *The Rape of St. Augustine*. In the end, Black organizers successfully stopped the celebration of segregation in St. Augustine. Civil rights leaders succeeded in calling for John F. Kennedy and Lyn-don B. Johnson's administration to withhold federal funds from the self-proclaimed "oldest community of the white race in the U.S." In fact, the national media's role in publicizing acts of white violence against Black demonstrators in St. Augustine is credited with pushing Johnson to sign the Civil Rights Act.

The story of the St. Augustine Movement does not end with the passage of the Civil Rights Act but extends from the attempt on Martin Luther King Jr.'s life in St. Augustine through his actual assassination in Memphis as he became ever more outspo-ken about "the giant triplets of racism, extreme materialism, and militarism."[73] As monuments to the civil rights Foot Soldiers go up and Confederate monuments begin to be taken down, it is tempting to subsume this story into a comforting national mythos of progress toward racial harmony. Yet to see the story of the St. Augustine Movement as ending triumphantly with the passage of the Civil Rights Act would be to foreclose a broader critique of racism and colonialism.

The St. Augustine Four, along with thousands of young activists, paid a heavy price for leading the fight for freedom in St. Augustine. Audrey Nell Edwards's arrest record followed her for her entire life, barring her from employment opportunities. Sam and Willie Carl refused to speak about what happened to them at the Florida School for Boys. "Audrey Nell, don't ask me about Marianna. I'm serious. Don't ask me about Marianna anymore," Willie Carl had said anytime Edwards asked him about it. Sam said practically the same thing, she remembered. She could tell from the "unbelievable hurting" the boys carried around as adults that "something really, really bad happened to them there." Carrying around that pain was the main reason they were "gone too soon," Edwards reflected. "They took whatever happened to them there to their grave."[74] One can imagine how similar it might have been to the horrors experienced by Indigenous children at Fort Marion, at Carlisle, and at so many other federal Indian boarding schools. The extent of the brutal physical punishments and sexual abuse is only now being unearthed as the bodies of more and more young people are exhumed from the ground.[75]

Forts and Freedom

St. Augustine, Florida, was the first place enslaved Africans disembarked in the present-day United States, in 1565. Castillo de San Marcos (Fort Marion) was built by Black and Indigenous people forced to labor under Spanish, and then later U.S., military command. Its infamous reputation grew as neighboring forts that had been places of fugitive freedom, like the Black Fort, were crushed and covered over. The growth and expansion of U.S. prison imperialism not only captured and contained, it foreclosed other possible ways of being. The decimation of the Black Fort and the rise of Fort Marion, like twin historical vectors moving in opposite directions, reveal the centrality of racial violence to the long history of prisons. Together they represent two of the longest lasting and most dangerous elements of prison imperialism: preemptive strike and preventative detention used in the name of deterrence. These doctrines were woven into penal policy and foreign policy as those who sought to govern the prison, and the world, developed overlapping strategies for how to predict, incapacitate, and eliminate perceived threats.

U.S. prison imperialism relied on the continual production of in-between spaces of perpetual limbo; in a word, purgatory. People at the time knew it, even as they described it, or tried to hide it, in different ways. Between Richard Pratt's *Battlefield and Classroom* was the prison. Pratt and others like him would have gladly likened it to purgatory, believing as he did that he held prisoners suspended between savagery and civilization. The Cheyenne must have experienced it as a different kind of purgatory, seeing each successive river as they were transported east as among the four they would cross before the afterlife.

Carcerality is marked by its ability to spread beyond the physical walls of the prison itself. The history and practice of anti-carceral movement building and decolonial resistance also spread outward from its origin points, like rhizomes underground. The story of the St. Augustine Movement continued through place-making protests like the occupation of Alcatraz by the Indians of All Tribes (1969–71) to ongoing struggles like Standing Rock. As recent efforts to identify and repatriate the remains of children exhumed from burial sites at Indian boarding schools make clear, these histories have also been trapped in a kind of purgatory. Together with the bodies of the boys exhumed from the Dozier School for Boys in Florida, these human remains bear witness to undead colonial regimes of power. Still, as Black and Native American studies scholars and activists reiterate, to understand how racism takes place may also require us to see how freedom *is a place*.[76]

2

The Jefferson–Monroe Penal Doctrine

Neither slavery nor involuntary servitude, except in punishment for crime whereof the party shall have been duly convicted, shall exist within the United States, or any place subject to their jurisdiction.
—United States Constitution, Amendment XIII (1865)

At the dawn of the nineteenth century, Gabriel Prosser and hundreds of enslaved people in Virginia planned a revolt. Enslavers and local militia members discovered and thwarted the rebellion, amid a suffocating climate of white hysteria over the revolution taking place on the former French colony of Saint-Domingue, where enslaved people were engaged in a struggle against slavery and colonialism that would establish the first Black republic in the Western Hemisphere. In the wake of Gabriel's Rebellion, James Monroe wrote to Thomas Jefferson requesting he find a place to transport prisoners convicted of sedition, conspiracy, or insurrection "out of the limits of the U.S."[1] Although Jefferson and Monroe did not manage to purchase such a "noncontiguous territory" at the time, plans for a national Black penal colony recurred throughout the nineteenth century, leaving an indelible imprint on federal penal policy.

A century after Gabriel's Rebellion, John P. Foley claimed
that rising Black crime made "consideration of the old proposi-
tion very nearly imperative."[2] Searching for responses to what he
framed as a "race-crime problem" at the turn of the twentieth
century, Foley republished the series of correspondence between
Jefferson and Monroe on penal colonization. Foley was particularly zealous about their plan to establish a "black penal colony"
to punish enslaved people deemed rebellious after Gabriel's
Rebellion in Virginia. The penal colony was earnestly discussed
by state, federal, and foreign governments because Southern
states were "fully alive to the dangers of negro uprisings." Foley
reasoned that had the "territorial conditions" at the beginning of
the nineteenth century been what they were by the end it—that
is, had the United States "then been in possession of Alaska,
the Philippines, Hawaii, or any other islands"—Jefferson and
Monroe would surely have realized their plan. As a Thomas Jefferson aficionado who spent the better part of his life compiling
The Jefferson Cyclopedia, a ready-reference guide to his political
thought, Foley felt strongly about the continued use of what he
called the Jefferson-Monroe Penological Doctrine.

The Jefferson-Monroe Penal Doctrine provided an ideological justification for and captures many common elements of the
recurring schemes to establish a national penal colony.[3] Foley's
penal colonization proposal was one among many made over
the course of the nineteenth century, proposing forced transportation and territorial segregation of criminalized Black people.
The plans proposed acquiring new territory to banish criminalized segments of society and advocated that racial segregation
take territorial form. The fantasy that penal colonization would

advance white society's "manifest destiny" reoccurred frequently in debates over nineteenth-century prison expansion and criminal transportation in American empire, serving as a touchstone for changing ideas and policies on race, crime, and sovereignty.

Federal Policy's Reach

Proposals to establish a national penal colony reveal with striking clarity how slavery and empire shaped nineteenth-century federal penal policy. Focusing on criminal transportation and penal colonization rather than on brick-and-mortar prisons turns attention away from the traditional "rise of the penitentiary" story. Most histories of prisons before the Civil War have followed a kind of social-order paradigm, charting the growth of prisons in response to rising crime rates within the territorially bounded space of the nation-state.[4] This has limited our understanding of how slavery, settler expansion, and empire influenced federal penal policy. This is in part because much of federal penal policy typically falls under other historical headings, such as African colonization, interstate commerce, or "Indian removal." While the national government was not yet in the business of building brick-and-mortar penitentiaries in antebellum America, federal agencies became increasingly involved in defining and policing all sorts of crimes, particularly those that crossed borders. Think, for instance, of the way the Constitution's commerce clause tasked federal marshals with enforcing the Fugitive Slave Act or of how military troops invented new forms of punishment, confinement, and forced labor as they waged wars of conquest against Native Americans.

National penal colony proposals became particularly forceful after the Civil War, deepening the major political fault lines of Reconstruction: namely, the place of free Black, immigrant, and Indigenous peoples in the nation, the relation between state and federal government police powers, and the uses of newly acquired territories. After secretary of state William Seward's acquisition of Alaska in 1867, for example, many thought he purchased it for a penal colony, to become "America's Botany Bay."[5] The growth of the penny press and the rise of syndicated news outfits widened circulation and profoundly changed the role of the press in national debates over crime and prison reform. The economic downturn, known as the Panic of 1873, triggered a frenzy of interest in penal colonization, and labor unions pressured state legislatures to introduce legislation that would insulate them from competition with convict-made goods.

Opposition to penal colonization was led by abolitionists, peace activists, and journalists. African American newspaper editors were especially critical of penal colonization schemes, denouncing imperialism abroad and incarceration at home. Black abolitionists like Frederick Douglass, anti-imperialists like Charles Gano Baylor, and anti-lynching activists like Ida B. Wells fought against disproportionate imprisonment, disenfranchisement, and mob violence. Together they helped develop the intellectual foundations for a critique of prisons as imperial institutions. The struggles against criminal transportation and penal colonization serve as a reminder that the carceral state was built through a series of contingent public policy decisions based in shifting and contested sets of ideas about danger, deviance, and unfree labor.

African Colonization

The Jefferson-Monroe Penal Doctrine was first worked out alongside the transatlantic slave trade and African colonization schemes for transporting African-descended people out of the United States. Jefferson and Monroe first explored the possibility of sending Black people convicted of certain crimes to Caribbean islands and places on the African continent. Jefferson asked the U.S. foreign minister in London to take the proposal to the British Sierra Leone Company, which was already in the business of African colonization.[6] Coupling penal transportation with other colonization schemes might make the plan more successful, Jefferson suggested. Enlisting ship captains who could bring back "commercial articles" enough to turn a "sufficient profit" and cover the expense of the voyage would lower what he saw as the otherwise prohibitively high costs of long-distance penal transportation. The only commercial vessels outfitted for the forcible transport of large human cargoes were designed for slave trading. In practice, this plan sought to use the transatlantic slave trade from Africa to subsidize the cost of penal transportation to Africa.

Jefferson and Monroe worried over the racial composition of the young republic. "It is impossible not to look forward to distant times, when our rapid multiplication will . . . cover the whole northern, if not the southern continent, with a people speaking the same language, governed in similar forms," wrote Jefferson.[7] "Nor can we contemplate with satisfaction either blot or mixture on that surface."[8] "Should we be willing to have such a colony in contact with us?" They agreed that a penal colony should never be too close to the United States, then or in the future. Where, then, "could we procure land beyond the limits of the United States to form a receptacle for these people?" they wondered. Jefferson considered how it might affect relations with other empires on the northern, southern, and western frontiers before ultimately deciding that a noncontiguous territory, such as an island, would be best. Their imperial vision of expanding penal colonies across space was evidently part of a theory about extending white supremacy over time.

Federal control was needed not only to claim potential locations for a national penal colony but to raise revenue. Taxation was unpopular, and policy makers were evidently concerned that taxpayers across the republic would be unwilling to finance a national spatial solution to what was perceived primarily as a regional problem. As in his proposals for African colonization generally, Jefferson looked to expansion as the way out. When politicians in South Carolina and other slave-holding states appealed to the federal government in the wake of the Denmark Vesey conspiracy (1822), Jefferson proposed using the land market provided by western territories taken from Native Americans to pay for the removal of babies born into slavery in the South, as a racial population-control measure. Jefferson proposed appropriating territorial lands equivalent to the amount ceded by "the states needing this relief," which constituted about a quarter of the size of the United States at the time. He based his calculations on the cost of an enslaved infant being $12.50, which would cut his previous estimate of $600 million to $37.5 million needed to compensate enslavers for the colonization of African-descended newborns. In the Jefferson-Monroe

Penal Doctrine, as in Jefferson's colonization plans to avoid "blot or mixture," he effectively proposed that the land market serve as a mechanism through which the imagined costs of enslaved humanity be rendered equivalent to the supposed value of white supremacist racial purity.[9]

Unlike local and state control over criminal matters, sentences of transportation between states or territories, along with deportation or colonization abroad, required the federal government's powers over interstate and international affairs. The Constitution's commerce clause meant that the federal government was ultimately responsible for adjudicating the "chattel principle," policing the Fugitive Slave Act, and determining the future of slavery in the territories. The federal government's powers over interstate commerce and newly acquired territories proved vital to national penal colonization schemes. Criminal transportation, along with capital punishment, became a defining feature of federal sovereignty. Yet, for the most part this form of criminal transportation was mystified at the time as "interstate commerce," as human beings were sold via the interregional slave trade, and it largely has therefore been understood as part of the history of slavery rather than as part of the history of the expanding penal state.

The terror of family separation, being "sold down river" as punishment or deported beyond U.S. borders, was a form of control wielded not only on plantations but in courthouses and legislatures. Slave revolts like Gabriel's Rebellion and the German Coast Uprising in Louisiana in 1811 led even the fiercest slave-owning defenders of "states' rights" to beg for U.S. military intervention when local militias looked to be outmatched.[10]

Punishing freedom seekers increasingly relied on the expanding carceral power of state and federal governments. After Denmark Vesey's conspiracy in South Carolina (1822), for instance, forty-three enslaved and free Black people were transported out of the United States and thirty-five people were hanged.[11] Following Nat Turner's Rebellion in 1831, state legislators in Mississippi began requiring "certificates of character" from slave-exporting states verifying those being transported were not "criminals."[12] According to studies of states like Georgia, sentences of transportation, defined as "sale out of state," made up as much as one-quarter of punishments meted out against enslaved and free Black people before the Civil War.[13]

The ability to pursue such plans relied on the projection of diplomatic and military power in the hemisphere, commonly understood in terms of the Monroe Doctrine (1823). Having purchased the Louisiana Territory from the French in 1803 and having invaded and taken Spanish (Seminole) Florida in 1819, federal officials drew a hard diplomatic line between the Old World and the new, claiming the Western Hemisphere as an exclusively U.S. "sphere of influence." Still, they had vowed to respect international agreements with European powers, including agreements over the treatment of prisoners of war, even as they promulgated policies that ensured African-descended and Indigenous people would have "no rights which the white man was bound to respect." It was not only slaveholders "at the helm" of U.S. foreign policy who looked to Caribbean islands as possible sites for a national penal colony.[14] On the eve of the Civil War in 1861, Abraham Lincoln, in his annual message to Congress, urged that they consider acquiring new territories to fund the colonization of enslaved people freed under the first Confis-cation Act.[15] He even signed contracts to colonize Black people to Chiriquí, on the Isthmus of Panama, and to Île á Vache, off the coast of Haiti.[16] Lincoln's administration pursued coloniza-tion schemes in Latin America and the Caribbean much later than is typically known.

Invoking Jefferson and Lincoln was instrumental to crafting the legal architecture for what would become the most enduring statement of federal penal policy at the end of the Civil War. When Congress passed the Thirteenth Amendment in 1865, they determined more than the end of slavery. The language of the amendment's convict clause—outlawing slavery and invol-untary servitude *"except as punishment for crime"*—codified fed-eral authority over unfree labor. It applied, moreover, not only within the thirty-six newly reunited states but *"any place subject to their jurisdiction."* The phrasing prohibiting slavery and invol-untary servitude "except as punishment for crime" was drawn from the Northwest Ordinance (1787). While drafting the con-stitutional amendment, senators like Lyman Trumbull preferred the "Jeffersonian language" of the Northwest Ordinance to the "Radical Republican" senator Charles Sumner's proposal that did not include the convict clause, because the former was "free of foreign associations."[17] Trumbull and his allies also pointed out that the recent passage of the act banning slavery in the ter-ritories (1862) had also incorporated Jefferson's wording.[18] Legal scholars suggest that using Jefferson's language helped to win the support of War Democrats, including Lincoln's vice presi-dent, Andrew Johnson.[19]

The end of the African colonization movement did not put

a stop to calls for racial banishment. During Reconstruction, a new flood of proposals for criminal transportation and the creation of a Black penal colony were developed. These ideas about racial segregation again took territorial form when secretary of state William H. Seward purchased the Alaska Territory from Russia in 1867, as it was rumored that he had done so with penal colonization in mind. Vehement anti-Black racists and so-called Redeemers began reprinting Seward's statements on colonization. Rowan Hinton Helper promoted the publication of his book *The Negroes in Negroland* (1868), for example, by announcing it contained the views of prominent federal officials, featuring Seward's statement, "The great fact is now fully realized that the African race here is a foreign and feeble element, like the Indians, incapable of assimilation."[20]

Penology in a World of Empires

Public discussion of penal colonization drew on the emergent fields of criminology and penology during Reconstruction and the ensuing period of westward expansion. After the first National Prison Congress in 1870, U.S. delegates took a leading role in organizing the inaugural meeting of the International Penitentiary Congress (IPC) in London in 1872. Criminologists Enoch C. Wines and Theodore Dwight assembled a massive study on the U.S. prison system and looked to international examples to assess the "best course" for prison expansion and reform. This was a moment when "the world had not yet agreed whether transportation is on general principles a desirable substitute for imprisonment."[21] Indeed, at the IPC's first meeting,

U.S. delegates joined their counterparts from the British, French, Russian, and Dutch empires to debate the topic.[22]

The IPC's executive committee was made up of delegates from every European empire, except Portugal, along with the United States, Mexico, Brazil, and Chile. The United States sent sixty delegates, the most of any member country. Invoking a kind of penological Monroe Doctrine, these delegates claimed to speak for "the United States and Mexico."[23] In the IPC's discussion of transportation and penal colonization, examples from the British, French, and Russian empires featured most prominently. Although British convict transportation to North America and Australia was held up as a successful case, delegates were careful to show that they had since moved away from the practice. The Russian case presented some "definitional challenges," as the committee secretary put it, as "Russia might deny that deportation to Siberia was properly transportation and might call it inland colonization, just as if destitute children were sent from New York to some distant part of the Union."[24] Indeed, the United States had also been practicing its own form of "inland colonization" by forcibly transporting criminalized Native people to reservations, to jails in Indian Country, and to the ever-expanding network of federal boarding schools. Still, the recent establishment of French penal colonies in Algeria, Guiana, and New Caledonia was seen to provide the most salient contemporary case studies.[25]

The IPC's inaugural debate over whether transportation was "admissible and expedient in punishment of crime" proved inconclusive and ultimately left open to individual member states. The subcommittee agreed that transportation served both the need to "protect society" and the need to act as a deterrent, through the threat of banishment. They also agreed on the need to distinguish the earlier British mode of penal colonization, to America and Australia, from the more recent French one, to designated prison islands. The Dutch delegate argued that the "English system" should no longer be honestly considered because it "dooms natives to extinction." The Russian delegation, for their part, advocated transportation in circumstances where territory needed developing.[26] U.S. delegate Wines sided most strongly with the new directions being taken in British imperial penology, particularly the work of Alexander Maconochie's penal colony on Norfolk Island, off Australia, then being implemented by Sir Walter Crofton in Ireland.[27]

Wines had established the groundwork principles for the National Prison Association in the United States the previous year. In the "new science of prison discipline," Wines outlined his adaptation of Maconochie's "marks and credit plan" and Crofton's "Irish system" to American circumstances. These penological systems were based on two principles: satisfying the "necessity of labor" and harnessing the "prisoner's hope."[28] Crofton began developing his Irish system after an 1854 act of British Parliament substituted "conditional liberation" for transportation. Conditional liberation, as the term suggests, was a form of correctional supervision that set a series of limits on full freedom and was an early precursor to parole. Like Maconochie's prison "currency," it was the product of ideas about colonial governance that provided "incentives" for proving one's fitness for freedom through physical work and obedience. Together, these systems represented the "admiration, example, and chief hope" of the "new social science of prison discipline," according to the National Prison Association's executive committee.[29]

In the United States, news of the IPC meeting in London in 1872, along with an acute financial crisis, known as the Panic of 1873, unleashed new plans for penal colonization. Charles Nordhoff was foremost among these new champions, and his proposal "What Shall We Do with Scroggs?" in *Harper's Magazine*, referring to Alaska, was the most widely recirculated.[30] Nordhoff pointed directly to the IPC, quoting Italian criminologist Count di Foresta's position that "transportation with compulsory labor in a colony" was "the best punishment for criminals."[31] Maconochie's success with the penal colony of Norfolk Island, Nordhoff urged, proved it would work in Alaska. Nordhoff was persistent, even challenging delegates at the National Prison Association, including Wines's son, Frederick Wines, to debate the issue fifteen years after he had originally laid out his penal colonization plan.

Penal colony boosters in the United States framed it as a matter of national security and international competitiveness. Nordhoff argued, for instance, that the U.S. public should embrace the establishment of a penal colony in Alaska because "society would rid itself, by a natural and proper method, of the human beasts who prey upon it, and threaten its security." The nation's prison system was in crisis, he claimed, with state and local prisons overflowing and with rampant corruption at all levels. This was too high a burden for taxpayers to bear, especially as high rates of recidivism proved the system was not working to reduce the criminal population at large. Nordhoff calculated that 1 in 450 adults between the ages of sixteen and forty was in a jail of some kind. The claim that this ratio was ever increasing added particular urgency to his appeal. Convicts at the Alaskan penal colony would be reformed through *productive* labor. The bracing environment would spur industriousness, and outdoor work would be "good for their health." There was no lack of work for them to do clearing land, mining resources, felling and hauling timber, and building roads. By developing the territory, taxpayers would see a return on their investment from the Alaska purchase and the costs of the expanding criminal justice system. In this way, penal colonization was envisioned as a way to advance state and empire building, and the plantation model was held up as the best path for developing newly acquired land.

The White Press Calls for National Action

The press was instrumental in creating a national call to action on penal colonization as a federal response to crime. In fact, the rise of mass circulation daily, known as the penny press, was largely due to the popularity of stories about crime and prostitution.[32] Publications like George Wilkes's *National Police Gazette* specialized in this genre, while others like the *New York Sun* got their start in lurid crime reporting and later diversified their coverage. Even when newspapers were not using explicitly racial language, they were developing a set of terms that coded crime and criminality as black.[33] Terms used to describe those who should be sent off to penal colonies—scum, refuse, villains, vagrants, rascals, pests, beasts, fiends, brutes, lazy beggars, and dangerous classes—conveyed racial meaning to certain audiences, especially after the Civil War.

The press amplified the idea that penal colonization would be useful in claiming and developing new territories. When Wilkes's *Police Gazette* pushed the cause, for example, it was described as enabling prisoners to aid the "spread of civilization."[34] Redeeming the convict, in this formulation, was part and parcel of westward expansion. While the labor of imprisoned people—clearing land, planting crops, and building infrastructure—was often described as advancing civilization, they themselves were not. This mode of expansion was about acquiring new territory by sending dangerous or otherwise unwanted populations there to occupy and develop it. "The vast Pacific is dotted with a thousand locations where the scheme of transportation might be successfully carried out," suggested the *Police Gazette*, "and if we are not mistaken there are several islands off the coast of Oregon and California where this humane and necessary reform might be commenced."[35] Like Jefferson and Monroe's search for some noncontiguous "receptacle" to banish those perceived as a threat, this imperial formula involved staking claim to new land.

After the Civil War, penal colonies were put forward as a kind of halfway house between slavery and freedom. These penal colony proposals read like an American version of the apprenticeship system implemented by the British in the Caribbean colonies of Jamaica and Barbados after slavery was officially ended. The apprenticeship system of forced plantation labor in Britain's Caribbean colonies was advanced as more desirable than warehousing people in jails and penitentiaries without work, or making them perform "unproductive" labor on torture devices designed to replicate plantation labor, like the infamous "treadmill" used in Jamaican prisons.[36] Arguments in favor of penal colonization often employed the same set of terms used by advocates of the apprenticeship system: namely that convicts would learn obedience to law, cultivate habits of industry through hard physical labor, and benefit from the fresh air of outdoor work.[37] Penal colony boosters argued that penal colonies were a "natural" halfway house between slavery and freedom, "which sound well on the ear of slaves but are most repulsive to citizens free born."[38] These claims hinged on the racist idea that formerly enslaved people turned vagrants were unable to support themselves and would actually seek imprisonment as a form of freeloading. While the apprenticeship system claimed to "redeem" formerly enslaved people's souls by refitting them for free society, it actually served to compensate former enslavers who sought to redeem value from their lost "property" in human beings.

Press coverage of penal colonization proposals played an important role in uniting Northern and Southern policy makers, who worked to undo the political gains won by Black people during Reconstruction. For racist Southern Democrats known as Redeemers, penal colonization promised not only to banish criminals, unwanted Black politicians, and "colored carpetbaggers" —their derogatory term for Black people who relocated from Northern to Southern states during Reconstruction—but also to remove federal troops who occupied Southern states.[39] Penal colonization was seen as a way to advance their "Lost Cause" vision of white manifest destiny. Northern War Democrats, who supported President Andrew Johnson's plan to return control of the South to the defeated Confederates, saw a role for penal colonization as well. In his daily paper the *New York World*, for example, Democratic stalwart Manton Marble claimed that Alaska was purchased as a penal colony to fulfill the national mission of manifest destiny. "We rejoice at the acquisition of Alaska, because it is part and parcel of the mighty North American continent, every inch of which should belong to the United States, and the acquisition of which 'peaceably if we can, forcibly if we must' ought to be made a cardinal plank of Democratic platforms," he wrote. "Louisiana, Florida, Texas, and California were all acquired under Democratic administrations," he concluded, "so let this be the glory of Andrew Johnson's administration."[40] Referring to Alaska as a "field of Reconstruction," Marble likewise recommended sending newly elected Black politicians, Radical Republicans, and "colored carpetbaggers" who "infest the South" to the penal colony there.[41]

Strange Bedfellows

Labor organizations advocated for penal colonization as a means of fighting perceived competition from industrial and factory convict labor. The labor lobby protested that convict-made goods within U.S. borders suppressed wages and degraded the honest workingman. Their search for solutions to "the convict labor problem" relied on a hierarchy in modes of production established under racial slavery, by which convicts would be held at the bottom, being allowed to engage in only the most arduous manual labor—clearing forests, breaking rocks, harvesting crops—and reserving industrial and skilled work for free citizens. Local and national labor organizations, like the Knights of Labor, the Manufacturers' and Workingmen's Protective

Associations, and the Anti-Convict Contract Association, lobbied state legislatures to pass anti-convict contract legislation
and petitioned Congress to establish a national penal colony. As
W.E.B. Du Bois observed in *Black Reconstruction*, many white
workers derived a kind of "psychological wage" from discourses
of white supremacy even when it ran counter to their actual economic interests.[42]

The Knights of Labor were especially vocal in arguing that
penal colonization would instantiate the proper hierarchy of
productive labor. The views of prominent Knights of Labor
members from New York, Washington, DC, and Massachusetts
were collected and reprinted in newspapers, like the *New York
Herald*, that supported the idea. In their petition to the Michigan state legislature, for example, the Jackson Knights of Labor
pointed to the way other empires had used convicts to develop
new territories.[43] As master workman John E. Smallwood put it:
"Let us get rid of these men and women who here do absolutely
nothing for the good of their kind. Let them go to this new
country, develop its resources, and pave the way for a higher
order of civilization."[44] The Alaska Territory was perfectly suited
for a penal colony, proclaimed the New York Knights, because
it was still "wild."[45]

New York assemblyman Charles T. Trowbridge described the
penal colonization resolution he brought to the New York legislature (1879) as the only solution to the convict labor competition problem. "Trade unions and workingman's guilds from
all over the state are constantly protesting the legislature about
prison competition in the various trades," the *New York Herald*
reported. Trowbridge's scheme "will protect honest industry."[46]

The New Jersey legislature abolished convict "contract labor" at the same time as they passed the joint resolution recommending Alaska be used as a penal colony (1884).[47] When California state senator Edward Gibbons introduced joint resolution no. 34 to the state legislature (1874), he proposed that a penal colony in Alaska would "obviate the evil of bringing convict labor into competition with the labor of law-abiding citizens."[48] The Rhode Island state legislature, for its part, requested a congressional inquiry into a national penal colony.[49] A national penal colonization bill was introduced in U.S. Congress (1885) and referred to the Committee on Territories.[50] When the national Bureau of Labor made its report on the prospect of a national penal colony (1886), Commissioner Carroll D. Wright worried it might "increase the opportunity for the preparation of the criminal classes through heredity."[51]

By the end of the nineteenth century, policy makers continued to view penal colonization in racial and imperial terms, fretting over the place of criminals in the biological makeup of the growing republic. Penal colonization schemes relied on new statistical discourses about crime and "race science" (eugenics) that were ascendant in the field of criminology. Black and "foreign born" were operative categories of "writing race into crime," and Frederick L. Hoffman's *Race Traits and Tendencies of the American Negro* (1896) made statistical data on Black criminality central to framing the "Negro Problem" in modern race-relations discourse.[52] The use of birth rates and crime statistics compounded a set of racist and classist fears: namely that poor families "bred criminals" and that criminality could be inherited and passed down like a congenital disease.[53]

Fear that the growth of the "criminal classes," if left unchecked, would outpace the growth of the overall population was another proposed reason for establishing a national penal colony. "Public opinion" in Chicago, Boston, Philadelphia, Richmond, and Albany generally favored the creation of a national penal colony, according to news correspondents, because "the growth of the criminal classes is relatively more rapid than the growth of the population."[54] As Chicago mayor Carter Harrison put it to prison officers assembled for their national conference, the "progeny of the worst elements of society" have "taken from the blood of the parent the criminal taint" and are overflowing the nation's prisons.[55] When Prison Reform Association agent Alonzo A. Webb was sent to Alaska to report on the feasibility of a penal colony in 1887, he told the local paper he was there because "the criminal element is constantly increasing."[56]

Criminologist John D. Milliken was more explicit, listing sterilization and castration under the heading of "colonization" in his report for the National Prison Reform Association on the bill to establish a penal colony in Alaska.[57] Milliken claimed that scientists were in favor of the "asexualization" of certain classes as the most "humane and natural way of preventing crime." Indeed, his section on penal colonization summarized the racially specific castration laws on the books in various states and territories where any "negro" or "mulatto" convicted of attempting to "defile, rape, or compel a white woman to marry" was subject to "emasculation," as were "felons upon a third conviction."[58] John Milliken concluded his discussion of penal colonization, sterilization, and castration by suggesting the practices be seen as more scientific and humane alternatives to lynching.

The lynch mobs, he warned, sought to dominate public opinion and control the courts.

Lynching and Empire

At the dawn of the twentieth century, a white woman named Valley Younger was found raped and murdered in Corsicana, Texas. A Black man named John Henderson was lynched. The lynch mob fired guns into the homes of local Black residents, burned a Black schoolhouse, and warned "the negroes in the neighborhood . . . to leave in forty-eight hours."[59] A letter to the governor warning him not to try to prosecute the lynch mob was signed: "Every white man in Navarro County." The coroner's verdict written by justice of the peace H.G. Roberts pronounced Henderson dead at the hands of "outraged citizens and the best people of the United States."[60] Texas newspapers referred to Henderson's lynching as "a priceless heritage of the Anglo-Saxon race," which "commands that no one shall lay forceful hands on the body of a woman."[61] The members of the lynch mob were never prosecuted.

A retired Texas police magistrate instructed his wife, "Mrs. Magistrate," that her "sisters in the federation of clubs could discuss no greater topic" than how to create environments that would save those living in remote places from the fate of Mrs. Younger.[62] Together they dreamed up a "New Code" to be adopted by the "Outraged Citizens of the United States of America" while "Henderson was burning at the stake."[63] Imprisonment was not a sufficient cure for criminality, according to the police justice, as they inevitably polluted society again upon release. They dreamed that the criminal population be banished forever, shut out beyond the pale of civilization: "In a word, segregation is the only cure."[64] "This revolution in our methods of punishment," reported Mrs. Magistrate, was an issue fit for a presidential campaign. According to their plan, once the "New Code Party" had won under the leadership of an "intrepid President," the first order of business would be to establish penal colonies: "one in Alaska for male offenders, and one in Hawaii for female transgressors." Crime would be controlled, and society "saved."[65]

The details of the scheme invoked the historical imagery of the slave trade. Guards armed with clubs and revolvers oversaw the "human freight" as they faced the awful prospect of banishment, "a punishment a thousand times worse than death." The ship to Sitka, Alaska, was "built expressly for the convict service" and striped like the trains. "A leviathan monster that swallowed a thousand men at the mouthful, to drop them behind the awful walls of Alaska." As the guards escorted the prisoners into this "floating coffin," they saw it was not lined with cells but was rather just one "gigantic cage."[66]

The murder of Younger and the lynching of Henderson is what led Foley to propose a national penal colony. The only solution, according to men like Foley, was to banish Black men accused of the "most heinous" crimes, which he saw as "infiltrating" white womanhood. Otherwise, the contagion of Black criminality would "pollute" white society. This, in short, was how he came to propose territorial segregation as "the only cure." Foley reached back to the founders for ideological justification, invoking the Jefferson-Monroe Penal Doctrine to support forced transportation and penal colonization as a deterrent to the "criminal classes," and as an alternative to white vigilante mob rule.[67] Ideas about controlling white women's reproduction and eliminating criminality that might be inherited through "tainted blood" lay at the core of penal colonization schemes. At the dawn of the twentieth century, as U.S. troops deployed to Cuba, Puerto Rico, Colombia, Samoa, and the Philippines, penal colonization was held up as an answer to the "crime problem" and the so-called race problem at home. Imperial expansion made it easier to envision segregation taking territorial as well as legal and institutional form. This was a national spatial solution to what was imagined as an entwined problem of rising crime rates, the inheritability of criminality, and racial danger.

The Black Press Challenges Prison Imperialism

Ida B. Wells, who compiled the *Red Record* on racial terror lynchings, wrote that the real purpose of savage and cruel lynchings was to show Black people in the South they have no rights the law would enforce. Along with critiquing lynching and the unjust legal system, she also opposed the "belligerent expansionism" of U.S. empire. With the U.S. military invasions of formerly Spanish-claimed territories, prominent Black anti-imperialists like Charles Gano Baylor exclaimed that the same Anglo-Saxon tactics of "law and order" being used to put down the revolutionary movement of Black Cubans would likewise be carried out against Black people in the South, and that "liberty will lie bleeding under the heel of white minority rule." Black journalists and activists like Baylor and Wells, together with organizations like the National Negro Anti-Expansion, Anti-Imperialist, Anti-Trust, and Anti-Lynching League, made explicit the connection between imperialism and imprisonment, at home and abroad. Together they formed a key part of a Black protest tradition that linked white vigilante violence and disenfranchisement to a form of colonial rule, within and beyond U.S. borders, and sought to rework the meaning of what, and who, was "criminal."

The Black press condemned penal colonization schemes, even likening convict leasing and prison plantations in the South to penal colonies on dry land—just as Black abolitionists and newspapers in antebellum America had opposed the cruelty of slavery, imprisonment, and federal penal policy—particularly the border-crossing power of the U.S. Marshals Service policing the Fugitive Slave Act. It is these abolitionists, reformers, and organizations who laid the intellectual foundations for the critique of the police and prison system as an imperial institution enforcing a form of internal colonialism. African American newspaper editors denounced penal colonization, as they had with earlier Black colonization schemes designed by whites. Black newspaper editors condemned the Southern convict system as a disgrace to civilization worse than the penal colonies of the British, French, and Russian empires, simultaneously warning against attempts to replace it with U.S. penal colonies. Some sarcastically pointed to penal colonization as a way to banish white supremacists to various circles of hell, thereby flipping the script on other formulations of the so-called race-crime problem. As the postbellum era of white settler colonial expansion erupted into full-scale overseas war making, the Black press vigorously protested the racial subjugation of dark-skinned people at home and abroad.[68]

At the end of Reconstruction, some Black journalists used the popularity of the proposed Alaskan penal colony to decry racial violence and voter suppression. The *Weekly Louisianan,* for example, ran a story suggesting that the Alaska Territory be divided up into circles of hell, like Dante's *Inferno.* Louisiana's white supremacist "bulldozers" would be transported to their own special circle, called "Tensas parish," while the "Florida" circle would become synonymous with the "dishonest canvassing boards" carrying out Black-voter suppression after the recent withdrawal of federal troops from Louisiana, South Carolina, and Florida. "Breathett County," Alaska, would be home to the "Kentucky murders," forever symbolizing the evils of mob rule.[69] Indeed, forty-five people had been killed in the last rash of violence in Kentucky, leaving local papers to complain that the magistrates, sheriffs, jurors, and constables were all complicit in these violations of the law.[70]

Other Black-owned newspapers saw how penal colonization was being proposed as a replacement of the convict lease system, particularly after the widespread circulation of George Washington Cable's exposé *The Silent South* in 1885.[71] The *Huntsville Gazette,* for instance, pointed out that Alabama was agitating for a penal colony to replace their state convict system.[72] The *New York Age* and *Leavenworth Advocate,* meanwhile, called Georgia's convict system a disgrace to civilization ten times worse than Russian Siberia or French New Caledonia. At the heart of their critique were the issues of racial disparity in incarceration and the targeting of Black youth. "Of 1,649 convicts in its camps,

1,526 are Afro-American," reported the *New York Age* in 1891.[73] Southern white judges, the article explained, were in the habit of giving ten-year-old Black children ten-year-long sentences.

Along with the critique of criminal transportation and penal colonization, many Black newspapers began increasingly to equate the denial of rights and white violence in the United States to a form of colonial rule itself. As they had done by inverting the racial meanings of Alaska penal colony schemes, these articles denounced Anglo-Saxon law and order and "civilization" as mere pretense for racial despotism, if not thoroughly irredeemable concepts altogether. As the *Indianapolis Recorder* put it, "Anglo Saxon mastery" was again asserting itself in the name of humanity.[74] Responding to the most recent lynching in Georgia, a journalist for the *Iowa State Bystander* asked in desperation, "Are those white people insane?" If the action of the Southern states is called civilization, they continued, and the "frightful crimes" are not stopped, "then we had better close the school house, burn the books, tear down the churches, and admit to the world that Anglo-Saxon civilization is a failure."[75]

At the outbreak of the Spanish-American War, the *Cleveland Gazette* asked if "America is any better than Spain" in terms of enforcing colonial unfreedom on its subjects.[76] Anti-imperial activist Charles Gano Baylor published long letters in the *Richmond Planet* arguing that Anglo-Saxon law and order was invoked to put down the Black Cuban political challenge to Spanish rule and the U.S. invasion. "The American Negro cannot become the ally of Imperialism without enslaving his own race," he proclaimed. "Freedom under Sovereignty Referendum government, being once firmly established in Cuba, will then be asserted in South Carolina, Mississippi, and Louisiana where liberty now 'lies bleeding' under the heel of a ferocious white minority race rule."[77] In other words, just as racial violence was exported outward, new tactics of colonial rule would be imported back into the Southern states.

Or, as the *Coffeyville American* reframed it, strategies of colonialism pioneered in the South were now being extended in the name of civilization: "It would be deplorable to have . . . the people of Cuba or Puerto Rico ruled as the Negroes of the South have been ruled . . . this kind of 'civilization' ought never to be extended to new territory."[78] Lewis H. Douglass, son of the famed abolitionist, extended this critique to President William McKinley's Philippine policy, saying that Filipinos should not be governed as vassals, serfs, or slaves. "No sane, honest man in the country believes that equal and exact justice . . . will be had where race hate is indulged in by the men who denounce Filipinos as 'niggers' and only fit to be subjected to the white race has full sway," he wrote. "Now its expansion means the extension of race hate and cruelty, barbarous lynchings and gross injustice to dark people."[79] Centering anti-Black racism as the source of violence, political subjugation, and the miscarriage of justice provided the foundation for further critiques of the U.S. legal system's culpability in producing forms of internal colonialism.

It also required redefining who, and what, was seen as criminal. The *Cleveland Gazette, New York Age, New Orleans Southern Republican,* and *Washington Bee* all ran stories describing the forcible annexation of Cubans and Filipinos as "criminal," while the *Richmond Planet* called the war in the Philippines one of the "foulest crimes" ever attempted.[80] Overseas war making not only was wrongfully slaughtering freedom fighters, it was unjustly imprisoning broad swaths of the civilian population, argued the *Philadelphia Defender*.[81] Imperialism abroad was inextricably linked to the same sort of ruthless aggression that was causing lynchings at home, which were described as the "basest and most atrocious crimes known to criminology."[82] This twinned critique of the criminality of lynching and imperialism underscored political organizations like the National Negro Anti-Expansion, Anti-Imperialist, Anti-Trust, and Anti-Lynching League in Chicago. In staking out his opposition, league president W.T. Scott called out lynching and mob rule as both criminal and imperialist.[83]

The single greatest force in systematically redefining lynching as a criminal act was Ida B. Wells. Speaking out against mob violence in the North and in the South at the National Afro-American Council in Washington, DC, in 1899, she also called on Black people to oppose belligerent expansionism.[84] Referring to the recent rash of lynchings as "the reign of outlawry," in her work *Lynch Law in Georgia*, Wells explained that "the real purpose of these savage demonstrations is to teach the Negro that in the South he has no rights that the law will enforce."[85] In denouncing lynching, disenfranchisement, and second-class citizenship, activists like Wells, along with the Black press, likened the treatment of African Americans in the South to overseas war making and colonialism. Appeals to justice figured prominently in the growing argument against slaughter, imprisonment, and rule without the consent of the governed. Lynching, convict leasing, and racial disparity in the penitentiary system all conspired to subjugate Black people like colonial subjects. From this tradition of thought and organizing comes the insight that prisons might in fact be best understood as imperial institutions, designed to produce different classes of political subjects.

The Penal Colony That Wasn't

The federal government never did establish a national penal colony; Alaska did not become "America's Botany Bay." The Alaska Purchase (1867) did trigger a host of state and federal legislative penal colony proposals, however. By the California and New York State legislatures in 1874 and 1879, for instance, and by the New Jersey and Rhode Island legislatures in 1884. The penal colonization bill introduced to the U.S. Congress went as far as the Committee on Territories (1885). These were serious proposals, tracing their ideological origins to the Jefferson-Monroe Penal Doctrine and given weight by the professionalizing fields of criminology and penology. In other words, they now had experts. Ultimately, plans for a national penal colony served as a way for certain groups of people—such as the Redeemers, nativists, white nationalists, and eugenicists, as well as labor leaders, policy makers, and newspaper editors—to imagine a greater role for the federal government in the growing prison system. By conflating what they called the "Negro Problem" with a supposed "crime problem," they looked to racial banishment and empire building as they wrestled with the future place of free Black people, American Indians, and immigrants in the postwar world. The national penal colony served as a symbol through which they envisioned a national spatial solution to what many white people referred to as the "race problem": through empire.

In the penal colony, as in Thomas Jefferson's search for a non-contiguous territory to avoid "any blot or mixture," racial segregation could take territorial, not just institutional, form.

The network of federal penitentiaries has always been more widely spread out than local jails and state prisons. As federal officials had realized when imprisoning Native Americans from the Southwest in Fort Marion, on the far eastern edge of Florida in St. Augustine, they did not necessarily need a formal penal colony to use criminal transportation as a form of counterinsurgency. After the Census Bureau announced the "closing of the frontier" in continental North America, the United States went to war with Spain over its colonies in the Caribbean and the Pacific. As the federal government took control of Puerto Rico and the Philippines, they expanded the use of criminal transportation and incarceration as a linchpin of U.S. counterinsurgency during war making and as a strategy of colonial rule in its wake.

Prisons in the Philippines During U.S. Occupation

Laoag

Bangued
Vigan   Tuguegarao
Bontoc   Ilagan

Bayombong

Lingayen

Tarlac   Cabanatuan
San Fernando
Balanga   Malalos
           Pasig
Fort Mills   Bilibid

Bantagas   Butan   Naga

Catbalogan

Tacloban

San Jose   Iloilo

Cebu

Bohol   Surigao

Iwahig

Cagayan

Malaybalay

San Ramon   Davao

Cotabato
Zamboanga

Jolo

©compass cartographic

3

Geographies of Counterinsurgency

Bilibid prison in fact could be likened to a faucet which
though used day and night was never without water.

—*Awit* (beggar's song)[1]

The Philippine Revolution began as an armed uprising against
Spanish colonial rule (1896) and continued as a protracted struggle against U.S. occupation for decades after the outbreak of the
Philippine-American War (1899). It was led by the Katipunan,
a revolutionary brotherhood and mutual aid society organized
to fight colonial control and promote *kalayaan* (liberty), a vision
of sovereignty based on an ethic of collective care. Soon after
Emilio Aguinaldo, president of the newly independent Philippine Republic, and his supporters celebrated liberation from
Spanish rule, U.S. troops occupied the Philippines. The U.S.
military waged an all-out offensive on the new nation. Two hundred thousand Filipinos were killed in the first three years of
this colonial war. Devastated by the death toll, the Katipunan
brotherhood was forced underground, where they continued to
organize for independence. After declaring an end to the war

and transfer from military to colonial rule, U.S. officials continued their counterinsurgency campaigns against uprisings that
sprang up around the archipelago but shifted from military to
police personnel.

Perpetually afraid that the rise of a "messiah" capable of
leading the Katipunan would unite ongoing popular uprisings
around the archipelago, U.S. officials used criminal transportation to separate messianic figures from their networks of belonging. Thousands suspected of belonging to the Katipunan were
arrested and jailed. Bilibid Prison, in Manila, became the hub as
colonial governors and police commissioners forcibly transported thousands of people around a vast network of jails across the
archipelago, even extending to nearby islands, like Guam. As
officials engineered the rise of a massive police and surveillance
state in the Philippines over a half century of U.S. occupation
(1898–1946), they came to rely on criminal transportation as a
practice of colonial domination.

The colonial war itself had roots in a prison. In late January
of 1899, anticolonial revolutionaries had planned a revolt inside
Bilibid Prison. Manuel Xerez Burgos, working as a physician
inside the prison, informed Philippine president Aguinaldo that
"it is absolutely necessary that an order be received here per-
mitting the uprising of those in prison before the movement is
begun anywhere else."[2] Jacinto Limjap, imprisoned for financ-
ing the revolution against the Spanish colonizers, drew up the
plan for arming prisoners with rifles taken from the U.S. Army
barracks directly across from the prison. As commander of the
"volunteers inside the penitentiary," he coordinated with Aguinaldo's general, Teodoro Sandiko, on the outside.[3] Aguinaldo

and Sandiko stationed six hundred troops, called *sandatahan*, on the outskirts of Manila in preparation. U.S. officials, who had intercepted their communications, feared a simultaneous attack from inside and outside the city before reinforcements could arrive.[4] On February 4, 1899, U.S. troops fired on a sandatahan patrol on the edge of Manila; the patrol returned fire, and the exchange marked the start of war. The ensuing U.S. attack left five hundred Filipinos dead and pushed Aguinaldo's forces out of Manila.

Fearing the Flood

The thwarted Bilibid Prison revolt became a cornerstone of U.S. justifications for war. Major John R. Taylor put the prison plot at the heart of a coordinated uprising in Manila that would have "slaughtered every American in sight," when explaining the outbreak of hostilities to the U.S. War Department back in Washington, DC. It was not difficult for Limjap to find volunteers to "rob, to burn, to rape, and to murder," Taylor claimed, because that was why they were sent to prison in the first place. He argued that as the uprising spread from Bilibid across Manila, servants would rise up and kill their masters, insurgents disguised as civilians would fall on U.S. Army barracks, and white people would be massacred in the streets. "If the plan had been carried out," Taylor reported, "no white man and no white woman would have escaped."[5] For officials like Taylor, the narrative that a dangerous prison revolt would lead to widespread anticolonial uprising figured prominently in the "prose of counterinsurgency": that is, the need to characterize insurrection as irrationally violent to justify colonial law and order.[6] The specter of prison revolt was repeatedly pointed to as the prime example of how Filipinos were treacherous, irrational, uncontrollably violent, and hence unfit for self-rule. According to this colonial logic, it was prison revolt igniting mass urban uprising that proved Filipinos were motivated only by malicious "savagery" rather than by "any fixed determination on their part to push for independence to the bitter end."[7] From the inception, as accounts like Taylor's illustrate, prison revolt lay at the core of white supremacist fantasies of race war in the Philippines.

The U.S. military, and then colonial government, developed and deployed criminal transportation and incarceration as twin counterinsurgency strategies. First they transported the most prominent leaders of the revolution beyond the archipelago altogether. During the war, the U.S. military captured scores of revolutionary leaders and nationalist political writers. Those who refused to swear a loyalty oath to the United States, such as Apolinario Mabini, Artemio Ricarte, Maximo Hizon, Pio del Pilar, and Pablo Ocampo, were exiled to the U.S.-controlled island of Guam.[8] In so doing, U.S. officials were following the precedent set by the Spanish system of deporting political prisoners to far-flung islands, such as Guam and the Mariana Islands.[9] After U.S. colonial officials exiled better-known figures, they sought to systematically reclassify significant portions of the ongoing anticolonial struggle as "bandits" rather than as members of lesser-known and long-misunderstood movements led by those who refused to assimilate into either U.S. colonial or Filipino nationalist regimes.[10] Afraid that revolts would trigger widespread uprising, U.S. officials used transportation

within the archipelago as a strategy of colonial domination. Bilibid Prison was the hub of the network of prisons U.S. colonial
officials inherited from the Spanish. Under U.S. colonial rule,
that network grew to include San Ramon Penal Farm in Mindanao, Iwahig Penal Colony on the island of Palawan, Bontoc
Prison in Mountain Province in Northern Luzon, Fort Mills
on Corregidor Island, and a host of provincial jails, temporary
facilities, and detention sites listed in colonial reports merely as
"other stations."

The U.S. counterinsurgency relied on maps and population
studies as well as on boots on the ground. Frustrated by ongoing
uprisings, military officials sought to map the unfamiliar terrain.
At first, they used existing Spanish atlases, and then they began
creating their own survey maps. Along with these maps, U.S.
colonial officials conducted a census and studied the population
by measuring prisoners inside Bilibid. Together, these tools of
governance produced a lasting set of ideas about religious, racial,
and regional difference that were mapped onto explanations of
crime over the first decade of U.S. occupation.[11] The *Census of
the Philippine Islands* presented a series of staged photographs of
people from various islands arranged along a gradient of supposed "civilization."[12]

Studying the people incarcerated inside Bilibid Prison became
central to the U.S. counterinsurgency strategy because the people there were transported from all over the archipelago. Daniel Folkmar set out to classify Bilibid prisoners in his *Album of
Philippine Types*.[13] Taking detailed measurements of the head
was part of the prevailing belief in phrenology that the outer
surface of the cranium bore signs of inner character. There was

an eerie parallel between how officials in command of the counterinsurgency campaign imagined the topography of the skull and the topography of the land, each with presumed regions of localized deviance.[14] Mapping and population studies were combined with criminal statistics to target suspected perpetrators for forced transportation.[15]

The early reports of the secretary of commerce and police reveal how this kind of thinking about subject populations and criminality informed counterinsurgency strategy. Secretary Luke E. Wright described the fear that *ladrones* and gangs of robbers would swoop down and prey on the rest of the population before taking refuge again in the "mountain fastnesses."[16] Formidable bands of "considerable magnitude" had sprung up in the provinces of Rizal, Cavite, Albay, Iloilo, Cebu, Surigao, and Misamis, according to Wright. Their leaders managed to evade capture by concealing themselves in the remote mountains.[17] Ultimately, different classifications of people—as insurgent or criminal versus civilian or subject—allowed for drastically different levels of violence to be enacted on them. As Wright put it, "The speedy killing and arrest and punishment . . . of outlaws has already produced a most beneficial effect and has borne in on the minds of those likely to depart from the path of peace in future."[18]

Being the Flood

Breaking out of prison as an act of individual liberation leading to collective salvation was a recurrent theme throughout the various waves of revolutionary activity in the Philippines.

In 1902, U.S. officials tried to propagate the fiction that war had ended by prematurely declaring a handover from military to civil government. Governor-General William Taft led the Philippine Commission in passing a series of legislation to try to render abstract sovereignty into actual jurisdiction on the ground. The sedition and bandolerismo laws (1902) provided the legal architecture for hunting down and locking up all remaining "insurgents," suddenly reclassified as outlaws and bandits rather than as anticolonial freedom fighters.[19] The years following the U.S. transfer from military to colonial government were marked by what the Philippine Constabulary referred to as the period of "papal resistance."[20] These militant religiopolitical movements were led by messianic figures, called "popes," and traced their origins to the Katipunan. According to the constabulary, grassroots resistance organizations included the Santa Iglesia, Tulisans, Dios-Dios, Colorados, Cruz-Cruz, Cazadores, Colorums, Santo Niños, Guardia de Honor, Hermanos del Tercio Orden, and Babaylane.[21]

Felipe Salvador was the leader of the Santa Iglesia. He had defeated three thousand Spanish with an army of three hundred at the Battle of San Luis in Pampanga in 1896, captured one hundred Mauser rifles from the Spanish, and led a triumphant march through Candaba after Pampanga had been liberated from the Spanish in 1898.[22] He had amassed an enormous following and was routinely tracked by U.S. intelligence forces. Ensnared by the new laws, he was captured in Nueva Ecija on charges of sedition and transported to Bilibid Prison in 1902. But when they passed Cabiao en route, he escaped. To his followers, Salvador's escape was seen as an individual act in the service of communal freedom. He had predicted it, telling his followers he went to jail voluntarily and would walk free when he chose.[23]

Salvador's escape was one among a series of prophecies featuring imprisoned leaders as harbingers of liberation that had deep roots in the original Katipunan. During the war against the Spanish, Salvador promised the return of the revolutionary hero Gabino Cortes, along with seven archangels to shield them from the bullets.[24] In preparation for war against the Spanish, anticolonial leader Andrés Bonifacio had ascended Mount Tapusi to write "long live Philippine independence" in chalk on the wall of the Cave of Bernardo Carpio. King Bernardo, "hero of the Indios," was said to be "imprisoned in the cave, awaiting the day when he would break loose and return to free his people."[25] During Salvador's escape, he too ascended a mountain top. After wandering in the nearby forests and swamps, Salvador climbed Mount Arayat and returned with a prophecy: a great flood would wash away nonbelievers and precipitate the impending battle for independence.[26]

Tulisan leader Ruperto Rios, self-proclaimed "Son of God" and "Deliverer of the Philippines," was targeted as another potential messiah. He and his followers articulated a vision of independence that was forged through their experience being surveilled, hunted, and imprisoned. While being interrogated, a wounded Tulisan prisoner told his captors there was a box inscribed with "independencia." It was in the box, he told them, but had now flown away back to the pope to be enclosed again in a new box. "The fanatic rolled his glistening eyes as he drank in the thought of the approach of the millennium," wrote Vic

Hurley, chronicler of the Philippine Constabulary. "'When independence flies from the box, there will be no labor, señor, and no jails and no taxes . . . and no more constabulario,'" explained the prisoner.[27] Here was a vision of freedom defined in opposition to imperial notions of law and order, predicated on the abolition of policing, prisons, taxation, and labor. Messianic leaders like Rios and Salvador were promising total revolution in the Philippines, social transformation rooted in a collective experience of criminalization.

The revolutionary impulse carried forward the metaphor of the flood. Two years after Salvador's escape en route to Bilibid, for example, the Philippine Commission intercepted a call to arms. Writing to Dionisio Velasquez and all members of the Santa Iglesia, estimated to be fifty thousand strong, Salvador asked them to assemble and to ready the soldiers: "'I therefore request that you do all you can in order that we may have our self-government within the month of October.'"[28] The constabulary believed he was using the old Spanish Weather Bureau's infrastructure to circulate predictions of floods and typhoons.[29] The Detective Bureau believed Manila to be continually in danger. "This city has always been the storm center of these political typhoons, and the least variance of sentiment or feeling of unrest is at once noted," wrote secret service chief C.R. Trowbridge.[30] Although Salvador's plan for an uprising did not come to pass in 1904, revolutionary forces continued to muster and would again break out in the People's Rising, in 1910. By that time, it was clear not only that Salvador's followers believed the prophecy of the great flood but also that U.S. colonial officials thought in terms of fluid dynamics about the revolutionary currents. If Manila was the storm center, as we shall see, Bilibid would again be its epicenter.

Valves of Revolutionary Pressure

U.S. officials increasingly relied on incarceration and convict transportation as the linchpins of their counterinsurgency strategy. First, they exiled political prisoners to Guam. Then, over the first decade of U.S. rule, they built a network of prisons around the archipelago and moved prisoners to different locations to separate them from regional affiliations and bases of support. Hard labor served to deplete their revolutionary energy, literally disorienting, working, and starving them to the point of total exhaustion. In moving these prisoners around, police secretary W. Cameron Forbes sought to uproot political prisoners from local ties and to design new systems of racial management.[31] Convict transportation and forced labor on public works created a spectacle of degradation that clearly stuck "criminals" at the bottom of the social hierarchy.[32]

Forbes was the force behind this expanding element of prison imperialism, using transportation and forced labor as tools of governance. Read alongside police and prison reports, Forbes's journal reveals the extent to which he saw himself as a mastermind of convict transportation in the Philippines.[33] He began by using Bilibid as a valve: redistributing revolutionary pressure around the islands by transporting prisoners to a network of far-flung jails and prison labor projects, such as Iwahig Penal Colony on Palawan Island. Officially, the colonial government started using convict transportation to relieve the overcrowding

at Bilibid, which they blamed for the unsanitary conditions and
rampant disease that periodically killed hundreds of prisoners.
But reading Forbes's journal alongside the police and prison
reports reveals how criminal transportation was developed as a
technique of colonial rule.

Police and prison officials like Forbes considered the ability
to move people around forcibly and to compel them to work
defining features of colonial control. Still, transporting prisoners to labor on public works began haltingly. When Governor
Taft and the Philippine Commission declared their intention
of making Baguio their summer capital (1901), they brought in
Major L.W.V. Kennon to take over construction, to make the
Benguet highlands "accessible to the white man."[34] He experimented with convict labor when 200 prisoners were sent from
Bilibid to Twin Peaks that year but reported less than promising
results. Disease ravaged them, many died, and others escaped
because they could not be shackled while working above the
nine-hundred-foot sheer drop, called Devil's Slide, without risk
of falling off the cliff.[35] Forbes persisted. In 1904, he sent 1,000
prisoners to General Leonard Wood to build roads in Mindanao, and another 500 to General Henry Allen in Albay to
work the Tabaco-Ligao Road.[36] Months later, Wood requested
an additional 250 prisoners to work on a railroad from Over-
ton to Marahui, in Mindanao, and 1,000 prisoners were moved
from the Tabaco-Ligao Road to Jovellar to begin work on the
Guinobatan project.[37] To these colonial officials, criminal transportation and forced labor were seen as the keys to preventing
uprisings in the prison, as well as across the archipelago. Bilibid's
first warden, George N. Wolfe, reported that a revolt of some

200 detention prisoners was caused by "lack of work."[38] When authorities captured the "inciter of a riot in Samar," Forbes suggested hard labor as the proper cure for such rebelliousness.[39]

Independencia

In the *awit*, or beggar's song, Bilibid Prison was characterized as a faucet with an unending supply of criminalized subjects flowing through it. Over the first decade of U.S. rule, it became used as a valve for distributing revolutionary pressure around the archipelago. Mass criminalization was central to the colonial logic of control, which maintained that Filipino subjects were unfit for freedom or self-rule. Through selective criminalization, U.S. officials sought to remove particular threats from their support bases, to cut off and isolate revolutionary leaders from their networks of belonging. Through convict transportation, officials exploited regional differences, rendering them into practices of race management. These transportation schemes relied on a theory of sovereignty as absolute power, not just to decide on the exception or to hold the monopoly on violence but to manage life by forcibly moving people around and compelling them to work. This vision of colonial control was most clearly evident in the administration of colonial prisons.

Felipe Salvador's prophecy of a flood leading to independence can be seen in the waves of anticolonial revolutionary movement against this version of U.S. sovereignty. First, there was the recurrent theme that imprisoned leaders—Bernardo Carpio, Andrés Bonifacio, Gabino Cortes—would return as harbingers of liberation. Next was the growing sympathy for fugitives from law-and-order "justice"—Felipe Salvador and Julian Montalan—rooted in the collective experience of criminalization under U.S. colonialism. Prison revolts were seen as triggers of widespread uprising. And the revolution—whether Salvadorist or Aglipayan—was said to wash away established hierarchies of wealth and power. These popular independence movements in the Philippines must not be subsumed into a singular elite-nationalist narrative but rather must be understood in terms of the meaning of revolution to the masses, including the vitality of the messianic and millennial visions within these movements.[40] These revolutionary movements opened a new experience of sovereignty, based in *kalayaan*, understood as "freedom from the necessity of labor and the violence of law."[41]

Prison revolt in the Philippines can be seen not only as an affront to U.S. sovereignty but as an alternative practice of freedom itself. Those alternate ideas and practices of freedom were shaped by experiences with U.S. prison imperialism. If the Philippine Revolution opened a more miraculous experience of sovereignty as the "evanescent opening of an entirely new life," prison revolt symbolized a radical break from one condition and an entrance into another state of being.[42] As symbol of anticolonial struggle, it unworked the mechanism by which freedom fighters had been transformed into "outlaws." Through revolt, the imprisoned could be turned back into anticolonial revolutionary leaders, reversing the process of criminalization.[43] Perhaps this is what the Tulisan prisoner was pointing to in his definition of *independencia* as the abolition of police, prisons, taxes, and labor.

Empires use distance to punish, and the practice has proved

more resilient than might be expected.[44] Consider Project Exile, the twenty-first-century "tough-on-crime" program, for example, designed to deter gun crime in major U.S. cities by imposing harsher mandatory minimum sentences that transport people to distant federal prisons, farther away from family, friends, and networks of support. Organizations like Families Against Mandatory Minimums have condemned Project Exile for the way it targets certain neighborhoods and disproportionately impacts communities of color. Since the Bureau of Prisons and U.S. Marshals Service have joined with Immigration and Customs Enforcement to create the Justice Prisoner and Alien Transportation System, the U.S. federal government forcibly moves over a quarter-million people each year. Now the United States not only has the highest incarceration rate, it also has the largest prisoner transportation system in the world.[45]

Gamboa Penitentiary, Panama Canal Zone

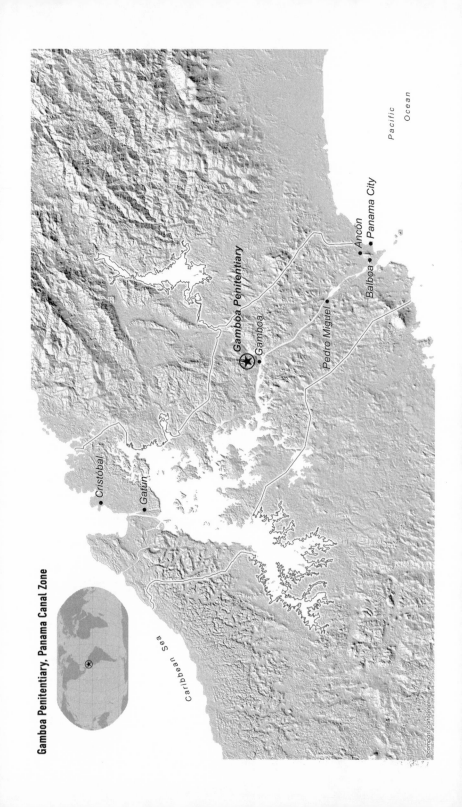

Pacific Ocean

Panama City

Ancón

Balboa

Pedro Miguel

Gamboa Penitentiary

Gamboa

Cristóbal

Gatún

Caribbean Sea

Eumaps cartographic

4

The Strange Career of the Convict Clause

*The road is a cemetery. . . . For some, it is civilization and
progress, but for me it is the grave where the ravenous hunger
of wildlife who descend from the mountains to confront modern civilization dies forever.*

—Joaquín C. Beleño[1]

Clearing, cutting, grading, leveling, draining, filling—each
stage of the roadbuilding process presented its own arduous
challenges. The work was grueling for the prisoners forced on
to the first "road gangs" of the Isthmian Canal Commission
(ICC) in the Panama Canal Zone, as they graded a sixty-foot
slope leading to a bridge they would have to build over the Mira-
flores dump. But perhaps even that gang, averaging one hundred
daily, did not envy their fellow prisoners who were sent to fill
swamps at West Culebra in the blazing mid-August sun.[2] By fall,
the prisoners had begun work on the section of road between
Empire and Paraíso, and the road gang was moved to a new convict labor camp on the side of Gold Hill. When ICC chief engineer George Goethals announced the opening of the "Highway
to Empire" in his "Notes on Progress" (1910), it had taken over
a year for prisoners to build the 18,392-foot-long, 18-foot-wide

stretch of roadway. They had excavated some 17,457 cubic yards of material for the subgrade and laid 2,563 cubic yards of gravel and another 2,860 cubic yards of stone in the process.[3]

Taking stock of the roads the U.S. government forced the Gamboa Road Gang to build in the Panama Canal Zone fifty years later, Panamanian journalist Joaquín Beleño likened them to a death-dealing graveyard. His *Gamboa Road Gang (los forzados de Gamboa)* offered an extended critique of U.S. modes of imprisonment and forced labor in the Canal Zone, echoing themes from Aimé Césaire's *Discourse on Colonialism*, published five years earlier. Born in Martinique at the apex of canal construction, Césaire described a geography of exploitation stretching from Africa to the Caribbean, where he saw the United States aggressively asserting control. He particularly warned against being duped by claims of civilization and progress. Colonists talk about "achievements," they throw "facts at my head, statistics, mileages of roads, canals, and railroad tracks," Césaire wrote emphatically. "But American racism!" He proposed looking instead at what lay behind these massive infrastructure projects, what they killed off and covered over. "I am talking about societies drained of their essence, cultures trampled underfoot, institutions undermined, lands confiscated, religions smashed, magnificent artistic creations destroyed, extraordinary *possibilities* wiped out." By the time canal construction was complete, the United States was gearing up to "raid every colony in the world," he predicted. And "American domination" is the only domination "from which one never recovers."[4]

The American-style chain gang was brought to the Panama Canal in the aftermath of racial slavery. W.E.B. Du Bois

famously condemned the convict labor system that took hold
in the U.S. South following formal emancipation there as the
"spawn of slavery."[5] That system of slavery and involuntary servitude to continue as punishment for crime was authorized by
the "convict clause" in the Thirteenth Amendment of the U.S.
Constitution. Historians of the convict leasing and chain gang
era have characterized it as "worse than slavery" and "slavery
by another name."[6] While most studies have focused on the
U.S. South, the convict clause itself applied not only within the
United States but to *any place subject to their jurisdiction*."[7] Following the Civil War, those places came to include territories
across western North America, Alaska, Hawaii, Guam, the Philippines, Puerto Rico, and the Panama Canal Zone. As the convict clause has come to symbolize systems of racial domination
within the United States over time, its imperial career reveals its
expansiveness across space.

African-descended people living and working in the Panama
Canal Zone became acutely aware of the way the penal system
was used to support the ICC's efforts to establish and maintain
racial segregation and hierarchy. Over the first decade of canal
construction, Black workers from neighboring islands of Barbados, Jamaica, and Martinique were targeted by a set of bogus
new "morality" laws banning things like swearing, cohabitation,
gambling, and other ways people had lived their lives without
causing harm—like the infamous vagrancy laws in the U.S.
South—and soon found themselves representing 80 percent
of the prison population. Like Beleño and Césaire, Caribbean
labor organizers and workers protested the anti-Black racism of
the U.S.-imposed prison system. Drawing on anticolonial and

Pan-Africanist thought and organizing, Afro-Panamanians and Caribbean migrants vigorously protested U.S. prison imperialism, constructing positive visions of Blackness as solidarity and race pride to shield themselves from white supremacist practices of racial domination in the Canal Zone. Their efforts offer insight into the U.S. carceral state's imperial dimensions and enduring lessons for movements struggling to broaden the meaning and experience of freedom in the face of slavery's recurrent afterlives.

Highway to Empire

When U.S. troops occupied the Isthmus of Panama and the Hay-Bunau-Varilla Treaty was signed (1904), President Theodore Roosevelt issued a series of executive orders to establish the legal architecture for the Canal Zone. The treaty provided the United States with "all rights, power, and authority which it would possess and exercise if it was the sovereign of the territory," and Roosevelt's orders created an outline for the criminal legal system. He gave the ICC and Canal Zone governor sweeping exclusion and deportation powers and initially chose not to extend the right to jury trial. He did choose to extend the convict clause, the Thirteenth Amendment's provision allowing for slavery and involuntary servitude to be used as punishment for crime.[8] As Canal Zone district attorney William Jackson described it, the sources of law included an eclectic mix of executive orders, congressional acts, local ordinances, criminal codes, and military doctrine, all of which were designed to ensure labor productivity.[9]

The expansion of federally funded convict roadbuilding was

worked out in explicitly racial and imperial terms. The Canal Zone's legal architecture was created with Black labor migration in mind, as well as with an eye toward those who were already there. Tens of thousands had migrated from Jamaica, Antigua, Barbados, St. Lucia, Haiti, Martinique, and elsewhere to work on the French Canal and Panama Railroad between 1850 and 1904.[10] Hundreds of thousands more migrated from the Caribbean, Latin America, Europe, Asia, and the United States during the period of U.S. canal construction. The so-called problem of freedom, or how to compel formerly enslaved people and their descendants to work certain hard-labor jobs, still dominated policy discussions in the United States and other empires.[11] In the years since the Civil War, thousands of former Confederate soldiers and other white Southerners had become managers, foremen, and overseers on plantations and infrastructure projects in the U.S. South and West and across Latin America, the Caribbean, and the Pacific Ocean.[12] In the Panama Canal Zone, white officials and engineers from the U.S. Northern states were also eager to establish a racialized division of labor. The Canal Zone's legal system was designed to maximize labor productivity and to police morality and enforce racial segregation.[13] Canal officials set up "Gold Roll" and "Silver Roll" employee designations to structure racial hierarchy in the Zone. Gold Roll employees received untaxed income, free housing, utilities, health care, schooling, sick leave, and paid vacations. Silver Roll employees, on the other hand, received no such government benefits and paid taxes that supported public services.[14] Beneath gold and silver status lay an ever-present third metallic metaphor, the convict's iron ball and chain.

The ICC convened a Special Committee on the Employment of Prisoners in the Panama Canal Zone in 1908. Proposing that convicts be forced to build roads, the committee's stated aims were threefold: to reimburse the government for the expense of maintaining its penal system, to open the fertile valleys of the Canal Zone to development, and to improve the condition of the prisoner.[15] The convict roadbuilding program began in March of 1908, when Governor Joseph Blackburn authorized the transport and housing of prisoners outside the Culebra Penitentiary.[16] As a Kentucky plantation owner and former Confederate officer in charge of an independent command in Mississippi, he was familiar with regimes of forced labor as well as with military-style work camps. On his order, Canal Zone police established a portable camp at Brazos Brook and moved half of the penitentiary population there to be near the work at all times.[17]

Reimbursing the government for the expense of maintaining the penal system was one of the three central aims of the ICC Special Committee on the Employment of Prisoners. Monthly police reports made the financial record of prisoners' labor publicly available.[18] The system of accounting for the value of prison labor used a fixed hourly wage rate and then subtracted the cost of their subsistence, clothing, and guarding. At the program's inception, the chief of police reported that the Division of Municipal Engineering credited the Department of Civil Engineering 80¢ per day for each convict employed on the roads. He was proud to report that the experiment was proving profitable: "The Department of Civil Administration finds that the revenue from its prisoners is greater than the expense of keeping them."[19] Yet that was not the total cost of maintaining the penal system;

the payroll for 150 members of the police force was still listed at ten times the value of road work performed by about the same number of prisoners.[20] One year later, the monthly value of prisoner roadwork was reported as $1,821.55, while the cost of subsistence was $857.75, clothing was another $378.80, and guard payroll was an additional $1,473.76.[21] By 1914, the value of work surpassed the cost of "prisoner maintenance."[22] The costs involved in road building, meanwhile, were reported in local newspapers in a such a way as to reinforce the idea that their work was already a naturally unpaid, and presumably unobjectionable, part of the equation. It was estimated, for example, that the Empire-Gamboa Road would cost $17,952.98, "exclusive of convict labor."[23]

Once incarcerated and designated for roadwork, Canal Zone prisoners were made to clear the ground, build portable camps, haul water, prepare food, and clean. The force "does its own cooking and takes care of the sanitation of the camp," claimed one monthly police report.[24] By making them responsible for their own social reproduction, such as it was, colonial officials and prison guards sought to turn prisoners into pure surplus. In 1913, a photographer from the Keystone View Company captured one of these "convict corrals" in the background of a stereograph postcard of a "Thatched Roof Native Home." Of course, the caption read, "This corral is a temporary structure because these convicts are transported from point to point, according to where their labor is needed."[25] Intrigued, the photographer captured the camp itself. "We have a closer view of the corral partially seen in view 21740," they wrote. "The corral is the temporary quarters for the prison convicts, who are here employed in building a macadam road." The image depicts the barbed-wire enclosure and an officer "brandishing a revolver," described as "necessary assistants in such camps," as well as the prisoners' mess table shown in the foreground.[26]

The stereograph's caption explained how "the roads are being built by the United States Government and the convicts here located are prisoners sentenced for misdemeanors done in the Canal Zone."[27] Perhaps in an attempt to portray the prison system as racially unbiased, the Keystone View Company's writer added, "Naturally these prisoners are of all races and colors." But in fact, the prison population and road gangs they were looking at were disproportionately Black.[28] "In the Canal Zone is to be found, doubtless, the only place where the National Government uses convicts for road construction," they noted, while in some Southern states, "convict labor is the usual one employed in building roads." The practice had not yet been taken up in the nation's federal penitentiaries. Postcards like these, together with photographs in news reports and exhibitions like the 1915 World's Fair, were instrumental in constructing the visual representation of the Canal Zone's prison labor program to the U.S. public.

Another goal of the Special Committee on the Employment of Prisoners was to open the fertile valleys to cultivation and development, by which they meant to white settlement. When Governor Blackburn first authorized the prison road gangs, ICC officials explained it this way: "The intention is to locate these roads away from the railroad so as to develop the agricultural resources of the country to as great an extent as possible."[29] The roads were designed to facilitate settlement and plantation-style agriculture both within the Zone and in the neighboring Republic of Panama. Zone administrators pressured their government counterparts in Panama, urging them also to employ convicts to build connector roads outside the Zone. As civil engineer J.G. Holcombe told the *Daily Star and Herald*, he intended to get to work at building roads throughout Panama and would use prison laborers wherever possible so they would cost a minimum outlay.[30] The *Daily Star and Herald* reported that a highway would be built from the town of Empire, in the Canal Zone, through to La Chorrera, in the Republic of Panama: "From Empire to Arraijan the trail traverses one of the best agricultural sections of the Zone and a large amount of fruit and produce is brought over it by pack horse and marketed in Empire." It was nine more miles, however, from the edge of the Zone boundary to the "native village" of La Chorrera, a town of about 3,500 people, with "many farms of considerable extent" growing corn and other produce and raising cattle. The government of Panama has given assurance, a reporter told readers, that it will continue the highway built to the Zone line into La Chorrera, "thereby making the entire section of country accessible to Empire."[31]

Expanded Deportation Powers

The Canal Zone prison roadbuilding scheme cut through an ongoing debate over labor migration, settlement, and depopulation in the Canal Zone. Those who favored settler colonialism in the Zone advocated roads be built to connect agricultural plantations to markets. As Canal Zone governor George Goethals told it a few years later, the group in favor of establishing a white settler colony asserted "that Americans should be permitted to take up land, provision being made for homesteading it as an inducement . . . the assumption being that they would have farms or plantations worked by West Indian negroes; the general idea amounted to opening up the land to 'gentlemen farmers.'"[32] Goethals himself, however, opposed settlement in favor of depopulation after work on the canal was complete: "I did not care to see a population of Panamanian or West Indian negroes occupying the land, for these are non-productive, thriftless, and indolent." According to his racial nightmare, they would not only act as unproductive squatters but also drain government resources by congregating in small settlements and costing the government money for sanitation and police.[33] As his theory about the increased cost of policing suggests, he speculatively criminalized those he lumped into the category of unwanted surplus once their labor was no longer needed on the canal.[34] The irony was that throughout the canal construction period, only Black Silver Roll employees paid income tax that supported such public services, while white Gold Roll employees paid no income tax and received a range of free and subsidized government benefits.

Police and prison officials routinely deported people from the Canal Zone throughout the period of canal construction (1904–14). When George Shanton was appointed police chief, he saw deportation as his first order of business. He had gathered veterans of Theodore Roosevelt's Rough Riders and other "American gunmen" to round up any "bad men" in the newly occupied territory, even before he was expressly granted expanded deportation powers.[35] "We went after them and some we found necessary to kill off but the great majority were gradually rounded up and placed in the stocks, later being put into bull-pens which we constructed," he told the *Boston Globe* years later. "The next thing to do was to get them out of the country altogether, but we were in a position where we could not legally deport them. So we rounded up some old three masters [. . .] and, bundling the birds all aboard, shot them off to the Islands thereabout." His nonchalance masked a more systematic process of targeted depopulation that combined Spanish-speaking Afro-Panamanians, French-speaking Martinicans, and English-speaking Jamaicans and Barbadians under the general category of "negro criminal," who were then indiscriminately sent off to neighboring Caribbean islands. "With them out of the Zone," Shanton wrote, "we were then in a position of refusing them entrance should they attempt to return."[36]

Many Canal Zone officials believed Black workers to be indebted because they had covered some of the costs of labor migration. Canal Zone district attorney Jackson, for instance, argued that the "great expense" the government had incurred by paying to transport some twenty thousand workers from Barbados "abundantly justified" expanded powers of deportation and judicial cost savings measures.[37] The Canal Zone government paid the cost of deportation, he added, and recouped the "enormous expense incident to jury trials."[38] As with other labor recruitment contracts, some officials worried they were skirting a line too near slavery and involuntary servitude. Responding to John Steven's request to import more Chinese laborers, for instance, secretary of war William Taft wrote, "Peonage or coolieism, which shortly stated is slavery by debt, is as much in conflict with the Thirteenth Amendment of the Constitution as the usual form of slavery."[39] Despite apparent ambiguities in charting these degrees of unfreedom, Canal Zone officials knew for certain that the Thirteenth Amendment's convict clause provided that those convicted of crime could become slaves of the state. Evidently paying the passage of a small fraction of the total Canal Zone workforce had metaphorically, if not contractually, already indentured much wider segments of the population in the eyes of certain administrators.

Allegations of Black people's supposed indebtedness began well before they were actively criminalized by the police and in the legal system, or even arrived in the Canal Zone. For many former slave owners and their offspring, the debt Black people owed white society stemmed from the "crime" of freeing themselves through the greatest general strike turned slave revolt in modern history during the Civil War.[40] Former slaveholders jealously recounted the £20 million the British government had paid their counterparts for the loss of wealth in the form of enslaved humanity in the Caribbean colonies of Jamaica and Barbados. It was no secret that the legal system in the American South was being used to try to extract value from the formerly enslaved. In a sentiment echoed by Black-owned newspapers across the South, the attempt to revive slavery using local jails was nothing more than "a shrewd device of the ex-slaveholders to get compensation for the loss of their slaves."[41]

With expanded imprisonment and deportation powers, federal officials pushed the logic of disposability, already present in the domestic prison system, to new extremes. In a declassified record from the ICC's Executive Office at the end of canal construction, officials noted that in addition to those they had deported and those they had "removed in the course of depopulation," the ICC planned to begin transporting people who were now out of work "as a police measure."[42] Their justification for mass deportations revealed the logic at work in speculatively criminalizing unemployment and poverty. "Any increase in crime always occurs where conditions cause a large number of men to be without employment," wrote Police Chief Mitchell, expressing what seemed like a timeless, race-neutral truism. Yet he and Mr. Copeland knew exactly what group they were targeting: "Nearly all police cases in Panama for wounding, sneak thieving, robbery and fraud," he speculated, "are those of Jamaicans who are out of work on account of termination of canal work."[43] They were also clearly ambivalent about those they deemed surplus, whose lives they evidently did not consider very valuable. While Mitchell proposed removing all "unemployed aliens" from the isthmus if the U.S. government "had to take care of them," for example, he added that they actually might need all available labor, adding that *such labor could be forced.*"[44]

Imperial Practices and Personnel

The police and prison guards charged with implementing the forced labor program brought their own ideas about punishment and work. Racialized labor control schemes had been vitally important to their jobs throughout American empire. Zone policemen like Harry Franck and Robert Lamastus remarked that their fellow officers were mostly Southerners and almost

all were military men.[45] Police Chief Shanton, for instance, had
served in the Rough Riders during U.S. wars in Puerto Rico and
the Philippines. His successor had been a Confederate blockade
runner, and the police chief after him was a former U.S. marshal in Indian Territory.[46] Their lived experience with colonial
violence shaped how they thought about mastery, adventure,
and the course of their own lives. Colonial officials, meanwhile,
used expanded legal power and discourses about racially differentiated labor capacity and fitness for freedom to design and
justify new convict labor regimes. In places like the Canal Zone,
the federal government took an active role in promoting white
uplift through Black immiseration by promising to turn convicts' alleged debt to society into a "public good," literally paving
the way for capitalist development, tourism, and other forms of
profit and pleasure seeking.

Lamastus, who was put in charge of working prisoners outside
the penitentiary, exemplified many of the experiences guards
brought to the road gangs. With his family back in Kentucky
heavily indebted after the Civil War, he had gone fortune seeking in the far reaches of the Northwest, joining the army in
Alaska. He dreamed of striking it rich prospecting for gold or
purchasing land to clear and cultivate. Yet his letters home made
clear that he envisioned himself directing rather than perform-
ing hard physical labor. Referring to farm work, for example,
he exclaimed that there were "plenty of easier ways of making
a living besides working like a slave for it."[47] Lamastus joined
the police force in 1907 and was rapidly promoted. Within two
years he was making $107.50 per month, five times what he
earned when he first enlisted in the army, and the following

year he received an additional $10 a month to serve as labor foreman over prisoners at Culebra. "We are building roads with them," he wrote home. "I start work at 7 in the morning and I am through 5:30 in the evening."[48] After successfully completing his roadbuilding assignments in the town of Empire, he was made assistant deputy warden in charge of all outside work. "I was promoted on the 19th of Dec. my pay is $125 per mo," he proudly wrote home.[49] In addition to their salary, white police and prison officers like Lamastus, as Gold Roll employees, received the full range of government benefits, including paid housing, health care, and vacations. The racially segregated social and economic hierarchies he and his colleagues helped establish in the Canal Zone, therefore, ensured that white American men, as a group, would stand to gain the most from the incarceration and forced labor of Zone inhabitants. Their vision of white settler colonial agricultural development depended on roads being built throughout the Zone and across Panama. It provided prison administrators and guards a unique avenue of upward social mobility. After a career commanding prison labor in the Canal Zone and directing the Panamanian prison colony on Coiba Island, for example, Lamastus went on to set up coffee plantations in Boquete, Chiriquí, that have remained in his family to this day.

Pan-American Highway

The Canal Zone convict roadbuilding program created the cornerstone from which Good Roads Movement boosters pushed for the Pan-American Highway stretching from Alaska to

Argentina. The Pan-American Highway was shrouded in the rhetoric of hemispheric harmony, and the Good Roads Movement as encapsulating "the very essence of true Pan-Americanism."[50] Movement champions within the United States lobbied for massively increased federal support for public transportation infrastructure and extolled the benefits of using convict labor. Proclaiming that "the convict on the road is a slave of the state," they joined prison reformers in calling for an end to the privately controlled convict lease system.[51] Public control of convict labor became a convenient way to appease urban progressives and agrarian populists by aligning the interests of cities, towns, and rural areas. The demise of the private convict lease system and the rise of public road gangs in places like Georgia was used to redistribute the spoils of Black convict labor more widely beyond the wealthy few who controlled monopolies on the lease.[52]

This sea change in the use of convict labor took place throughout American empire over the first two decades of the twentieth century. The convict roadbuilding scheme in Panama began the same time that chain gangs were deployed on public roads in Southern states like Georgia, western territories like New Mexico, and island colonies like Puerto Rico and the Philippines. Imperial personnel and practices moved between these sites, as military men became police and prison guards. As a group, they brought personal experiences of slavery and the Civil War and colonial expeditions from Indian Country to places like Alaska, Cuba, Puerto Rico, the Philippines, and Panama.

The foothold created by these roads built by people imprisoned in the Canal Zone enabled colonial officials, army engineers, and politicians in the United States to train their sights on a Pan-American Highway. Convict roadbuilding in Panama became part of the massively increased federal support for convict roadbuilding projects across states, territories, and colonies under U.S. jurisdiction. Federal officials, meanwhile, pushed their modernizing agenda for prisons and roads at the convenings of international organizations like the Pan-American Union (PAU) and the Pan-American Prison Congress. E.W. James, chief of the Inter-American Regional Office of the Public Roads Administration, promised the highway would open up great tracts of land and offer U.S. motorists scenes of "exotic interest," discovery, and adventure.[53] Probably "no white man" has ever traveled between Central and South America overland, he wrote, referring to the Darién Gap between Panama and Colombia.[54] He provided a list of voyages along portions of the highway, including that of *Zone Policeman 88* by Harry A. Franck.[55] At the Panama-Pacific International Exposition, the 1915 world's fair held in San Francisco, the U.S. Office of Public Roads staged the most comprehensive road exhibit to date.[56] By the end of World War II, the Inter-American portion between the United States and Panama included 1,557 miles of paved roadway, 930 miles of all-weather road, 280 miles of dry-weather road, and 567 miles of trails. "The last quarter century in the Western Hemisphere has been preeminently an era of road building," James proudly concluded.[57]

In the United States, local officials looked to the example the federal government set overseas as more federal funding became available in the form road subsidies and police, jail, and prison funding. When the Commercial Club of Mobile, Alabama, wrote to ask Panama Canal warden and police chief

Shanton about the convict roadbuilding program, for instance, Shanton proudly informed them it was the "most practicable and humane" method of handling prison labor.[58] Reporters and globe-trotting penologists remarked on the growing U.S. role in promoting this new era of "progressive" penology compared with other preeminent empires. Missouri journalist Samuel Fox even advocated that the federal government import convicts from the United States for canal construction in Panama. Apparently, the U.S. Department of Labor and Commerce found the proposal convincing enough to instruct Fox to forward it to the ICC for consideration.[59]

The expansion of federally funded convict roadbuilding was worked out in explicitly racial and imperial terms. As Blake McKelvey put it, prison expansion in the "Great West" was essential to the "institutional conquest of the last frontier."[60] Up to that point, the federal government had "scarcely shown sturdy leadership in territorial penology," he wrote. "The same government that was so soon to take up proudly the 'White Man's Burden' across the seas, and there, incidentally, to learn some progressive penology."[61] According to McKelvey, the Good Roads Movement had found the perfect solution: it drew on funds from the East, the demise of the private convict lease system in the South, and experiments with convict labor on public roads in the Western territories.[62] McKelvey tried to distinguish convict roadbuilding from older modes of racial domination, as to him "penal slavery" stopped at the "borders of the black race" in the South.[63] Road camps, as Colorado warden Thomas Tynan put it, were not to be confused with Southern contract camps, "where men are sold at auction to the highest bidder."[64] Yet, despite these statements to the contrary, the chattel principle embedded in the convict clause ensured that "slaves of the state" would continue to be imagined as Black well beyond the U.S. South.

Protesting Prison Imperialism

A collective experience of unjust, racially targeted persecution by police, judges, and prison guards was instrumental to the politicization of the labor movement, culminating in a massive Silver Worker strike of some twelve thousand to sixteen thousand people (1920).[65] Barbadian William Stoute and Afro-Panamanian Eduardo Morales emerged as local labor leaders because of their ability to articulate a positive program of "Race Success," a claim to Black solidarity forged in opposition to the structural racism of the U.S. policies of penal servitude and unequal exposure to danger and death.[66] Both of them were members of Marcus Garvey's Universal Negro Improvement Association (UNIA), which had chapters in Panama City and throughout the Caribbean. During the strike, Stoute wrote to Garvey and thanked him for his leadership in opposing the "unspeakable oppression of our race by the whites."[67]

Garveyism had deep roots in Panama, and Garveyite organizers were intimately familiar with how the U.S. and British states used surveillance, espionage, jailing, and deportation to try to control Black labor and suppress protest movements. Amy Ashwood's parents had left Panama and returned to Jamaica because of the substandard education she was receiving there ten years before she co-founded the UNIA with Garvey (1914).[68] Having lived in Panama himself, Garvey summed up the conditions he saw in the Zone: they were dominated by prejudice, discrimination, and oppression of Black people by the white race. "Most of the American foremen, superintendents, and officials were rabid Negro-hating Southerners," he wrote, who were busy segregating employment and "Jim-crowing" on work trains and public institutions.[69] The arrival of UNIA's international organizer Henrietta Vinton Davis aboard the Black Star Line's SS *Frederick Douglass* likely provided a triumphant counterpoint to the specter of the British convict ship *Success*, which was paraded through the canal by white officials en route to the Panama-Pacific International Exhibition (1915).[70]

The road gang serves as the main motif of Joaquín Beleño's novel *Gamboa Road Gang (los forzados de Gamboa)*. Beleño based his protagonist Atá on the actual case of Lester Greaves, who became a "symbol of apartheid justice" in the Zone.[71] Greaves was sentenced to fifty years at hard labor on the road gang after he was arrested and charged with the rape of a white woman, who he maintained was his lover. Beleño ends his narrative with a powerful scene of Atá, after suffering a kind of nervous breakdown from being forced to work on the roads, walking off in protest. "*Son of a bitch. HALT!*' yelled the gringos as they raised their rifles, aiming," writes Beleño. "Still, Atá is slowly heading down the Golden Highway. . . . No one can stop him. Nothing can stop him. The rifles are still fixed upon him. *'HITT . . . !!!'* came the voice of the guard again," Beleño continues. "The guards fire three shots, mount new rifles and open fire again. Atá's legs tremble, he shakes all over. The blood saturates his shirt, but still he does not fall to the ground." Finally, "he stumbles, stretches out his arms and staggers slowly down the road, dying."[72] Beleño writes, "So long Atá! At last you are free! You are safe!"[73] This final protest feels like a gesture toward what one contemporary Black political theorist calls "planetary violence." Invoking the term *poblacion chatarra* (disposable people) from Latin American social movements, theorist Ronald Judy applies it to conditions of violence that tend toward annihilation rather than redress.[74] That is to say, forms of violence that are produced by conditions of utter disposability.

"The road is a cemetery," Beleño concluded. "For some, it is civilization and progress, but for me it is the grave," he wrote, that swallows all natural life who dare confront it.[75] In juxtaposing claims of civilization and progress with the violent reality of colonial domination, he amplified a central theme of Césaire's *Discourse on Colonialism*. As with Beleño's critique of convict roadbuilding as a symbol of civilization, Césaire's indictment of colonialism centered state violence. Colonists kill, torture, and imprison, Césaire wrote. From the vantage of the colonized, there exists only "relations of domination" that turn the colonizer into "an army sergeant, a prison guard, a slave driver."[76] Césaire's theory of the boomerang effect of colonialism was also about policing and prisons. Colonization works to decivilize and brutalize the colonizer by stoking violence, race hatred, and moral relativism: "The gestapos are busy, the prisons fill up, and the torturers standing around the racks invent, refine, discuss."[77] In the flight of the boomerang, by treating the colonized like a beast, the colonizers themselves become the animal. The civilization that justifies colonialism is morally diseased,

Césaire proclaimed, and will progress, one denial after another, to fascism. This is what he meant when he wrote that a society that chooses to close its eyes to the most crucial problems of the day is a sick one. And a society who plays fast and loose with its principles is a dying one. For Stoute, Beleño, and others, what Césaire said of colonialism in general could likewise be said of U.S. prison imperialism in particular.

Sovereignty and Servitude

In the Panama Canal Zone, as in the U.S. South, officials used highly visible and degrading forms of hard physical toil to try to fortify the equation of Blackness and criminality.[78] U.S. officials used the criminal legal system not only to extract value through regimes of forced labor but to produce and structure racial hierarchy in the Zone. Through a process of targeted criminalization, the Canal Zone prison roadbuilding program turned a supposed "debt to society" to a "public good," even a "surplus." The costs and benefits were neatly tabulated and celebrated as economic progress. There was profound violence in transfiguring alleged Black indebtedness into whites-only welfare benefits through legalized racial domination.[79] That violence helped establish racial hierarchy, along with white supremacist claims to sovereignty. Prison imperialism was not just an economic response to the demand for unfree labor driven by an invisible and almighty profit motive, it was a means by which to transport U.S.-style structural racism around the globe.[80]

The story of convict roadbuilding in the Panama Canal Zone over the first half of the twentieth century is just one chapter in the imperial career of the convict clause. The convict clause may now actually be the longest-lasting and farthest-reaching aspect of federal penal policy, stretching back before the Constitution and up through the present. The constitutional provision for slavery and involuntary servitude as punishment for crime predates the Constitution itself. It originated with the Northwest Ordinance (1787), which outlawed slavery and involuntary servitude, "except as punishment for crime," in lands claimed northwest of the Ohio River. It also provided that any "fugitive" from slavery could be "lawfully reclaimed and conveyed" to their enslaver, which, together with the Fugitive Slave Act, bound federal police power to uphold racial slavery not only in the U.S. South but throughout the American empire. When the Thirteenth Amendment to the Constitution was drafted (1865), the convict clause ensured that slavery and involuntary servitude would continue as punishment for crime not only within the United States but also in *any place subject to their jurisdiction.* Following the Civil War, the infamous images of Black chain gangs in the U.S. South can likewise be found in places like Panama, Puerto Rico, and the Philippines. The Black road gang in the New South appears little different from the Gamboa road gang in the Canal Zone during the same period. Prison labor at Parchman Farm in Mississippi was similar to plantation labor at the Iwahig Penal Colony in the Philippines. As the convict clause perpetuated slavery and involuntary servitude forward in time, it simultaneously projected it outward across space.

The federal government used "slaves of the state" to build infrastructure, establish racial hierarchy, and consolidate power within *and beyond* U.S. borders. If the rise of the carceral state is considered a continuation of slavery and the Jim Crow racial caste system, it has also always been a strategy of empire building. The chain gang was, and is, an imperial institution, long used to produce and maintain racial hierarchy overseas, as at home, to "govern difference, differently."[81] This history suggests that anti-imperial along with antiracist movement-building strategies are necessary to reckon with the living legacies and ongoing forms of racial domination in the modern-day prison system. Ultimately, a more complex framework for understanding the roots of anti-Black carceral violence within and beyond borders might open a wider range of alternate solutions. This could begin, returning to Beleño's epigraph, with the choice of how to see the highway itself: as a symbol of civilization and progress or as a death-dealing graveyard.

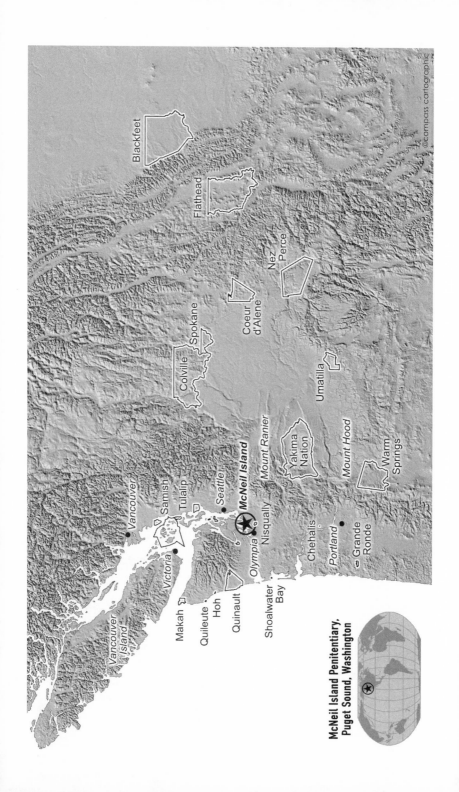

**McNeil Island Penitentiary,
Puget Sound, Washington**

5

The Prison Without Walls

The federal government had scarcely shown sturdy leadership in territorial penology—the same government that was so soon to take up the "White Man's Burden" across the seas, and there, incidentally to learn some progressive penology.
—Blake McKelvey (1933)[1]

The most remarkable prison in the world. The "prison of tomorrow," it was called. Acclaimed by globe-trotting criminologists for its progressive penology, the "prison without walls" held a tantalizing promise. In contrast to walled institutions that relied on physical punishment and control, this prison purported to use a set of incentives, stages of confinement, and an invisible supervision system to maintain order. By the 1920s, two federal institutions claimed this mantle: McNeil Island Federal Penitentiary in the Puget Sound, off the coast of Washington State, and the Iwahig Penal Farm, a U.S.-run penal colony on the island of Palawan, in the Philippines. As model institutions, they were designed for immigrants and colonial subjects deemed deviant or otherwise unfit for freedom.

Progressive Era penologists found the fullest expression of

their desire for control through hard work and stages of supervision in the prison without walls. These world-traveling experts looked to prisons in American empire as the leading edge of penology. By the 1930s, they held up the Iwahig Penal Colony as the poster child prison without walls. "The most remarkable prison in the world," they called it at the meetings of the American Prison Association at McNeil Island (1927) and of the International Prison Commission in Prague (1930). At Iwahig, prisoners could progress from the Barrack Zone to the Home Zone to the Free Zone, based on compliance and "good behavior." At McNeil, also designated a wall-less island prison, they might earn the privilege of working the Honor Farm.

Over the years, McNeil and Iwahig locked away some of the strongest challengers to empire, from those who fought to defend their lands from white settler attacks and encroachment, to those who crisscrossed changing territorial, state, and international boundaries, to those who protested racism, economic exploitation, and war making. Among them were members of the Colville Confederated Tribes, Chinese and Japanese migrants, Mexican anarchists and revolutionaries, Filipino anticolonial fighters, and white conscientious objectors and labor organizers. Some drew on organizing traditions like emancipatory internationalism to make common cause with anticolonial movements throughout the Global South; others used Marxism to confront capitalism and imperialism; while others invented new intersectional forms of solidarity.[2] Ultimately, their interwoven critiques of imprisonment and imperialism reveal the more hidden contours of America's carceral empire building during this period.

"Crimmigration" at McNeil

Abraham Gervais, labeled a "half-breed" in the prison log, stepped, or perhaps was dragged, into the cell house on McNeil Island when it was first completed in 1875. He had been transported there by boat, as the territorial prison sat on a small island in the Puget Sound, across the water from Fort Steilacoom. The cell house was situated directly on top of an old homestead that had been donated to the federal government by a white settler turned prison guard in 1870. Together with other so-called half-breeds and squaw men whom U.S. marshal Edward Kearney imprisoned there, Gervais was convicted of selling liquor to Indians.[3] Indian Prohibition Laws had given U.S. marshals license to patrol newly established Indian reservations in the Pacific Northwest, like nearby Colville, as they sought to regulate the boundaries of racial belonging around the perimeter.[4] The U.S. military was waging an ongoing series of genocidal Indian Wars in the Pacific Northwest, and marshals and Indian agents were increasingly making their police presence felt. These two processes overlapped. As an imperial outpost, McNeil was used to regulate and accelerate the process of American empire building. Federal agents policed all sorts of things that crossed borders, be they people, goods, or ideas. The prison acted as both container and valve—used to eliminate perceived threats and to dispense with surplus laborers or those periodically deemed unwanted. Referred to as America's most heterogeneous prison, it would come to incarcerate people from just about every race and nation under the sun.

In the depression that followed the economic crises of the

1870s, white vigilantes went on an "expulsion" rampage in the Pacific Northwest, massacring people at Rock Springs, murdering more in Squak Valley, and burning homes and businesses. In eighteen months of "pure hell," anti-Chinese racial violence spread like arsonists' fire up and down the Pacific coast. White mobs rioted in the streets of Seattle and protested when their ringleaders were detained at McNeil. The vigilantes declared victory, proclaiming that the federal government had endorsed their "Tacoma Method" of burning down Chinatowns because it had authorized the deportation of Chinese migrants under the Exclusion Act (1882). What they sought to do was to collapse the distinction between lawful and unlawful immigration and between vigilante expulsion and federal deportation.[5]

Beginning in the 1880s, U.S. marshals imprisoned thousands of immigrants on McNeil Island on charges of being in the country unlawfully. Once there, Chinese prisoners were crammed into congregate cells, attacked by racist white prisoners, and made to do hard labor while awaiting deportation. The prison's daily log reveals how Chinese prisoners were systematically assigned more feminized or degrading tasks, made to scrub the guardhouse, cook, wash, and clean.[6] Guards used labor, food, and sleep deprivation as forms of torture, alongside the dreaded "dark cell." One wrote, "Chinamen all crying" after being confined in their cells all day on "bread and water" for making complaints about the food.[7] For some, like On Gee, it was too much. In the middle of winter, he hurled himself off the wharf and into the freezing cold water. Guards immediately pulled the "crazy Chinaman" into a patrol boat. Later that year he fell ill, "lying in a stupor . . . evidently insane." A year later, he made his escape: let out after supper to clear the empty dishes, telling the guards he was going to gather some herbs in the yard, he disappeared.[8]

McNeil Island was the early epicenter of what has come to be known as the rise of "crimmigration," the toxic melding of criminal and immigration law enforcement that now systematically disappears half a million migrants from society each year.[9] Over the first sixty years, between 1880 and 1940, more than 20 percent of "foreign born" people were imprisoned on McNeil Island for immigration offenses.[10] At first, it was not at all clear that immigration violations, like entering the country without authorization or being in the country unlawfully, were imprisonable offenses. But in *Wong Wing v. United States* (1896), the Supreme Court argued that immigrant "detention" without due process was not "imprisonment in the legal sense," thereby providing the legal grounds for caging people charged with immigration offenses.[11]

Violence directed at immigrants was the match that sparked the modern era of "crimmigration" and the solder that has glued it together. Exclusion and imperialism went hand in hand. The plenary power doctrine evoked in the Exclusion Act was used to strip power from Native Americans, curtail the rights of Chinese people, and deny constitutional guarantees to U.S. nationals in places like Puerto Rico. As such, it erected barriers against "outsiders" within U.S. territory, whether they be "alien, native, or colonial."[12] By drawing strict racial boundaries around citizenship domestically, the plenary power doctrine lessened the racial anxiety of those who worried expansionism would contaminate the purity of the white American racial stock that had temporarily helped hold overseas imperialism at bay. After 1898, as the U.S. military expanded into Puerto Rico, Cuba, Hawaii, Guam, and the Philippines, all of which had sizeable Chinese communities, they carried these exclusionary policies and practices with them.[13]

McNeil Island Federal Penitentiary was used to contain perceived threats to U.S. empire building, especially those that crossed borders. During the Mexican Revolution, Partido Liberal Mexicano (PLM) leaders and anarcho-socialists, like brothers Enrique and Ricardo Flores Magón, routinely crossed the Rio Grande in their extended campaigns against Porfirio Díaz's dictatorship. The magonista movement was "a rebellion born of U.S. imperialism," historian Kelly Lytle Hernández explains, and incarceration was increasingly used in counterinsurgency on both sides of the border.[14] An old photo in the anarchist newspaper *Regeneración* depicts Ricardo Flores Magón, Enrique Flores Magón, Anselmo Figueroa, and Librado Rivera as "*la junta para McNeil Island.*"[15] The junta were PLM leaders fighting against the Díaz dictatorship during the Mexican Revolution. Indeed, Díaz had agents like Enrique Creel tracking Ricardo Flores Magón all over the United States and Canada. Yet, when Ricardo Flores Magón was imprisoned at the Los Angeles County Jail, he spoke through the bars to his supporters on the outside. Still, repeated imprisonments worked to eliminate Ricardo Flores Magón from the post-1910 rise of the Mexican Revolution, after the ousting of Díaz. Only Emiliano Zapata "carried the flag of Land and Liberty into battle," writes Hernández, while Magón remained in Los Angeles. After the outbreak of the first world war, during the so-called Red Scare, the United States aggressively criminalized dissent and targeted labor militancy. Officials arrested Ricardo Flores Magón on charges of sedition for his antiwar writing and sentenced him to twenty-two years at Leavenworth. He died in his cell in November 1922, of a lung condition, according to Leavenworth officials; yet his cell neighbor maintained they were covering up his murder.[16]

Federal prisons became a "convergence space," of radical internationalist traditions, a microcosm of antiracist, anti-capitalist, and anti-imperialist struggles during this time.[17] Magón believed the Mexican Revolution could inspire "new global visions of liberation across the color line. [. . .] If the color line could penetrate prison walls, a movement confronting it would need to do the same."[18] Indeed, it was a moment of solidarity building in opposition to the forces of racism and militarism, as many working-class Black people supported the impulse of the Mexican Revolution, and Black IWW labor organizers, like longshoreman Ben Fletcher, were heavily surveilled by the FBI for signs of "negro agitation."[19] Fifty-two imprisoned Wobblies at Leavenworth wrote an open letter to President Warren Harding likening themselves to Mexicans, always portrayed as villains in the movies, and insisting on collective rather than individual clemency.[20]

Uncle Sam's Devil's Islands

"It seems like a terrible nightmare," Nesta Wells wrote to her friend after returning from McNeil Island, where she had been prevented from visiting her husband, Hulet, and delivering food she had made. "He has spent twelve days in that terrible place," she continued, referring to the "black hole" isolation dungeon where he was confined on bread and water. Being suspended in chains by the wrists, manacled to the wall, was standard punishment for refusing to work, a painful and physically exhausting form of forced immobility. The warden told her he would not release Hulet until he agreed to go back to his work assignment cutting wood. Like so many women in the antiwar and labor movements, Nesta knew how to sustain a movement, both through the unpaid work of social reproduction like preparing meals and through broad-based protest strategy. She wrote letters to sympathizers all across the country, instructing them to lobby their congressmen and President Woodrow Wilson and to push for the humane treatment and release of political prisoners, people like her husband, convicted under the Espionage Act. Hulet Wells had been convicted of conspiracy to obstruct the Selective Service Act, for printing twenty thousand "No Conscription League" circulars, essentially of sedition for opposing the draft.[21]

As a union organizer, Wells knew the importance of his individual work stoppage, a prison labor strike, and collective action. Fortunately for him, he had the backing of Seattle's labor movement. As they rallied and protested in the city streets, Seattle Labor Council secretary James Duncan took the matter to federal court, forcing the judge to grant a medical inquiry. Clearly sympathetic to the cause, Dr. Lane's report concluded that Wells had been "assigned tasks beyond his endurance" and had been tortured for his refusal to do them. "Frail Man Brutalized," the national news story declared, emphasizing Wells's slight stature. Indeed, according to his prison intake record, the forty-one-year-old postal worker stood 5 feet 7 inches, weighed 138 pounds, and had brown hair, gray eyes, and "medium" complexion.[22] One can only imagine how much weight he lost after two weeks on only fourteen ounces of bread and water per day. "If they will do this to Hulet, to what lengths will they not go in punishing men who have no friends on the outside!"[23]

The collective action and political pressure proved successful. The national scandal got the warden fired and Wells released early, in 1920. Appealing to President Hoover to remove his status as a convicted felon, Wells situated himself in firm solidarity with other people imprisoned for opposing the war. The wrongs wreaked by a "war-crazed majority" were inflicted "on us *as a group*," he wrote. "The reparation," therefore, "should be made to the group."[24] Other members of the group he envisioned included fellow Wobblies, conscientious objectors, and members of the Socialist and Communist Party of America. The red-baiting of the so-called Red Scare whipped up a toxic mix of militarism, white nationalism, and xenophobia that stigmatized antiwar protesters as criminal subversives. The category of "criminal," and "alien" if they were foreign born, was racialized, even for white labor organizers.

As Philip Grosser explained in *Uncle Sam's Devil's Island: Experiences of a Conscientious Objector in America During the First World War* (1933), his account of being imprisoned in Alcatraz Federal Prison, guards told them they were not white men anymore but "yellow men," and they would treat them as such when they broke the rules.[25] The guards said they could not understand them, and thus chose a slur to liken them to an "inscrutable oriental," and a "yellow-bellied coward." Grosser also refused to work and was likewise thrown in "the hole." It was dark, damp, and rat infested. After they were no longer allowed to hang prisoners by their wrists, the guards built iron "coffin cages," twenty-three inches wide by twelve inches deep, and alternated between standing the conscious objectors up in these iron maidens and confining them alone in the hole. Grosser endured it for two months and then, realizing that his "brain and body could stand no more," gave in and was released from the torture cage and made to work breaking rocks.

Wells's complexion—his skin privilege—did matter, however. Black, brown, and Asian anti-imperialists were not able to evoke similar sympathies, get wardens fired, or be pardoned by the president. Despite the national torture scandal, by the end of the decade, America's Devil's Island in the Puget Sound, the famous prison without walls, was still said to be one of the world's finest penal institutions, among the most "successful and far-reaching experiments ever known."[26] Indeed, in printing the first official history of McNeil, *The Prison Without Walls,* the Justice Department intended to present it as a model prison to a global audience, providing the McNeil Island *Lantern Press* funds to distribute it, free of charge, around the world. They boasted of reaching readers in Australia, Africa, China, Indian, and every European country.[27] Yet to some of the globe-trotting penologists who gathered at the convenings of the American Prison Association and International Penal and Penitentiary Congresses, it was only in taking up the "white man's burden" that the federal government learned some "progressive penology," pointing across the Pacific to another wall-less prison, the Iwahig Penal Colony in the Philippines.[28]

Iwahig Penal Colony

U.S. government officials in the Philippines began sending prisoners from Bilibid Prison, in Manila, to the Iwahig Penal Colony on Palawan Island in 1904, following the transfer from military to colonial rule there. According to the colony's first superintendent, John R. White, they shipped over one thousand prisoners there during the first four years. The vast majority of those selected to be transferred were men between the ages of twenty and forty, whose professions were listed as "farmers" and "day laborers." Fishermen, seamen, traders, washermen, clerks, barbers, cigar makers, shoemakers, engravers, shopkeepers, and students were also among those sent to the penal colony. Unknown numbers had belonged to the Katipunan revolutionary brotherhood and to local messianic movements around the archipelago, like the Tulisans, Santa Iglesia, Dios-Dios, and the Guardia de Honor. Indeed, significant numbers had been convicted of political crimes like bandolerismo, sedition, treason, and insurrection. As a group, the men selected for transfer tended to be those nearing the end of long sentences, as a kind of "privilege" that could easily be revoked.[29]

Once they arrived at the island, by boat, and made their way to Iwahig, on the outskirts of Puerto Princesa, they were put to work clearing, draining, deforesting, and planting the land and constructing the buildings they would live in. Along with small home farms near the barracks and out-stations to grow food, they were forced into hard agricultural labor on several permanent plantations—devoted to cacao, coffee, kapok, cocos, maguey, rubber, ilang-ilang, papayas, and pineapples—producing cash crops for export. The prisoners were divided into five grades, "colonist Classes" 1–5, and given designations of skilled workman, assistant squad foreman, and chief foreman. They were assigned to a work "division"—farming, construction, forestry, roads, transportation, serving, executive, health, out-stations, and police—each with its own overseers who reported on them.[30]

The Iwahig Penal Colony was designed to represent a different stage of supervision than used for confinement in the overcrowded Bilibid Prison in the middle of urban Manila. Yet, the two depended on each other. According to police and prison commissioner W. Cameron Forbes and Superintendent White's plan for Iwahig, the primary "features of control" at Iwahig were the threat of being returned to Bilibid, the impracticality of escaping off the surrounding island of Palawan, and the ability for prisoners to earn "good conduct time."[31] White documented the number "returned to Bilibid on account of bad behavior" in his monthly and annual reports. He felt "the long detention period in Bilibid where the offender is habituated to habits of industry and discipline" worked to deter "bad conduct" at Iwahig. He believed that a year or two at Iwahig "in a semi-free, hard-working, agricultural community has excellent moral and physical effect." Still, Forbes worried that it not appear too soft: "Jail must be made a very real and awful thing to the criminal classes and that the amelioration of prison like must never be such as to publicly palliate crime."[32] Discipline, he concluded, rested on the "absolute and unquestioned authority" of the superintendent, the secondary authority of foremen and overseers, and the power to transfer prisoners back to Bilibid.[33]

When penologist John Lewis Gillin visited Iwahig as part of

his international tour of prisons, he characterized his visit to the two most famous U.S. prisons in the Philippines, Bilibid and Iwahig, as moving "from certain hell to kingdom come." "You are assured that Iwahig is only possible because of the experience the prisoner has had in Bilibid," he told his readers in *Taming the Criminal: Adventures in Penology* (1928). Contrasting Bilibid's high walls with Iwahig's wall-lessness, he concluded that prison authorities evidently realized that a "taste of hell" is necessary to produce the "proper appropriation of kingdom come."[34] At Iwahig, prisoners could progress from the Barrack Zone to the Home Zone to the Free Zone, based on compliance and "good behavior." They would be demoted for infractions in an instant, of course, and the threat of being transferred to a higher security prison constantly loomed over those chosen for relative latitude within confinement. Gillin concluded that the "Indian, Filipino, and Negro criminal" suffered from a "slave morality" learned over centuries of oppression.[35] Like many Progressive Era penologists, he articulated a deeply held set of assumptions about criminality, inferiority, and racial hierarchy even as he blamed historical, cultural, and environmental factors along with biological heredity. To his mind, the "Indian, Filipino, and Negro criminal" were "the problem" in need of fixing, uplifting, even saving.

The plan for Iwahig was modeled on that of the George Junior Republic, a reform school for "delinquent" and "dependent" immigrant children removed from New York City. The experiment was founded by Progressive Era penologist William Ruben George, with the backing of Theodore Roosevelt, who served as the city's police commissioner at the time (1895–97). While designed in theory to be a kind of simulacrum of self-governance and capitalist production, the school was always "fated to remain a junior republic undergoing endless tutelage."[36] Indeed, before Iwahig and McNeil emerged as twin poster children for the prison without walls, Thomas Mott Osborne, a progressive penologist turned warden, oversaw a parallel experiment in adult prisoner "self-government" at Sing Sing State Prison in New York (1914), which ended in the widely publicized scandal of him being accused of sodomy and removed from his post. In the Philippines, as in other sites of American empire, prison expansion incorporated experience in military combat and overseeing unfree labor alongside emergent forms of penological expertise as it widened the "carceral continuum," extending forms of supervision and control beyond the physical walls of the prison itself.

*   *   *

This logic of control through stages of supervision underpinned debates over "indeterminate sentencing" and federal "good time," probation, and parole laws, together known as the "great triplets." U.S. delegates to the International Prison Congresses argued for a perpetual, rather than transactional, relation between lawbreakers and the state. As with colonialism generally, at issue was a struggle over where the authority to determine "readiness for release," or fitness for freedom, would be located. Rather than the state compelling a person to "pay a debt," these penologists maintained the prisoner would be detained until "fit for liberty." Still, they believed, "criminality must be exterminated" before a prisoner can be released. Drawing on examples from overseas prisons like Iwahig, penologists and policy makers argued that discretion to determine when someone was fit to reenter society should not lie with judges at sentencing, but rather with criminological experts. They argued this would mark a major advance from a system based on retribution to one based on the principle of rehabilitation. Ironically, these advocates for what was called the "indeterminate sentence" ended up pushing for longer sentences, seeing them as "windows of time" within which to work on rehabilitating the prisoner, who might be able to "release themselves" through their good behavior. This form of "net-widening," the process of extending social control through the carceral system, often in the name of reform, is rooted in the colonial logic of prison imperialism.

Stages of Supervision

A series of federal laws established stages of supervision for those deemed criminal within the United States and across the American empire. Federal good time, probation, and parole systems were envisioned as working together from the start. Congress passed the federal good time law in 1902 and parole in 1910. Probation, introduced in 1909, was passed in 1925. The "triplets" as penologists called them, "gave meaning to each other"; they were designed to create stages of supervision before, during, and after imprisonment.[37] These calculated attempts to control time were part of broader national and international conversations and were influenced by imperialist theories of development. In explaining new policies such as parole, prison administrators borrowed literature and techniques from "insular possessions" like the Philippines, debated the comparative advantages of different "convict colonization" schemes, and worried about the standing of their prisons in the community of "civilized nations."

Theoretically, original federal parole law made prisoners eligible for early release after serving one-third of their sentence. McNeil's *Rules and Regulations* explained that parolees would remain under the legal custody of the warden until the expiration of their sentence, "minus good-time earned."[38] The federal parole boards were composed of the warden, prison physician, and superintendent of prisons and met each January, May, and September at Atlanta, Leavenworth, and McNeil Island Penitentiaries. The board had the power to revoke and reincarcerate parolees, with or without restitution of the prior good time they had earned in prison. The U.S. Marshals Service was tasked with supervising federal parolees and executing warrants for parole violators. The board, it reminded prisoners, would fix the limits of residence for parolees and had the power to issue warrants based on any reliable information that the parolee had violated the terms of their parole.[39] This form of "conditional release," as it was called, relied on a speculation about a parole applicant's future: whether they were likely to live without violating the law and whether their release would be compatible with the welfare of society.

As with good time, prison officials made clear that parole was not a "vested right," as Robert Stroud put it in his prison writing from McNeil at the time, but that it could be changed or taken away. This made things confusing and unpredictable for prisoners and parolees who were continually counting down the days. Indeed, when McNeil Penitentiary's newspaper, the *Island Lantern*, set out to explain that those paroled before the

end of July 1932 would serve the remainder of their minimum
sentence, while those paroled after would have to serve the rest
of their maximum, the editor concluded exasperatedly: parole
is not a right "but an act of grace."[40] Stroud was furious that
the modification of the law also disqualified good time sentence
reductions for parolees. Making them serve the remainder of
their original maximum sentence on parole rather than serve
the reduced sentenced earned by good behavior he felt was like
making them serve their good time all over again. Any prisoner
serving less than ten years "who is not an idiot," he suggested,
should knock out the first person who looks at him sideways,
forfeit his good time, serve his sentence straight up, and go free
rather than be paroled.[41] As Stroud recognized, the modified law
also created parallel time horizons for prisoners serving shorter
sentences: one timeline anticipated release based purely on good
time sentence reduction; another was based on serving one-third
of the original maximum sentence. Which came first depended
on how long a prisoner was serving. Amidst the confusion, one
thing was made clear: prison officials held the power to turn
back time, erase good deeds, and reset the clock.

The prison's newspaper did more than get word out to prisoners about things like changes in the parole law. Begun in 1924, it
served to connect the federal prison to national and international discussions in penology.[42] In covering parole, for instance,
the editor remarked that while "it seems strange that one of
our insular possessions should be the home of so authoritative
a chronicle of progressive penology as the *Philippine Prisons
Review*," it contains "the best statement of parole."[43] The article
reprinted from the Philippines explained that the idea of parole

had originated in the British Empire when convicts were given a ticket-of-leave and served out the remainder of their sentences in Australia. It went on to describe the current system of parole in terms of civilizational standing: "The prevalent practice in almost every civilized country of the world of releasing prisoners under certain conditions prior to the expiration of their respective prison sentences."[44] Indeed, colonial administrators were well practiced at creating policies full of timelines and stipulations for partial freedoms.

The imperial borrowings became most pronounced when prison administrators at McNeil Island anticipated hosting the annual American Prison Association Conference in 1927 and prepared a 140-page special issue of the *Island Lantern* in French and English for the International Penal Congress in Prague three years later. Evidently concerned about their position among those "civilized nations," the prison newspaper ran stories comparing European and American prisons and solicited articles from experts on prisons from around the globe. American prisons had been accused of being lax on punishments and were compared unfavorably with Europe in terms of escapes, one story announced shortly before the conference.[45] One of the American Prison Association delegates said that American prisons had been "branded as the worst in the world."[46]

When the 350 delegates came to visit McNeil Island in August 1927, Warden Finch R. Archer proudly toured them through Honor Farm, established just one year before. He had also prepared the first official history of McNeil Island Federal Penitentiary and called it *The Prison Without Walls*.[47] According to the honor system, prisoners earned the privilege of working on the farm and enjoyed a relative degree of freedom, without guns trained on them, for instance. Although he did not state it explicitly, Archer was evidently well aware of the original prison without walls, the name of the Iwahig Penal Colony. Indeed, shortly before he endeavored to create Honor Farm, the *Island Lantern* ran a story on Iwahig. "This colony is the most novel experiment ever tried out in the reformatory treatment of criminals," it proclaimed.[48] Only prisoners with good records at Bilibid Prison, in Manila, had earned the privilege of becoming "colonists" at Iwahig, where prisoners served as police and were even given an allotment of land and allowed to be joined by their families "under certain conditions."[49] McNeil's prison chaplain, C.W. Burr, had attended the International Penal Congress in London, where he would have heard the report on Philippine prisons firsthand.

During the Progressive Era, American penologists led an international movement away from determinate sentences, with determined lengths of time set by judges, toward indeterminate sentences, with no fixed end. The idea, Samuel J. Barrows explained to the International Penal and Penitentiary Commission (IPPC) members, was to have the release date be determined by when the "criminal" had been rehabilitated. This would be decided by jailers, wardens, and criminological experts working directly with people inside prison. The principle was no longer that "punishment should fit the crime," but that "punishment should fit the *criminal*."[50] When Zebulon Brockway, the "father of American parole," first introduced indeterminate sentences and conditional release in Detroit, Michigan, and Elmira, New York, the principles were based on a grades and incentives system that the State Board of Charities found to lengthen jail time arbitrarily and coerce people to serve as informants after their release.[51]

The indeterminate sentence was first used for "juvenile delinquents," "prostitutes," and "wards of the state." Under this "historic new principle," power was given to a Board of Guardians and release was based on "evidence of improved character." The definite sentence, Barrows maintained, was about the completion of a transaction between the state and the lawbreaker. But with one of its "delinquent subjects," their "condition should change only when he changes, not before." These types of people had been "sentenced to [the Board of Guardians'] custody to become subject to their control, instead of being merely sentenced to the institution." Their relation to the state was "perpetual." "They are not those of debtor and creditor, which will cease when the penalty is 'paid.'"[52]

These Progressive Era penologists pushing One World penology believed it absurd to think that a judge could tell in 1900 whether someone would be ready to rejoin society in 1905. They advocated instead for discretionary authority to be shifted to prison administrators, wardens, jailers, and criminologists. Rather than the state compelling a person to "pay his debt," they maintained, the person merely would be detained "until he is fit for liberty." Their freedom would be "postponed" until their "fitness for liberty can be ascertained." This movement from a "retributive system," which rested on force, to a "reformative system" would align the interest of the prisoner with that of the state. Still, "criminality must be exterminated before [the prisoner] can be released." The criminal, delinquent, and ward of the state would no longer be in an antagonistic relationship with their jailers, the theory went, because they would be working toward a common goal. Through self-interest, self-discipline, and self-control "he may release himself."[53] Ultimately, this framework promised to give longer sentences, out of proportion with the crime, in order to give the jailers and experts time to work within that window.

At McNeil Island, good behavior could earn prisoners transfer to the Honor Farm, a kind of prison without walls within the prison without walls. At Bilibid Prison, obedience could earn them transfer to Iwahig, the one-hundred-acre plantation prison and, by 1920, the largest penal colony in the world. On the plantation, prisoners could earn further privileges, such as moving from the Barrack Zone to the Family Zone. With parole, it was imagined that these stages of supervision might extend even more: neighboring towns, cities, and entire regions might become part of the prison without walls. This has been a recurring fantasy of colonial governance.

Widening the Net

Parole was originally conceived of as "conditional release." It was not necessarily conceived as a way to let people out early or to relieve overcrowding, as is commonly believed, but as a way to give more control to certain agencies and experts. The inequities in the parole system, and the underlying logic of colonial control, were not lost on people in prison. In fact, when the Citizen's Inquiry on Parole and Criminal Justice Commission, headed by Ramsey Clark and Coretta Scott King, set out to investigate parole in the 1970s, they found in interview after interview that people in prison called it the "ultimate weapon of degradation." The supervision system, the commission found, was full of demeaning restrictions, arbitrary reporting, and constant fear. In their final report, *The Prison Without Walls*, Chairman Clark found "parole inequity" to be "a primary source of tension" in the Attica Prison uprising. Indeed, the McKay Commission's report on Attica had also found parole inequity to be a main cause of the famous prison rebellion, and most brutal repression, in U.S. history. "Those who love justice," the Citizen's Inquiry final report concluded, must "strive to change all this."[54] Their recommendation came down to brass tacks: abolish parole.

By the 1970s, the movement seeking to abolish parole condemned it as a "prison without walls," critiquing the way a carceral logic of control spread beyond the prison itself. Today, some prison reformers and journalists have revived the idea of the wall-less prison to promote the idea of electronic monitoring, positioning the prison without walls as a more humane alternative to bars and cages.[55] Pointing out that fully two-thirds of convicted people are not behind bars but on "supervised release," such as probation or parole, this argument claims that "by nearly any measure such 'prisons without bars' would represent a giant step forward for justice, criminal rehabilitation, and society." Inside America's open-air panopticon, a B.I. Incorporated monitoring hub in Indianapolis, one journalist marveled at the ability to summon a screen detailing the movements of someone through "exclusion zones" or "inclusion zones" in places as far away as Guam.[56] Yet, as those most directly impacted, together with scholars, activists, and prison abolitionists, have demonstrated, this kind of "prison by any other name" still has the effect of growing the apparatus of punishment and control with devastating consequences.[57]

These activists and grassroots groups challenging the spread of "e-carceration" have shown how it has been created in a global political economy and security industry. This global system has been developed to track people and has been used to repress social movements in places like Palestine and South Africa.[58] Several of the largest U.S. and multinational electronic monitoring companies are based in Israel, where they carry out experiments on Palestinians. Yet, it is not just private companies that are to blame, as James Kilgore and Ruth Wilson Gilmore point out, because this is a political project that has come to target the most "criminalized sector of the working class," namely Black and Indigenous people, migrants, and people of color.[59] Electronic shackles expand the police state into every corner of people's lives, they explain, and all the data being collected is joined together in "the cloud" and is used to make money and to deepen systems of punishment and control.[60] The prison without walls has now become a way to control and punish targeted populations through e-carceration.

This form of net widening is shaping the new era of crimmigration, marked by the dramatic rise in jailing migrants. E-carceration technologies, like ankle shackles, GPS trackers, facial recognition software, hotspot mapping, risk assessments, and predictive algorithms, combine and share data between private companies and government agencies in the criminal, legal, national security, and immigration control systems. When the U.S. Border Patrol began a new initiative named Operation

Streamline (2005), they found an old and rarely enforced legal provision in federal immigration law that made unauthorized border crossing a jailable offense. Not only are e-carceration technologies increasingly used in border police operations, but in some places a "shell game" has emerged whereby jail space that has been vacated by releasing people on electronic monitors who are awaiting trial or are on probation and parole is being filled with people arrested on immigration charges, with a daily per-bed fee paid by the federal government to state and local officials. Alongside the rise of migrant detention at home, the federal government and private companies are exporting this toxic combination of crimmigration and e-carceration abroad: pushing U.S. border control technologies for check points and crossings on other countries around the world in an ever-expanding "empire of borders."[61]

The rise in jailing migrants is part of the federal government's "prevention by deterrence" doctrine. Under the Trump administration's "zero tolerance" policy (2018), separating families was proposed as a "deterrence method," with the detention of parents in federal custody triggering "an automatic family separation." This is the earliest instance of family separation being proposed as a way to deter migration to the United States, writes one investigative journalist, even as it has been shown to increase the danger and harms to people seeking to cross the border that these policies claim to be trying to prevent.[62] The threat of separating families as a strategy of racial and colonial control is not new. It can be traced back through the Jefferson-Monroe Penal Doctrine, the birth of the Indian boarding school system at Fort Marion, the deportations from the Panama Canal Zone, and the rise of crimmigration at McNeil Island Federal Penitentiary.

Net widening, the process of extending social control through the carceral system, often in the name of reform, has its roots in the colonial logic of prison imperialism. If the indeterminate sentence shifted power from judges to criminologists, the mandatory minimum sentence was then used to shift power from experts to policy makers. During the "tough on crime" and War on Drugs eras, this meant that politicians had an outsized influence on how long people would be imprisoned for things like petty drug charges. The indeterminate sentence was a form of colonial tutelage, while mandatory minimums revealed the return of the use of retribution against those who had been most systematically criminalized. By the 1970s, the movement to abolish the parole system called parole the prison without walls. Even as it was once described as the hallmark of relative freedom in confinement, its roots were deeply planted in the racial violence of empire building. Today, the rapid proliferation of ankle monitors, trackers, facial recognition, and surveillance cameras marks the age of e-carceration, dubbed the "newest Jim Crow."[63] This is prison imperialism's next frontier.

Chief Osceola

Felipe Salvador

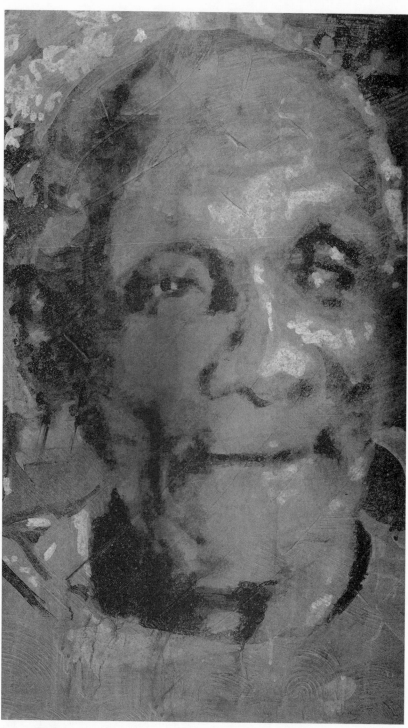

Lester Greaves

Claudia Jones

Blanca Canales

Lolita Lebrón

Assata Shakur

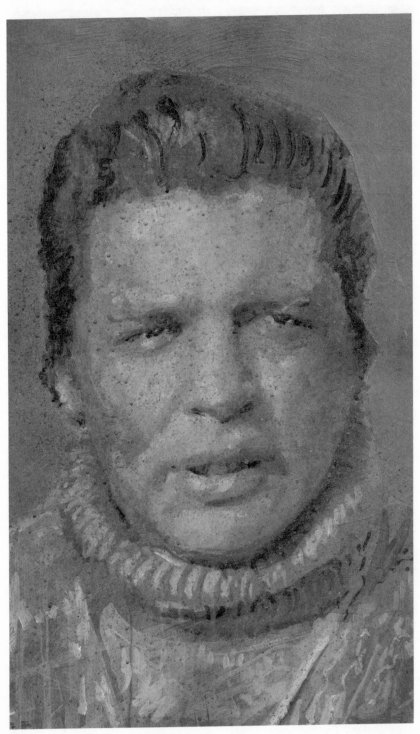

Richard Oakes

Jalil A. Muntaqim

Black Lives Matter (BLM) protestors

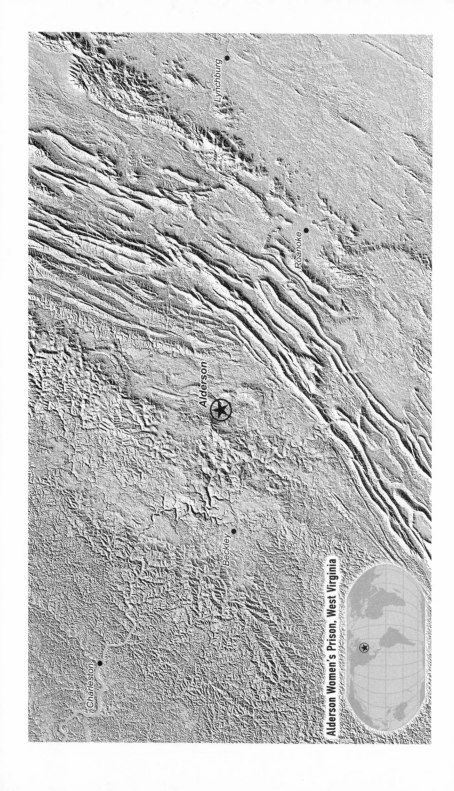

Alderson Women's Prison, West Virginia

6

The Imperial Boomerang

From the colonial sections of the world, it can be learned how they are striving to throw off the yoke of exploitation and oppression and trying to establish people's democracies, socialism, and self-determination—in other words to become masters of their own destiny.

—Benjamin J. Davis[1]

When Charlie Weems, Ozie Powell, Clarence Norris, Olen Montgomery, Willie Roberson, Haywood Patterson, Eugene Williams, and brothers Andrew and Leroy Wright were yanked off the freight train by the local sheriff and his deputized posse of angry white men in Paint Rock, Alabama, the nine teenagers had no idea their cause would become a touchstone of antiracist and anti-imperialist protest in the United States and around the world. They were joyriding and had gotten into an altercation with some white teens, who tried to throw them off the train. Two white girls aboard the train falsely accused them of rape, and later recanted, admitting they had made up the story. But by that time, the Scottsboro Boys had been tried and convicted by an all-white jury and all but the youngest had been sentenced to death (1931). Thirteen-year-old Leroy Wright, sentenced to life in prison, remained locked in an Alabama jail for the next six years as the trial of the other eight dragged on and up through the appeals process to the Supreme Court.

The defense campaign for the Scottsboro Boys, organized by the International Labor Defense (ILD), attracted many working-class Black people to the Communist Party USA. The Scottsboro defense, along with their position on the "Negro Question," supporting self-determination in the Black Belt, and their opposition to fascist Italy's invasion of Ethiopia (1935), demonstrated the Communist Party's willingness to help defend Black lives at home and abroad.[2] Groups like the ILD, the Scottsboro Defense Committee, and the Provisional Committee for the Defense of Ethiopia brought together working people, feminists, and communists in meccas of Black intellectual and political activity, like Harlem and Atlanta, and across the South. Black Communists who were active in these campaigns, like Angelo Herndon, Benjamin Davis, and Claudia Jones, found themselves targeted for censure and imprisonment. Sharpened through their experiences in prison, these political prisoners developed a powerful critique of what Jones called "Prison Jim Crow," the expanding use of prisons to maintain white supremacy and control movements for self-determination. Through their organizing to defend Black lives, they theorized how racism was rooted in the economic exploitation of global capitalism expanded through U.S. foreign policy and how techniques of colonial repression overseas were increasingly being implemented domestically.

The imperial boomerang of coercive social control through policing and imprisonment had returned home with full force over the preceding decade with the Red Scare, targeting socialists, communists, and ethnic communities. The modes of counterintelligence, incarceration, and criminal transportation that had been experimented with in empire were now being deployed against Black and Puerto Rican movements for self-determination within U.S. borders and on the island of Puerto Rico.[3] The colonial counterinsurgency tactics developed in the attempt to repress the rise of a "messianic leader" capable of uniting the Katipunan in the Philippines—where U.S. officials amassed index cards on 70 percent of Manila's population—now came to characterize the rapidly expanding American surveillance state.[4] Alabama labor organizer Angelo Herndon found himself arrested on an old insurrection statute, while prominent Black Communists like Benjamin J. Davis, his defense lawyer, and Claudia Jones were named to the FBI's key figures list, arrested, and imprisoned under the new anticommunist and anti-immigrant Smith and McCarran Acts (1940 and 1950).

The boomerang struck Puerto Rican nationalists fighting for self-determination at the same time. Leaders of the anticolonial movement for independence in Puerto Rico found themselves persecuted with similar tactics and prosecuted under similar statutes, like Executive Order 9835, a loyalty oath program (1947), and Law 53 (1948), *ley de la mordaza* (Gag Law), based on the Smith Act, which made it illegal to own or display a Puerto Rican flag. Puerto Rican Nationalist Party leader Don Pedro Albizu Campos pushed for a change in strategy from electoral politics toward armed struggle for independence following the violent repression of the nationalist movement at the massacre of Ponce (1937). Blanca Canales led the Puerto Rican Nationalist Party's raid of a fort in Jayuya (1950), and nationalists held the town for three days while others led uprisings in eight other cities across Puerto Rico. The rise of anti-communist hysteria of McCarthyism in the midst of the Cold War led to the arrest of thousands of nationalists and the mass killing and incarceration of frontline revolutionary fighters. Some anticolonial leaders, like Lolita Lebrón, took the fight to the U.S. Capitol, where she fired shots at the ceiling in Congress to protest the banning of the Nationalist Party (1950) and the passage of Public Law 600, which declared Puerto Rico a commonwealth under U.S. jurisdiction (1952).[5]

What Black communists, Puerto Rican nationalists, and anticolonial activists were able to point out in comparisons between Black and Puerto Rican struggles was the rise of a new era of prison imperialism, featuring the return of surveillance state tactics and the use of imprisonment to suppress movements for self-determination. The constituent elements of this critique of state violence at home and abroad came out of movements for collective self-defense, self-determination, feminism, and peace. Key leaders of these two linked struggles against colonial and carceral state violence—Claudia Jones, Blanca Canales, Lolita Lebrón, and, later, Assata Shakur—all became imprisoned at the Alderson Federal Prison for Women, in West Virginia. There they developed an intersectional analysis of oppression as rooted in imperialism and capitalism that presaged the Black Power and Third World Liberation movements.

Defending Black Lives at Home and Abroad

The Scottsboro defense campaign made direct connections between racism and imperialism at home and abroad. In his speeches and pamphlets, Angelo Herndon compared the rise of

white vigilante terror campaigns like railroading the Scottsboro
Boys and riding hooded on horseback through Atlanta's Black
neighborhoods, as the American Fascist Order of the Black
Shirts did, to the spread of fascism worldwide.[6] "It was at this
time that the rape of Ethiopia by the Italian Fascists was being
justified at great length by the white capitalistic newspapers in
this country because, they said, it would result in making the
Abyssinian savages 'civilized.'"[7] His commitment to fighting
oppression led Herndon to labor organizing, and his support for
self-determination in the Black Belt got him arrested on a pre–
Civil War slave insurrection law.

Herndon had gone to work in the coal mines in Lexington,
Kentucky, and Birmingham, Alabama, at the age of thirteen
and joined the Birmingham Unemployed Council to start labor
organizing in 1930. In Birmingham, Herndon received death
threats and was harassed by local police and arrested. He was
reassigned to Atlanta in 1931 and became active in the Scottsboro Boys defense campaign and organized an unemployed
protest at the county courthouse, for which he was arrested
and charged under the Georgia insurrection statute in 1932.
Herndon was initially sentenced to death, then his sentence was
revised to twenty years on the chain gang. His case was taken
up by the ILD, where secretary William L. Patterson directed
his defense to Atlanta lawyers Benjamin J. Davis and John Greer.
His case made headlines worldwide as an example of racial
injustice in the United States.[8]

Herndon was arrested and charged under Georgia's insurrection law for leading an unemployed demonstration for jobs and
relief at the Fulton County Courthouse in 1931. The statute was

passed in 1861 to prevent slave rebellion and was revised during Reconstruction to apply to Black and white "insurrectionists." The state based the prosecution on two pamphlets in his possession, one containing his article "Everything Is Peaches Down in Georgia" (*Daily Worker*), a satire about lynching, police brutality, peonage, unemployment, starvation, and repression imposed on Black people and poor whites, and the other *The Communist Position on the Negro Question*. The prosecutor took special issue with the slogan "Self-Determination for the Black Belt" in Herndon's trial because, as his defense lawyer Davis put it, "it would mean curtains for the lynchers, the poll-taxers, the Ku-Kluxers, the white supremacists." Throughout the trial, Davis challenged the prosecution's "verbal lynching" of Black people before the all-white jury, calling out the Jim Crow system of racial hierarchy. He called for a mistrial when both the prosecution and the judge referred to Black people as "darkies," "niggers," and "wards of the state." The white prosecutor, judge, jury, bailiffs, and spectators in the courtroom were shocked that Davis would challenge these racial slurs as prejudicial. Raising the specter of the "godless assault" of "communist and negro domination," the prosecutor, who was also a preacher accustomed to "condemning souls to purgatory," tried to conjure connected fears of slave insurrection at home and anticolonial revolts abroad.

Herndon was sentenced to eighteen to twenty years and spent the next few years in and out prison as his case went back and forth on appeal, before it was finally overturned by the Supreme Court (1932–37).[9] His time in prison was formative. His "racial status as prisoner" became inseparable from his "convict status as laborer and labor organizer," confirming and consolidating his "outsider status in relation to American capitalism and its unjust institutions." Out on bond, Herndon continued fighting unjust imprisonment, writing and distributing his pamphlets *You Cannot Kill the Working Class* (1935) and *The Scottsboro Boys: Four Freed! Five to Go!* (1937).[10] After the Supreme Court overturned his conviction, he moved to New York, where he edited the *Negro Quarterly* with Ralph Ellison, and then to Chicago. His prison memoir and autobiography *Let Me Live!* (1937) articulated his theory of radical Black activism that would speak to oppressed masses around the world: "To urge hundreds of millions of others like him across the globe—the poorest of the poor, the economically exploited, the socially outcast, those politically dismissed and lawfully persecuted—to actualize this praxis by joining in open rebellion against their own degraded status." His time in prison confirmed and sharpened his beliefs. When released, he proclaimed: "All that has happened to me thus far has been for me a sort of apprenticeship in the revolutionary struggle—a kind of prelude to life, as I must live it."[11]

Self-Determination in the Black Belt

The very idea of self-determination for the Black Belt was on trial in the Herndon case. As the prosecutor put it, "This is not only a trial of Angelo Herndon, but of [. . .] every white person who believes that black and white should unite for the purpose of setting up a nigger Soviet Republic in the Black Belt." Raising the old specter of race war, the prosecutor told the jury they could not sit idly by while "Angelo Herndon is organizing his army to march into the state to murder, kill and assassinate all white people, take away their property, and set up a 'nigger kingdom.'" An old Black worker interrupted him from the back of the courtroom: "Horse feathers! He only asked for bread for the unemployed and got it—that's all." As the courtroom rocked with laughter, Judge Wyatt flushed red with fury. Herndon knew that fighting in the white man's court was symbolic and took comfort from and was deeply moved by the pride that elders who had lived through slavery took in seeing him and Benjamin Davis take on an unjust system, reflecting that "through him spoke all the tribulations and the dreams of redemption of the Negro people."

Davis, the "Communist Councilman from Harlem," was originally from Atlanta, Georgia. Son of an influential news-paperman, he had gone to the best schools and was well connected by the time he moved home and set up his law practice. His family's prestige and connections did not protect him from formative experiences with racism, however, like the time he was roughed up by a "red-necked cop" and arrested for moving to the whites-only section of the Atlanta trolly after giving his seat to a pregnant woman. Nor was he protected from threats, attacks, and racist epithets that were hurled at him in and out of the courtroom as he practiced law. In Atlanta and across the Black Belt South, he reflected in his prison memoir, he could feel the weight of Justice Taney's dictum that Black people had no rights that the white man was bound to respect, which many whites considered the "white man's code of honor." As Davis put it in his memoir, "What I had not found at Morehouse, Amherst and Harvard I discovered in a dingy Georgia courtroom whose realities were far more penetrating than the abstractions of classical scholarship." Indeed, when he took up Herndon's defense, it became necessary for him to be physically protected by members of Atlanta's Black community.

Despite his own direct experience with virulent white racism in the South, Davis described his home in the Black Belt as a "Negro World," complete with all the beauties and strengths and inherent ability and power to fight for its own eventual liberation. Following on the expert witness testimony of Emory professors who showed how students would peg Thomas Jefferson and Abraham Lincoln as insurrectionary, Davis made the point that white people, too, had been colonial subjects. "If the prosecution was right, the American colonists who were against the colonial system of economics—then dominated by the British Crown—and who advocated political and economic independence from Great Britain could be indicted under the Georgia insurrection statute." The way Herndon and Davis saw it, the ruling elite was afraid of the unity displayed by the poor people's movement and did what they could to break it. As Herndon put it in his speech to the jury, "All I can say is, that no matter what you do with Angelo Herndon, no matter what you do with the Angelo Herndons of the future, this question of unemployment, the question of unity between Negro and white workers cannot be solved with hands that are stained with the blood of an innocent individual."

Davis drew a direct line between the insurrection statute against which he defended Black Communist organizer Herndon, the support for Black self-determination, and his own trial under the Smith Act. In his own case, it was enough simply to be accused of "conspiring," "teaching," or "advocating" the overthrow of the government by force and violence. The real purpose, he maintained, was to "intimidate and terrorize" militant Black and poor people fighting for liberation. Writing from a federal prison cell, Davis reflected on the anti-Black and anti-Communist persecution that landed him there. He was charged along with ten leaders in the Communist Party USA (CPUSA) under the Smith Act (1940) and given the maximum sentence. The Smith Act presaged McCarthyite and House Un-American Activities Committee (HUAC) hysteria, in what Davis described as an exercise in fascist policing and thought control. It was essentially an updated version of the old slave-insurrection statutes used to prevent revolts of enslaved and poor people, he argued, by charging them with seeking to overthrow the government by force.

In his prison memoir, *Communist Councilman from Harlem: Autobiographical Notes Written in a Federal Penitentiary*, Davis explained how prison shaped his perspective on the relationship between struggles for self-determination at home and abroad. "The struggle for peace is decisive for Negro and colonial freedom; it will be with us as long as capitalism, imperialism and human enslavement exist. The prison-enforced inability to participate actively in this supreme issue of our century throbs so acutely in one's mind that one is driven to find a task that has a meaning in this context."[12] In his correspondence with fellow Black Communist organizer Claudia Jones, Davis elaborated his position on the "national question." "The deterioration of the colonial system and its effects on the whole question of peaceful co-existence, on economic issues, on the whole political struggle—is the biggest thing in the world picture. We have yet to deal with that question fundamentally over here."[13] "From the colonial sections of the world, it can be learned how they are striving to throw off the yoke of exploitation and oppression and trying to establish people's democracies, socialism, and self-determination—in other words to become masters of their own destiny."[14] He developed this framework out of discussions on the "national question" with Black intellectuals and CPUSA members and sharpened it through his direct experience with political repression, surveillance, imprisonment, and the expanding violence of the carceral state.

Prison Jim Crow

Claudia Jones campaigned vigorously in defense of Davis and the CPUSA 11, the high-profile Communist Party members who were first targeted for arrest under FBI director J. Edgar Hoover's scheme to neutralize them. According to her FBI file, she and Davis were considered the leading Black officers in the CPUSA, for which she had been added to the FBI's key figures list. They had been tracking Jones for years, recording her speeches in New York and Detroit on victims of the Smith Act. In her speeches, as in her writing, Jones called for the nullification of the Smith and McCarran Acts, lambasting McCarthyism as patently racist, as much anti-Black as it was anti-peace and anti-democracy. In her defense of Davis, she took aim at "prison Jim Crow," centering the penitentiary in her broader critique of the rise of white nationalism, fascism, and imperialist war making. The FBI was especially concerned with the way Jones critiqued the federal government's framing of the "Negro Question" as one of "inter-racial difficulty," highlighting how she believed that it should be seen instead as one of "national oppression."[15] Framing Black oppression as a problem of inter-racial difficulty, she explained, falsely placed equal responsibility on Black and white. The so-called Negro Question was a question of national oppression she maintained. She deftly shifted the "Negro Question" out of domestic race relations and moved it to an international analysis of the rise of white nationalism and fascism. In so doing, she articulated a version of "internal colonialism"—the nation-within-a-nation thesis—that would gain wider traction in the Black Power era and would offer the building blocks for a decolonial theory of justice.[16]

Jones became involved with American Communism through the CPUSA's defense of Black teenagers in the Scottsboro case and the defense of Ethiopia against the Italian invasion. Through these mass defense campaigns, Black left feminists such as Jones, Louise Thompson Patterson, Grace Campbell, and Audley "Queen Mother" Moore were able to defend Black lives locally and globally, building Black women's interna-tionalism that was on the vanguard of social change. By fore-grounding a theory of "triple oppression," they demonstrated that women's liberation could not be separated from Black liberation, colonial liberation, and poor people's liberation.[17] Through her organizing work on the defense campaigns for the Scottsboro Boys, Rosa Lee Ingram, Angelo Herndon, and Benjamin Davis, Jones developed a critique of racism, sexism, capitalism, and imperialism with the prison at the center. She recognized how policing and prisons were increasingly being used to silence and eliminate threats to the state's legitimacy and how the expansion of the carceral system was becoming increasingly central to state making and empire building within and beyond U.S. borders.

Jones's thinking on the "Negro Question," like the thinking of fellow Black left feminists who studied Marxist-Leninism at the time, was inseparable from that of the "Woman Question."[18] She was also careful to situate Black women's political organizing as the leading edge of revolutionary change, as they experienced triple oppression as racially stigmatized women and workers. In her call to build an antifascist and anti-imperialist coalition, in *An End to the Neglect of the Problems of the Negro Woman!* for instance, she demonstrated why Rosa Lee Ingram's case was a key issue in the struggle. In her effort to organize a million-signature international campaign to free the Ingrams, she argued that no case dramatizes the oppressed status of Black women better than that of Ingram, who was sentenced to death for defending herself and her two sons from "the indecent advances of a white supremacist." How could the Truman administration claim to be exporting democracy and human rights to the world, Jones wrote, while keeping this courageous Black mother "under lock and key." It was only through the work of the Black women who organized the National Committee to Free the Ingram Family, sending ten thousand Mother's Day cards and a 25,000-signature petition to President Truman, that Ingram and her two sons were eventually released from prison, after twelve years. As Mariame Kaba puts it: "This would not have happened if not for the consistent agitation and organizing on their behalf by thousands of people across the world, and particularly Black women. It was that organizing that saved their lives."[19]

In her pamphlet defending Harlem's Black Communist councilman, Benjamin Davis, Jones explained how none better than
Black people could understand how it came to be that he was
framed for his political beliefs. "A people like ours can easily
understand that the Government is perfectly capable of framing
fighting Negro leaders like Ben Davis," she wrote. "The history
of more than 300 years of our people stands up to charge America's rulers with unpunished and monstrous crimes." Along with
Jim Crowing Black people's social, economic, and political life,
the government, Jones points out, was also guilty of lynchings,
bombings, court-martials, frame-ups, and persecutions of the
Scottsboro Boys, Angelo Herndon, W.E.B. Du Bois, Paul Robeson, and others. Black people stand up to charge America's rulers with "*the crime of genocide*," she pronounced, "springing from
the racist intent to destroy a national or religious group, entire
or in part."[20]

The treatment of Black people inside prison was both a microcosm and an intensification of U.S. racist oppression. Jones
wrote "be not afraid or dismayed" even in the face of "prison
Jim Crow."[21] Davis's legal work from inside of the federal prison at Terre Haute thoroughly exposed "the genocidal practices
of prison life" for Black people in America. She also knew, in
a deeply embodied way, how prisons slowly killed even those
sentenced to relatively short sentences, having herself suffered
repeated heart failures while imprisoned and being diagnosed
with hypertensive cardiovascular disease upon her release. This
"brazen practice of prison Jim Crow is another stench in the
noses of democratic Americans" she wrote, which further expos-
es the "hypocritical prattlings" of the State Department's claims

of Washington being the moral capital of "a 'free America in a free world.'" Despite the hard work of the Harlem Committee to Free Ben Davis and of the delegations led by the likes of Paul Robeson and William L. Patterson to the Federal Parole Board, Jones exclaimed: "HE IS STILL NOT FREE!" "Free Ben Davis and demand amnesty for all political prisoners," she thundered.[22]

Centering political repression, arrests, and imprisonment as technologies of racially targeted mass murder in charging the United States with genocide, Jones placed "prison Jim Crow" and "the genocidal practices of prison life" into a global human rights framework. In so doing, she was perhaps the first person in the modern anti-prison movement to center the prison as the core technology structuring racial domination and death. She might be considered the lodestone for subsequent Black human rights critiques of the prison system, much in the way the Civil Rights Congress's *We Charge Genocide* (1951) petition has been seen in efforts to charge the United States with genocide for police killings, racial violence, and premature death. Through her own imprisonment and through her prisoner defense committee organizing, Jones developed a critique of the U.S. prison system as genocidal by design. Responding to the persecution of Black Communists under the McCarran and Smith Acts, Jones herself was arrested for her political activism and was imprisoned four times between 1948 and 1955, before being deported from the United States altogether. They imprisoned and then deported her, but she continued her political activism from her new home base in London, leading her biographer to characterize her as "beyond containment."[23]

Alderson Women's Prison

"The politicals," as imprisoned Communist organizer Elizabeth Gurley Flynn fondly referred to them, at Alderson Federal
Prison for Women included Claudia Jones, Blanca Canales, and
Lolita Lebrón. Jones and Flynn were arrested and indicted along
with other members of the Communist Party USA on charges of
violating the Smith Act and stood trial as part of the now widely
discredited McCarthy era persecutions of the early 1950s. Inside
Alderson, Jones strengthened her bonds of solidarity with other
anti-imperial intellectuals and activists, and together they sharpened their decolonial framework for challenging, and ultimately
repairing, the injustices of the rapidly expanding carceral system
at the center of U.S. state building. In her poem to Puerto Rican
independence activist Blanca Canales, Jones expressed what
Africana studies scholar Carole Boyce Davies describes as her
theory of "anti-imperialist feminism."[24]

It seems I knew you long before our common ties—of
conscious choice
Threw under single skies, those like us
Who, fused by our mold
Became their targets of old[25]

With this first stanza, Jones cinched tight the threads that
wove the two of them together in common cause, as anti-
imperialist feminists and socialist revolutionaries. These bonds
of solidarity were chosen, she reiterates, even as they became
overdetermined by the targeted criminalization of Black and

Puerto Rican activists. Calling forth a long tradition of anti-carceral feminism stretching back to the likes of Ida B. Wells, Jones goes on to distinguish between "*their* justice" and real, actual justice. In so doing she weaves together the personal, political, and global, reclaiming the concept of justice by separating it from the targeted criminalization, political repression, and colonial practices mistakenly classified as criminal "justice" systems.

Anti-anti-fascistas!
That was your name
I sang your fame
Long 'fore my witness to your bane of pain

[. . .]

Oh wondrous Spanish sister
Long-locked from all you care
Listen—while I tell you what you stain to hear
And beckon all from far and near

We swear that we will never rest
Until they hear not plea
But sainted sacrifice to set
A small proud nation free

O anti-fascist sister—you whose eye turn to the stars still
I've learned your wonderous secret—source of spirit
    and of will
I've learned that what sustains you heart, mind and
    peace of soul

Is knowledge that their justice—can never reach
  its goal![26]

Imprisoned Black, Puerto Rican, and white intellectuals
and activists like Jones, Canales, and Flynn forged an antifascist sisterhood at Alderson. As Flynn described it in *The Alderson Story*, she first met Canales through Jones: "I saw a stout
little white-haired woman, who spoke with a Spanish accent.
She smiled and smiled at home with such cordiality that I felt
she must be someone special. When I described her to Claudia she said, 'That's Blanca, one of the Puerto Rican Nationalists.' I had often heard Claudia speak of this woman, whose
beautiful face resembled Dolores Ibarruri of Spain, known as
La Pasionaria. Claudia wrote a poem in tribute to Blanca called
'My Anti-Fascist Friend.'" She was known as Blanca Torresola
in the prison, although her family name is Blanca Canales Torresola. "Like us, she was a political prisoner, serving a five-year
sentence." Canales was transferred to do a life sentence at the
Puerto Rican women's prison at Vega Alta.[27]

In Puerto Rico, Canales was a well-known social worker
who belonged to a leading family. She was a member of the
revolutionary Nationalist Party of Puerto Rico, led by Dr. Pedro
Albizu Campos, who himself was sentenced to life in prison.
Canales was also said to be one of the best dressed women in
Puerto Rico. She told Flynn she had been arrested for taking a
U.S. Post Office in her hometown and hoisting a Nationalist flag
over it to protest commonwealth status. She had never been in
the United States before being transferred to prison and suffered
because of the cold winter. She wore a knitted stocking cap and

an oversized trench coat that came down to her ankles.[28] She had led the Nationalist Party's raid of a fort in Jayuya (1950), when nationalists held the town for three days while others led uprisings in eight other cities across Puerto Rico. This was during the height of Cold War McCarthyism, and the anticolonial revolutionary action led to the killing, arrest, and incarceration of thousands of frontline fighters.[29]

The Last Recourse

Soon after Jones was released from Alderson Prison, Canales was joined by fellow Puerto Rican nationalist Lolita Lebrón. When Lebrón arrived at Alderson, according to Flynn, Canales had not known her but was delighted to see her and took her under her wing, and they talked all day in Spanish. They even staged a successful protest inside the prison when guards tried to stop them from speaking in their native tongue. Lebrón looked so young that Flynn couldn't believe she was a grandmother. Her son had been killed in a car accident during her trial. Her elderly mother did not know she was in prison. Flynn asked why Lebrón had decided to fire shots at the ceiling rather than demonstrating with a banner drop at the Capitol. Lebrón responded resolutely, "I am ready to give my life for my country!"[30] It was part of her theory about "the last recourse," measures to be taken only in the face of extreme, systematic, and ongoing colonial violence.

The demonstration was part of a series of solidarity actions within U.S. borders. Lebrón, together with several other New York–based Puerto Rican nationalists, had unfurled a banned Puerto Rican flag, shouted "Puerto Rico libre," and fired warning shots at the ceiling from the gallery of the U.S. House of Representatives (1954) to protest Public Law 600, which declared that Puerto Rico would remain a commonwealth under U.S. jurisdiction, a continued colonial possession. Five congressmen were wounded. Lebrón was tried for attempted murder and sentenced to fifty-six years in prison.[31]

In "The Puerto Rican Struggle Continues," published in *Black Panther* (1976), Lebrón recounted the long history of struggle against U.S. colonial rule.[32] It began with the El Grito de Lares uprising, led by Mariana Bracetti (1868), and continued through the Jayuya Uprising against a fort in Puerto Rico, led by Canales (1950), and the People's Republic of Puerto Rico proclamations made by Lebrón (1954). Each act of anticolonial resistance has been "ignored by the oppressors, and their puppets and followers," she wrote. "We are called 'terrorists' by the U.S. government, but I tell you, United States of America, look inside your heart and see your atomic terror. [. . .] We will fight what terror we must fight, and we will win." Commenting on the asymmetry in military power, Lebrón explained, "You do not expect that Puerto Rico is going to, or would have been able to arm itself as other peoples do and confront the United States of America with a traditional war. No, it is not possible. We had made our war in the only way we've been able to." Armed struggle was the last resort: "We have been the most peaceful nation on earth, or as much as any other people on earth can be peaceful. But the centuries advance and the signs are here and Puerto Rico confronted its enemy in the only way it could have done because the enemy had no ears to hear." Campos, leader of the Puerto Rican Nationalist Party, taught that its "ears must be opened with guns." "The right to the last recourse is a recognized concept which has been used through history," explained Lebrón.[33]

Assata's Dream

Assata Shakur was transferred to Alderson Prison on April 8, 1978. Situated in the middle of rural West Virginia, the prison "seemed as if the mountains formed an impenetrable barrier between the prison and the rest of the world." The trip was especially expensive and difficult, and the family was allowed to visit only twice a year. "I had been convicted of no federal crime, but under the interstate compact agreement any prisoner can be shipped, like cargo, to any jail in u.s. territory, including the Virgin Islands, miles away from family, friends, and lawyers." She was held in the maximum security unit, a "prison within the prison," completely surrounded by an electric fence and the kind of barbed wire outlawed by the Geneva Convention. "This place had a stillness to it like some kind of bizarre death row."[34]

Soon after she arrived at Alderson, Shakur encountered Lebrón. "One day, as i was returning to davis hall, a middle-aged woman, with 'salt-and-pepper' hair caught my eye. She had a dignified, schoolteacher look. Something drew me towards her," Assata writes in her autobiography. "As i searched her face, i could see that she was also searching mine. Our eyes locked in a questioning gaze. 'Lolita?' i ventured. 'Assata?' she responded. And there, in the middle of those alderson prison grounds, we hugged and kissed each other." "For me, this was one of the greatest honors of my life. Lolita Lebrón was one of the most respected political prisoners in the world. Ever since i had first learned of her courageous struggle for the independence of Puerto Rico, i had read everything i could find about her. She had spent a quarter of a century behind bars and had refused parole unless her comrades were also freed. After all those years she had remained strong, unbent and unbroken, still dedicated to the independence of Puerto Rico and the liberation of her people. She deserved more respect than anyone could possibly giver her, and i could not do enough to demonstrate my respect." "Lolita had been through hell in prison, yet she was amazingly calm and extremely kind."[35]

Shakur had developed her own understanding of the imperial boomerang. By the late 1960s, the U.S. government, local police, FBI, and CIA had intensified the all-out war against people considered militants, particularly in Black and Puerto Rican communities leading the "people's movement against war, against racism."[36] It was when she was at community college that she awakened to socialism and to Third World solidarity activism, she recalled. She kept a picture of the My Lai Massacre in Vietnam as a reminder of the ugliness of war making abroad alongside the mental image of the assassination of Martin Luther King at home. "The Puerto Rican sisters and brothers who knew what was happening became our teachers. . . . I had hung out all my life with Puerto Ricans, and i didn't even know Puerto Rico was a colony. They told us of the long and valiant struggle against the first Spanish colonizers and then, later, against the u.s. government and about their revolutionary heroes, the Puerto Rican Five—Lolita Lebrón, Rafael Miranda, Andres Cordero, Irving Flores, and Oscar Collazo, each of whom had spent more than a quarter century behind bars fighting for the independence of Puerto Rico."[37] It was from them that she learned how "Black self-determination is a basic right, and if we do not have the right to determine our destinies, then who does?"[38]

After joining the Black Panther Party (BPP), Shakur was assigned as coordinator between the Harlem chapter and student movements in New York. BPP youth cadre member Mark Holder, who was fifteen years old when he first met Shakur, remembered how she had the gift of "holding court." She was able to connect with anyone, "to talk to the hustlers, and the street people, regardless of what scenario [. . .] she was able to engage them from a point where they were comfortable listening to her" because she was able to "deal with people from a point of compassion."[39] Together they met Puerto Rican activist and Young Lords leader Pablo "Yoruba" Guzmán and other student leaders. Shakur had a sophisticated knowledge of the world's struggles, of political history, and of revolutionary ideology, Holder explained.

Through her experiences organizing with the BPP and learning from the parallel struggles of the Puerto Rican movement for self-determination, Shakur developed a keen analysis of how the dynamics of colonialism shaped the growing carceral state. "One of the most important things the Party did was to make it really clear who the enemy was: not the white people, but the capitalistic, imperialistic oppressors. They took the Black liberation struggle out of a national context and put it in an international context," she wrote in her autobiography.[40] She believed that Huey Newton was wrong to move the discussion from the Black nationalist position that they represented an "oppressed nation" to the position that Black people in the United States represented "oppressed communities"; yet she also believed nationalism without internationalism can be dangerous. She wrote how developing a national consciousness was essential to developing a strong sense of collectivity, to being responsible for and to each other, and to exercising some measure of control over one's own destiny. "Any community seriously concerned with its own freedom has to be concerned about other people's freedom as well."[41]

Out of this framework for understanding how oppression was rooted in the racial inequalities created by capitalism and policed by the ever-circulating imperial boomerang of state violence, Shakur dreamed of internationalist solutions to it. After she was transferred from Alderson to Clinton Correctional Facility for Women, she was finally able to see her daughter, Kakuya, again. She describes her four-year-old's mixture of emotions—anger, sadness, and, most alarming, early signs of resignation. Kakuya told her mother she knew she could leave if she wanted to, pulling her little fingers against the bars. After the heart-wrenching encounter in the visiting room, Shakur remembers: "I go back to my cage and cry until i vomit. I decide it is time to leave."[42] In her poem to Kakuya, Shakur tells her how she wants more for her.

i have shabby dreams for you
of some vague freedom i have never known.

[. . .]

i can see a sunny place—
life exploding green.

i can see your bright, bronze skin
at ease with all the flowers
and the centipedes.

[. . .]

i can see a world where hatred
has been replaced by love.
and ME replaced by WE.
And i can see a world
where you,
building and exploring,
strong and fulfilled,
will understand.
And go beyond my little shabby dreams.[43]

Shakur's dream—"the abolition of racism all over the world"—
was neither shabby nor vague.[44] Yet, the clarity, calm, and confidence with which she tells her daughter how she can feel fulfilled
in building the world beyond speaks to the central tenet of abolition, which is not only to imagine a world without prisons, but
to construct its alternative.

Shakur's escape from prison on November 2, 1979, reverber-
ated across the world as an act of profound resistance. In her
statement to the UN Human Rights Campaign, she invoked
the long history of persecution. Every leader who has spoken
out for human rights has been killed or gone to prison, she
wrote. In order to build "a strong human rights movement,"
she explained, "We've got to build a strong prison movement.
We've got to build a strong Black Liberation Movement and

we've got to struggle for liberation." "Know what we are fighting against—namely genocidal treatment—now it is time to determine what we are fighting for: land and nationhood."[45]

Internal Colonialism

To combat the repression of Black and Puerto Rican movements for self-determination, activists and their allies developed an anticolonial framework for understanding state violence and alternative visions of placemaking. In individual struggles to be freed from prison, as with collective movements for self-determination, activists looked to how the colonized sections of the world, both within and beyond U.S. borders, were struggling to become masters of their own destiny, as Ben Davis put it. To understand decolonization within the U.S. prison movement, it is important to start with the theories of internal colonialism that came out of Indigenous, Black, Puerto Rican, and Chicanx protest movements in the 1950s and 1960s, and which had their greatest expression in the 1970s. Third World solidarity and anticolonialism provided the major inspiration for decolonization efforts in the era of Black, Brown, and Red Power. Internal colonialism provided a kind of "American theory of race."[46] Black and Puerto Rican nationalists and Chicanx radicals began using the concept of internal colonialism after studying Che Guevara, Marxist critiques, and dependency theorists out of Latin American social movements. They began to develop a theory of racial domination, subordination, and control by outsiders and to connect that to histories of stolen land, forced enslavement, and military occupation, connecting

"territorial concentration, spatial segregation, external administration," as well as "brutalization by police, toxic effects of racism, and second-class standing."[47]

The idea of internal colonialism had deep roots in Black
nationalist organizing and took particular shape in the imprisoned Black radical tradition. Black Communists like Claudia
Jones articulated it as a "nation within a nation" thesis in relation to the "national question" of self-determination for the
Black Belt. When Harold Cruse first used the term "domestic
colonialism" (1962), he argued that the Cuban Revolution was
an example of how Black people in the United States needed
a revolutionary nationalist movement to extend anticolonial
victories from the Third World to the United States.[48] Stokely
Carmichael and Charles V. Hamilton's manifesto *Black Power:
The Politics of Liberation* (1967) was the fullest elaboration of
the theory of internal colonialism of Black people in the United
States. The Black Power Conference in Newark (1967) asserted
independence. Viewing internal colonialism through a Marxist
and anti-capitalist lens helped shift the analysis of race and racism from a psychological framework to a structural one. Techniques of state repression that utilized policing and prisons, as
seen through the imperial boomerang, and oppression more
generally, was structural more than interpersonal, not only individual, but institutional.

Racial criminalization has been a primary tool of political
repression. It has been deployed not only with guns but also
through the weaponization of language, along the axis of damn-
ing key words like "criminal," "communist," and "terrorist,"
Angela Y. Davis has theorized.[49] As Black nationalist Robert

F. Williams pointed out, "Every American should realize that every movement for freedom, human dignity, for decency; every movement that seeks fairness and social justice; every movement for human rights is branded as 'communistic.'"[50] Out of this experience with political persecution and imprisonment has emerged a global framework for understanding root causes.

Decolonization as a theory of justice expands beyond the parameters of domestically bound "race relations"—long referred to by white policy makers and public as the "Indian Problem" and the "Negro Problem," and then later as the "Indian Question" and the "Negro Question." This is what Jones called out when she criticized the Eisenhower administration for framing the "Negro Question" as one of "inter-racial difficulty," mistakenly assigning equal blame and responsibility to Black and white people, rather than framing it as a question of national oppression. As Frantz Fanon put it in *The Wretched of the Earth* (1963), "Decolonization, as we know, is a historical process: that is to say it cannot be understood, it cannot become intelligible nor clear to itself except in the exact measure that we can discern the movements which give it historical form and content."[51] The United States has yet to fully reckon with global changes set in motion by decolonization, as Benjamin Davis pointed out in his letters to Jones. This is as true now as it was then.

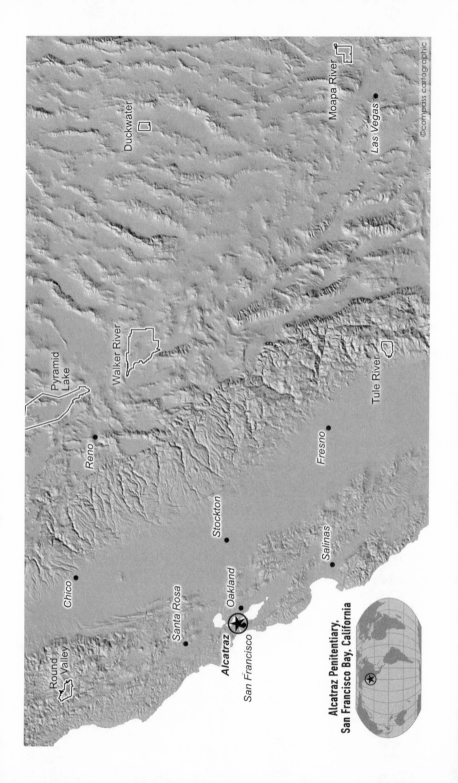

Round
Valley

Chico

Pyramid
Lake

Reno

Walker River

Duckwater

Santa Rosa

Stockton

Oakland

Alcatraz

San Francisco

Salinas

Fresno

Tule River

Moapa River

Las Vegas

©compass cartographic

Alcatraz Penitentiary,
San Francisco Bay, California

7

Protesting Prison Imperialism

We do not fear your threat to charge us with crimes on our land. We and all other oppressed peoples would welcome spectacle of proof before the world of your title by genocide.

—Richard Oakes[1]

We've got to build a strong Human Rights Movement.
We've got to build a strong Prison Movement.
We've got to build a strong Black Liberation Movement,
and we've got to struggle for liberation.

—Assata Shakur[2]

Before she was imprisoned and later escaped to Cuba, Assata Shakur stood with the Indians of All Tribes (IAT) during their occupation of Alcatraz, in San Francisco Bay. "Alcatraz had been taken over by Native Americans who were protesting against a long series of broken treaties, genocidal policies, and racist exploitation. Alcatraz symbolized the strength and dignity of Indian people as well as their resolve to fight to preserve their cultural traditions," she wrote in her memoir. Shakur was struck by the determination of the Indigenous movement for self-determination, protesting prison imperialism through an alternative vision of placemaking. "One old man who had spent many years in Alcatraz prison said that when he arrived on the island he had taken a sledgehammer and reduced the cell he had once been locked in to rubble. [. . .] The prison, one of the most infamous and sadistic ever to exist, loomed in the background." Ultimately, Shakur was inspired by the local and global implications of this form of direct action. "I will always be grateful for having had the opportunity to visit Alcatraz. I will never forget the quiet confidence of the Indians as they went about their lives calmly, even though they were under the constant threat of invasion by the FBI and the u.s. military."[3]

The Alcatraz takeover and Shakur's escape became lodestones for protesting prison imperialism precisely because these events internationalized the struggle. As a decommissioned federal prison, Alcatraz grounded American Indian movement activism in the concrete struggle over land deemed "surplus." Reclaiming surplus federal lands was an ingenious strategy predicated on restoring treaty rights by shifting the legal burden of proof for "criminal trespass" charges onto the federal government. The Alcatraz takeover then extended to other federal lands, as the "next Alcatraz" became occupations planned across Northern California and up through the Puget Sound, Alaska, and Canada. Even as it was grounded in local struggles over land, the Alcatraz occupation served as a platform for Native Americans' global appeal for sovereignty.

The Alcatraz Occupation

When the boat carrying fourteen Native American student activists approached Alcatraz Island in November 1969, Richard

Oakes jumped off to swim ashore. He was determined to get to the island first. After splitting into small groups, the students were eventually discovered and removed from the island. This was only the reconnaissance mission, they decided, and regrouped to return two weeks later. When they arrived on Alcatraz with eighty more people on November 20, 1969, they were able to hold the Rock for the next nineteen months. They reclaimed the Ohlone, Ramaytush, and Miwok land in the name of the IAT, a newly established intertribal organization. They claimed it by "right of discovery," and under the Fort Laramie Treaty (1868) provision that Indians could reclaim unused federal lands deemed surplus. While Oakes became the most recognizable face of the takeover, LaNada War Jack (Shoshone-Bannock) was the heart of the occupation, and John Trudell (Santee Lakota), host of Radio Free Alcatraz, became its enduring voice.[4]

Months before the occupation, activist LaNada War Jack (then known as LaNada Means) was arrested during the Third World Liberation Front student strike of 1969 and suspended from University of California, Berkeley. Undeterred, she occupied an abandoned section of a campus building, claiming it under squatter's right, and petitioned the university to turn it into a Native American Studies Center. She was the first Native American student admitted to Berkeley, and as chair of the Native American Students Association she had been leading the organizing to establish a Native American Studies Department there. Challenging the rules was not new to her. She had bounced in and out of Indian boarding schools as a child, being suspended and disciplined for speaking out against the prohibition on practicing Native customs and speaking Native languages. Upon arriving in the San Francisco Bay Area, she made deep connections with the Indian community there and was mentored by elder activists, like Belva Cottier (Rosebud Lakota) and Stella Leach (Colville-Oglala Lakota). She developed a framework of international Indigenous feminism, centering the Alcatraz occupation in a series of struggles for Indian self-determination during the Red Power era.

The idea for the occupation was worked out in the Indian Liberation course and Far Out Lab organized by War Jack and Jack Forbes (Powhatan-Renapé and Delaware-Lenápe) at UC Berkley, attended by San Francisco State students like Oakes (Akwesasne Mohawk). Cottier first explained the basis for the 1964 Lakota occupation of Alcatraz when she and forty others landed on the island and made their claim under the Fort Laramie Treaty. The acting warden had arrived and threatened them with felony trespass—a charge that would become central to the hundreds of ensuing occupations because it put the legal burden of proof on the federal government, or private landholder, to prove they actually held a title. Cottier and the other Lakota activists registered their claims with the Bureau of Land Management and took it to the courts. Ultimately, the courts ruled against them, arguing that the "Sioux" (Lakota) had not originally owned the land. But the example had been established.

Oakes was Akwesasne Mohawk from upstate New York. He was a tall, charismatic ironworker, whose Mohawk name—Ranoies—literally means "A Big Man." His wife, Annie Oakes, was from the Marrufo family, Pomo people, so they had family in Northern California. Oakes enrolled in the first Native American studies classes that came out of the Third World Student movement (1969) and helped recruit people for the

Alcatraz occupation with the IAT. The IAT was an example of urban, intertribal coalition building around direct actions that put land liberation at the center of claims of self-determination and sovereignty. They had a well-planned media strategy and legal team led by Aubrey Grossman. Oakes and Adam Nordwall's friend Tim Findley was a reporter at the *San Francisco Chronicle*, and Nordwall's connection to Findley was likely why the press arrived on Alcatraz in time for Oakes to read the preamble of the proclamation.

Alcatraz was a fitting site for an Indian reservation, according to U.S. government standards, the proclamation explained, because "the population has always been held as prisoners." The soil was nonproductive, there was no running water, and there was no subsoil oil or mineral rights, it continued, and the area was without adequate transportation, industry, education, and health care facilities. Still, it was strategically important. "It would be fitting and symbolic that ships from all over the world, entering the Golden Gate, would first see Indian land, and thus be reminded of the true history of this nation."[5] Oakes told reporters, "On one side of the country you have the Statue of Liberty, and this is the opposite, you have the true reality of liberty."[6] As they reclaimed the island, they sought to reclaim the meaning of justice: "There's a dual sense of justice in this country. We'd like a—end to this. And I think this here—manning the island of Alcatraz—is a positive step in that direction."[7]

The Alcatraz occupation was a direct protest against the federal termination policy. The policy consisted of a series of federal laws aimed at ending federal dealings with tribes by absorbing them into the general population. It was the realization of Henry

178   AMERICAN PURGATORY

Richard Pratt's fantasy—to "kill the Indian, save the man"—
through forced assimilation. As John Trudell put it in his radio
address from Alcatraz: "Termination is really a dirty word as far
as Indians are concerned." The question was asked: Why choose
to occupy an abandoned prison rather than a more desirable
land location? "The answers to that question are many and to we
Indians it is obvious. It is a symbol of what we have today and to
we Indians bears a remarkable resemblance to reservation life, as
neither has enough water, there are no natural resources, and the
federal government could find no use for it," Trudell explained.
"Thus Alcatraz became discarded land. We think it has more
value that than of a discarded prison. Yours is a competitive
society. And that's where the Alcatraz symbolism is. Alcatraz
was a prison, a symbol of what your society has produced. We
never needed prisons."[8]

Trudell began his first live broadcast from Alcatraz on Decem-
ber 22, 1969, with borrowed and donated radio equipment, from
the main cellblock building on Alcatraz, on the Pacifica Radio
Network on stations in Berkeley, Los Angeles, and New York.
Each episode began with a recording of Buffy Sainte-Marie
singing "Now that the Buffalo's Gone."[9] As the host of Radio
Free Alcatraz, Trudell interviewed prominent activists who
came to Alcatraz, like Sac and Fox citizen Grace Thorpe and
Jonny Bearcub, a member of the Fort Peck Assiniboine Sioux
Nation.[10] From the main cellblock, Trudell worked to internationalize the struggle, reframing the history of freedom and
placemaking. "You will forgive me if I tell you my people were
Americans for thousands of years before your people were. The
question is not how you can Americanize us, but how we can

Americanize you." In Trudell's telling, in the Native American way of life each has respect for the other's vision. "Because each of us respected his brothers' dream we enjoyed freedom here in America while your people were busy killing and enslaving each other across the water. [. . .] We have a hard trail ahead of us in trying to Americanize you and your white brothers, but we are not afraid." As Oakes put it: "We do not fear your threat to charge us with crimes on our land."[11]

The Next Alcatraz

The Alcatraz occupation inspired hundreds of grassroots takeovers of federal and corporate claimed places. As Trudell pointed out during the occupation of Alcatraz, the IAT members were also engaged in takeovers at Pit River and Clearlake, also in Northern California. When the final fifteen were removed from Alcatraz by U.S. marshals in 1971, some went almost immediately to occupy the federal Nike missile site and Bureau of Indian Affairs (BIA) offices in the East Bay. They inspired a groundswell of grassroots occupations and land liberations across the country. Over the next two years, Native American activists occupied seventy-four more federal facilities, culminating in a standoff at Wounded Knee on the Pine Ridge Reservation of the Oglala Sioux in South Dakota (1973).

Oakes called the Pit River occupations "the next Alcatraz."[12] The Pit River Rancheria consisted of 3.5 million acres of unceded ancestral land situated between four sacred landmarks: Mount Shasta and Mount Lassen, to the north and southwest, and Goose Lake and Eagle Lake, to the north and southeast. IAT members came to support the occupation of Rattlesnake Island, in Clearlake, which gave them momentum for a series of occupations on land claimed by the federal government, such as Lassen National Forest, and by the Pacific Gas and Electric company (PG&E). They then moved northward into the Pacific Northwest, where the United Indians of All Tribes (UIAT) attempted to occupy Fort Lawton, in Seattle. They were joined at their first attempt by the young activist Leonard Peltier, who helped people over the fence. Oakes was briefly arrested and jailed at Fort Lawton, but he maintained his promise: "This is the beginning of our fight for justice and self-determination—Alcatraz. Then Alaska, yes, Alaska is next."[13]

The symbol of Alcatraz lived on. Other Native American activists, like Russell Means, had learned from the example of the first Lakota occupation of Alcatraz (1964), led by Means's father, Hank Means, Belva Cottier, and others. As the strategy of reclaiming land spread across the country, Means participated in the takeover of the *Mayflower II* in Boston (1970), the occupation at Mount Rushmore (1971), carved into the Black Hills, a sacred site of the Lakota Sioux, the takeover of the BIA office in Washington, DC (1972), and finally, the occupation at Wounded Knee (1973–75).[14] In February 1973, the American Indian Movement (AIM) launched the occupation of Wounded Knee, on the Oglala Lakota Pine Ridge Reservation, in South Dakota. A determined group of about two hundred activists held the site of the 1890 Wounded Knee Massacre, in which the U.S. military slaughtered three hundred Lakota people over seventy-one days. The Wounded Knee occupiers established the state of Independent Oglala Nation (ION). After the lengthy standoff, the FBI launched a "second siege," resulting in the exchange of gunfire.[15] AIM activist Leonard Peltier was accused of killing two FBI agents and was sentenced to two consecutive life sentences.[16]

When the sentence was handed down, Peltier and his international defense committee knew that it was prison imperialism that should be on trial: "No, I'm not the guilty one here; I'm not the one who should be called a criminal—white racist America is the criminal for the destruction of our lands and my people; to hide your guilt from the decent human beings in America and around the world, you will sentence me to two consecutive life terms without any hesitation."[17] In his *Prison Writings*, he reflected, "When you grow up Indian, you don't have to become a criminal, you already are a criminal. You never know innocence. . . . We help give the American system of injustice the criminals it needs." As one Native American studies scholar puts it, "The prison is not just an apparatus of detention and punishment but a metonymic structure signifying the colonization, criminalization, and containment of an entire people."[18]

Through their strategy of occupying and reclaiming "surplus" federal properties, American Indian activists put their finger on a key dimension of prison expansion. The prison-building boom in California, as geographer Ruth Wilson Gilmore shows, relied on four types of surplus: surplus land, surplus capital, surplus state capacity, and in the context of deindustrialization and rising urban unemployment, "surplus" people.[19] Policy makers chose this response to economic crisis amid determined opposition from grassroots groups protesting increased criminalization, harsher drug laws, and mandatory minimum sentences.

Lawmakers sought a "spatial fix" to what they wrongly conceived as a race crime problem. Indeed, from the 1980s through today, California has built twenty-two prisons and only one public university. Native American activists advanced a spatial fix of their own. Efforts to stop the era of massive prison expansion are put into even starker relief by this series of direct actions by the IAT and other Indigenous people over the preceding decade. By occupying Alcatraz, they sought to open the ears, hearts, and minds of U.S. government officials to the fact that alternatives were, and still are, possible.

As Oakes put it in the IAT's message to the secretary of the interior: We "claim our traditional and natural right to create meaningful use of the Great Spirit's land."[20] The invocation of "use doctrine" was in part a tongue-in-cheek reference to John Locke's property rights theory, whereby English settlers had claimed land in North America. It also suggested a powerful and enduring truth: that this federal prison site could be better used as a Native American spiritual, cultural, and educational center. This place-based vision of justice, grounded on local land but making an international appeal, promised to undo rather than compound the ongoing impacts of prison imperialism.

Appealing to the World

Across the San Francisco Bay from Alcatraz, from inside San Quentin Prison, former Black Panther and renowned prison organizer Jalil A. Muntaqim began drafting his first appeal to the United Nations (1976). The petition gathered 2,500 signatures from prisoners across the country before it was filed in Geneva by Amnesty International lawyer Kathleen Burke.[21] Following Assata Shakur's escape to Cuba, Shakur answered the call to support the movement, issuing a "Statement to the UN Human Rights Campaign" proclaiming, "We've got to build a strong Human Rights Movement. We've got to build a strong Prison Movement. We've got to build a strong Black Liberation Movement, and we've got to struggle for liberation."[22]

Black prison organizers were well aware of the limits of using rights-based strategies to redress targeted persecution. With a hard-won understanding of the limits of state mechanisms to redress state violence, Black political prisoners appealed instead to the world. They hoped that an expanded human rights framework could be used to bring pressure on the United States. In a piece called "Let the People Speak to the United Nations" (1970), the BPP argued that petitioning against racism and genocide might expand the purview of the United Nations. Just as "Winston Churchill had no intention of presiding over the fall of the British Empire," they wrote, "these founders of the United Nations had no outlook that included the elimination of racism or its accompanying terror." Still, they believed in the promise it held as a global bully pulpit of public opinion. The UN must be made to work for the people everywhere, they argued, which begins by standing up to U.S. racist violence. This should be of paramount concern to the world, they warned: "American racism has become an export commodity spreading the germs of dehumanization." It is time to put an end to the "race wars this government is waging at home and abroad."[23]

The Malcolm X Doctrine

The strategy of appealing to the world to expose the injustices of the U.S. police and prison system had powerful precedent, stretching back through Black Panther and Republic of New Afrika (RNA) prison organizing, Malcolm X's Organization of Afro-American Unity (OAAU), mass defense campaigns for imprisoned Black activists like Claudia Jones, and the Civil Rights Congress's *We Charge Genocide* petition (1951), all the way to David Walker's *Appeal* (1828).[24] Among the imprisoned Black radical tradition appeals to the world formed an integral part of what RNA president Imari Obadele called the Malcolm X Doctrine.[25]

These principles of self-determination, appealing to the world, and global Black organizing were cornerstones of Malcolm X's OAAU human rights proposals. "Expand the civil rights struggle to the level of human rights, take it to the United Nations, where our African brothers can throw their weight on our side, where our Asian brothers can throw their weight on our side, where our Latin American brothers can throw their weight on our side."[26] Even as Malcolm X spoke of dragging the United States before the "world court," his organizing strategy was much broader than using international law as an end in and of itself. He used human rights as a means to build solidarity and connection with anticolonial liberation movements around the world. "Civil rights means you're asking Uncle Sam to treat you right. Human rights are something we're born with. Human rights are your God-given rights. Human rights are the rights that are recognized by all nations of this earth," Malcolm proclaimed in 1964. "So when we saw that we were up against a hopeless battle internally, we saw the necessity of getting allies at the world level," he wrote. As long as the struggle fell under the "jurisdiction" of the United States, it would be difficult for them to lend real support. "We decided that the only way to make the problem rise to the level where we could get world support was to take it away from the civil rights label, and put in the human rights label." In his *Appeal to African Heads of State*, Malcolm X explained that the OAAU had been sent to the historic African summit "to represent the interests of the 22 million African-Americans whose human rights are being violated daily by the racism of American imperialists." Tanzanian president Julius Nyerere proposed the summit pass a resolution condemning the mistreatment of Black people in the United States and support-ing the "freedom struggle for human rights."[27]

By framing the Black freedom movement as part of a world-wide struggle for human rights against colonialism, Malcolm X expanded the meaning and use of the concept. "The great-est weapon the colonial powers have used in the past against our people has always been divide-and-conquer," he explained. "America is a colonial power. . . . She has deprived us of the right to be human beings, the right to be recognized and respected as men and women." If the freedom movement is confined to the domestic boundaries of the nation-state, he reasoned, then Black people will be seen and treated as the minority. But if you look to the world stage, then "dark mankind" clearly outnumbers the so-called white population. "On the world stage the white man is just a microscopic minority."[28] This reality was deeply threatening to a white power structure who must have felt the moral precariousness of being a small settler minority on the world stage.

The RNA developed an internationalist analysis for how Black people in the United States had been treated like an internal colony, forming a nation within a nation and targeted with genocidal violence through policing and imprisonment. The FBI raided the RNA headquarters in Jackson, Mississippi, and arrested eleven members, who became known as the RNA-11, including RNA president Imari Abubakari Obadele (1971). Obadele spent twenty-one months in jail in Mississippi before being transferred and imprisoned in the federal penitentiary system, first at Terre Haute and then at Atlanta. Writing from federal prison in Atlanta, Obadele called out the hypocrisy of the U.S. human rights record in an open letter to Jimmy Carter (1978). "There is, Mr. Carter, a war of genocide being conducted against Black people, New Afrikans, in the United States." Pursuing policies that deliberately inflict conditions calculated to bring about the physical destruction of a group, in whole or in part, he continued, the U.S. government has also in particular targeted those Black people who resist poverty and oppression. Illegal FBI COINTELPRO raids, militarized campaigns, assassination plots, and imprisonment all suggest "to so much of the world that black lives mean less . . . than white lives."[29] When the New Afrikan Prisoners Organization proclaimed "We Still Charge Genocide" (1977), they outlined a decolonial theory of racial violence and oppression as well as an agenda for reparations that used the language of human rights while expanding it beyond UN definitions. The center of the RNA's political program was the demand to "free the land."[30]

Charging Genocide

As part of this international protest strategy, over the second half of the twentieth century Black radicals and their allies began repeatedly charging the U.S. police and prison system with genocide in an attempt to push open more narrow modes of redress offered by domestic and international legal systems. Drawing on the tradition of mass prisoner defense mobilized in support of the Scottsboro Boys, the Ingrams, Angelo Herndon, Benjamin Davis, and Claudia Jones, organizations like the Sojourners for Truth and Justice and the Civil Rights Congress further expanded the meaning and use of a Black human rights framework in their appeals to the world. This tradition was taken up and carried forward by the imprisoned Black radical tradition, who consistently fought for the freedom of U.S.-held political prisoners.

In their Black feminist manifesto *A Call to Negro Women* (1951), the Sojourners for Truth and Justice described the suffocating ubiquity of racism, making plain they could not eat, live, work, play, rest, or *breathe* free of racial discrimination and violence anywhere they went. "We cannot, must not, and will no longer in sight of God or man sit by and watch our lives destroyed by an unreasonable and unreasoning hate that metes out to us every kind of death it is possible for a human being to die," they proclaimed. "We have watched our husbands and fathers burned, quartered, hanged, and electrocuted by hooded and unhooded mobs. We have seen our brothers beaten, shot and stamped to death by police. We have seen our sons rotting in prison." Referring to the imprisonment of Rosa Lee Ingram in Georgia, they continued, "We have seen our daughters raped and degraded, and when one dares rise in defense of her honor she is jailed for life."[31] As they prepared to march on Washington, they beckoned: "Come, you widows of the legally lynched. Come you wives of those imprisoned and threatened with prison. Come you widowed by police brutality." The Sojourners for Truth and Justice was a veritable who's who of Black women activists, including Charlotta Bass, Shirley Graham Du Bois, Dorothy Hunton, Eslanda Goode Robeson, Alice Childress, Lorraine Hansberry, and Claudia Jones, who sent her support from confinement on house arrest. In their statement, they outlined a human rights framework that connected policing and prisons and state and vigilante violence as entwined forms of racist terror suffocating Black people.[32]

When the United States finally ratified the Geneva Convention on the Prevention of Genocide (1988), imprisoned Black radicals responded by pushing for a definition that included new "scientific forms of genocide" taking place inside U.S. prisons. Dr. Mutulu Shakur, Anthony X. Bradshaw, Malik Dinguswa, Terry D. Long, Mark Cook, Adolfo Matos, and James Haskins drafted *Genocide Waged Against the Black Nation* (1988), to circulate to political prisoners and for the Research Committee on International Law and Black Freedom Fighters in the United States to present at a human rights conference in Switzerland.[33] Written by those who experienced behavior modification firsthand, they chronicled the impacts of "psychological warfare" through techniques such as targeted segregation, isolation, sensory deprivation, drugging, and diet. "We specifically charge that the government of the United States is practicing genocide through behavior modification and counterinsurgency and low intensity warfare techniques in its penal system." Referring directly to the Geneva Convention on the Prevention and Punishment of Genocide, they argued that the behavior modification program in the U.S. penal system amounts to a "scientific form of genocide" waged against the Black Nation. Pushing for a wider international response, they explained, "The world can see what goes on in the tomb of America as Black people are being slowly strangled and suffocated to death." They concluded by putting it on permanent record before the world: "We charge the American Government with genocide. In clear, unequivocal terms, we charge the American Government with genocide against the captive Black people in America who are perpetually under siege."[34]

Decades of prison organizing resulted in *The Verdict of the Special International Tribunal: On the Violation of Human Rights of Political Prisoners and Prisoners of War in United States Prisons and Jails*, which charged the U.S. government, president, attorney general, FBI and CIA directors, Bureau of Prisons director, and state governors with human rights violations.[35] Responding to a series of new international resolutions against torture, genocide, and racism in the 1980s and 1990s, imprisoned activists, lawyers, and scholars pointed to the release of Nelson Mandela and political prisoners around the world and carefully made the case for the release of U.S. political prisoners and prisoners of war. Over the preceding year, delegations had petitioned the UN Human Rights Commission in Geneva, and now they were making the case in New York. Longtime movement attorneys Lennox S. Hinds and Jan Susler drew up the indictment, while

J. Soffiyah Elijah outlined the false convictions, excessive sentencing, and abusive conditions, including the targeted use of
control units, solitary confinement, and psychological warfare
techniques that political prisoners endured.[36] The tribunal drew
on UN conventions for human rights and genocide and made
the case for freeing all political prisoners and prisoners of war,
for their protection against genocidal practices waged by the
U.S. government and for self-determination for Black people,
Puerto Ricans, and Native Americans.

The Next Utopia

Appeals to international law, treaty obligations, and institutions
like the United Nations have had mixed results, even as the
language of human rights has been used forcefully to condemn
racist state and white vigilante violence in the United States.
Indeed, the mainstream version of human rights has had a vexed
relationship with the Black Freedom Struggle. In the early years
of the Civil Rights–Black Power Movement, many believed
that the United Nations' *Universal Declaration of Human Rights*
(1948) had the "language and philosophical power" to address
not only political and legal inequality but also underlying structural conditions in education, health care, housing, and employment. The ultimate tragedy was that Cold War politics twisted
the more robust definition of human rights into the narrowly
defined arena of abstract political and legal rights, forcing some
prominent Black activists and organizations, like the NAACP,
to remove the "Soviet-tainted" goals of economic and social
entitlements from their agenda. "The resulting inability to artic-

ulate the struggle for black equality as a human rights issue, doomed the subsequent Civil Rights Movement to 'a series of glorious defeats.'"[37] It was not until the 1970s that the "last utopia" of the modern human rights movement emerged, a broad social movement that promised to transcend government with a "moral displacement of politics," providing a "new paradigm of global aspiration." This last utopia was not enough, however, and it actually displaced competing global visions of safety, equity, and justice, namely in the forms of communism, socialism, decolonization, and Third World movements.[38]

In the Black-led anti-prison movement, appeals to the world have been used as a practice of world making, extending beyond the rights of individuals, international institutions, and a vastly unequal world order.[39] In the hands of imprisoned Black radicals, an alternate Black human rights tradition has been one of the primary means by which to internationalize the struggle against violence and domination and reenvision human flourishing. For many in the imprisoned Black radical tradition, human rights have actually been a way to mark the distinction between more thoroughgoing, revolutionary social change and more incremental, reformist, civil rights–based activism. Far from a bid for only legal recognition or redress, this tradition of human rights activism has sought to pry open the very underpinnings of the unequal world system and to ground a Black human rights tradition in a global theory of change.

Shakur's escape to Cuba was a literal, embodied appeal to the world for self-determination. She also carried forward a long tradition of Black political prisoners who have turned instead to international public opinion and global solidarity building. As

with the Black Communists persecuted under the Smith and
McCarran Acts in the 1950s, members of the BPP who were
persecuted by J. Edgar Hoover's illegal FBI COINTELPRO
program and crazed search to eliminate any potential "Black
messiah" capable of inspiring a mass movement for Black
self-determination, developed a deep distrust of the government
from personal experiences with unspeakable violence and trau-
matic loss. While it may have been more common to speak and
write in the language of internationalism during the New Negro
era of the 1920s and 1930s and in the language of solidarity with
Third World Liberation movements of the Global South during
the Civil Rights–Black Power era of the 1960s and 1970s, now
discourses and practices of police and prison abolition are ascendant in the latest phase of the struggle to overthrow global white
supremacy in the form of racist state and vigilante violence at
home and abroad.

In protesting prison imperialism, the imprisoned Black radical
tradition and former BPP members like Shakur and Muntaqim
have developed and deployed an expanded human rights framework that extends beyond flawed international institutions in
an unequal world system.[40] Beginning with his first petition to
the United Nations in 1976, Muntaqim has been at the center
of decades of international organizing from inside prison, bringing people together in the Jericho Movement and in his most
recent Spirit of Mandela campaign.[41] On the fiftieth anniversary of the Alcatraz takeover, LaNada War Jack was standing
on the front lines of the Standing Rock protest, an Indigenous-
led movement against the Dakota Access Pipeline. As War Jack
spoke with Red Nation cofounder Nick Estes (Lower Brule

Sioux) about the significance of the Alcatraz occupation to the ongoing Black and Indigenous movements for sovereignty, land rights, reparations, and abolition, they made clear how the process of ensuring the Spirit of Mandela and the Next Alcatraz are put into practice is both international and intergenerational movement-building work.[42]

Epilogue
Out of Purgatory

The only way to eliminate racism is to eliminate imperialism. The structure of imperialism means racism; the two are one thing.

—Richard Wright[1]

Three years before his release, Jalil A. Muntaqim launched the Spirit of Mandela campaign, in 2017 from inside a prison in New York, to convene an international tribunal to investigate violations of U.S.-held political prisoners' human rights. Invoking Nelson Mandela's imprisonment in apartheid South Africa, he called for the return of international jurists to reexamine the treatment of political prisoners in the United States under the United Nation's Mandela Rules. The coalition behind the campaign—including the Jericho Movement, the Campaign to Bring Mumia Home, the International Leonard Peltier Defense Committee, and the Incarcerated Workers Organizing Committee—views it as the latest action in a series of such global appeals. Along with the investigation itself, the campaign aims to expose the hypocrisy of the U.S. human rights record, broaden the base of antiracist and anti-imperialist unity, build international solidarity, create a commission to remedy FBI persecution under COINTELPRO, and provide an official report to the United Nations, and "hence to the world."[2]

The international tribunal is the latest in a series of international actions to support political prisoners within and beyond U.S. borders. Following the passage of the UN General Assembly resolution on the Right to Remedy and Reparation, the Jericho Movement pushed for congressional hearings on past and ongoing human rights violations. Comparing the documented torture of Muntaqim and many other prisoners to the victims of torture at Guantanamo Bay, Abu Ghraib, and Bagram Air Base, they called for a Truth and Reconciliation Commission to begin to "heal America's racial trauma."[3] This work was taken up and carried forward by coalitions using an expanded human rights framework to apply international pressure to push for reparations on the local level, in places like Chicago, where Jon Burge, former GTMO interrogator turned police commander, tortured false confessions out of over a hundred Black people during his decades-long "reign of terror."[4]

The Jericho Movement's defense campaigns include supporting world-famous political prisoners like Leonard Peltier and Mumia Abu Jamal, as well as lesser-known Black Panther Party, Black Liberation Army, and New Afrikan political prisoners, like Mutulu Shakur, Jamil Al-Amin (formerly H. Rap Brown), Ed Poindexter, Kamau Sadiki, Kojo Bomani Sababu, Ruchell "Cinque" Magee, Joseph Brown, and Rev. Joy Powell. They support those imprisoned in the corners of American empire, from the Caribbean islands to Indian reservations, like the Virgin Island Three—Abdul Aziz, Malik El-Amin, Hanif Shabazz

Bey—and the Water Protectors imprisoned for resisting the expansion of the Dakota Access Pipeline on the Standing Rock Sioux Reservation.[5]

Building on years of intergenerational organizing led by groups like the Jericho Movement, Black People Against Police Torture, Chicago Torture Justice Memorials, and Project Nia, a delegation of Chicago youth calling themselves We Charge Genocide (WCG) traveled to Geneva to testify to the UN Committee Against Torture (2014).[6] They were young people from a constellation of groups like Black Youth Project 100, Assata's Daughters, #LetUsBreathe Collective, Chicago Alliance Against Racist and Political Repression, and Women's All Points Bulletin. The delegation charged the Chicago police with genocide, while others testified about Jon Burge's torture cases, police rape of Black women, and the abuse and imprisonment of transgender women of color.[7] By advancing "A Human Right to Reparations," they then were able to bring pressure on the Chicago City Council to pass the historic Chicago Reparations Ordinance (2015).[8] This is the first reparations ordinance in the United States to specifically address the harm caused by torturous conditions of the police and the prison system.

Amid the worldwide Black Lives Matter (BLM) uprisings of some 26 million people in the United States alone, the United Nations issued a statement condemning systemic racism in the United States (2020).[9] What this means for those who have died and are dying and for those whose lives are daily threatened by unjust imprisonment during the ongoing pandemic remains to be seen. The uprisings are now considered the largest and broadest protest movement in U.S. history. They build on years of organizing for Black lives and have inspired solidarity protests around the world. Demands to free longtime political prisoners and to release all people from dangerous and unnecessary confinement in jails and prisons intensified as the COVID-19 virus was disproportionately killing people in prison. As new freedom dreams, policy proposals, and future-making practices take shape, many are looking to Black and Indigenous traditions of antiracist and anticolonial organizing and movement building for inspiration and lessons learned. Across the long history of the struggle against state violence, activists in the U.S. abolition movement have pushed for an international theory of change, rooted in a decolonial analysis of racial violence, and an expanded framework of human rights. Perhaps the global prison abolition movement will become the new human rights paradigm as we move from "the last utopia" to the next.[10]

Prison abolitionists have been organizing for decades to bring people together to imagine and build a world without prisons. Although sometimes wrongly characterized as concerned only with domestic campaigns to "defund" the police, prison abolition has always been a global coalition-building movement with an international theory of change. Drawing on a Black feminist genealogy linking Claudia Jones and the Third World Women's Alliance, organizations like INCITE! Women of Color Against Violence and Critical Resistance illustrate how triple jeopardy works along related axes of economic, racial, and gendered oppression from the most intimate to the most global scale. The *INCITE!-Critical Resistance Statement* (2001), a foundational document in the prison abolition movement, was a call to social movements concerned with ending violence

worldwide: "We seek to build movements that not only end violence, but that create a society based on radical freedom, mutual accountability, and passionate reciprocity."[11] As INCITE!'s
antimilitarism and community accountability toolkits circulate
around the world, they connect an increasingly global organizing ecosystem in places like Chicago, Manchester, São Paulo,
and Johannesburg.[12]

Abolition feminism, the driving force behind this organizing, operates from a global framework of power. As Angela Y.
Davis, Gina Dent, Erica Meiners, and Beth Ritchie explain
in *Abolition. Feminism. Now*: "It requires a respect for movements toward self-determination, recognizing forms of oppression across borders as an important context for redefining both
anti-violence work and freedom."[13] The framework of abolition
geography is similarly grounded in a global view of the problem
and solutions. Prison expansion was worked out in the context
of globalization, because "prison is the site where state-building
is least contested, yet most class based and racialized," abolitionist geographer Ruth Wilson Gilmore explains. "The struggle
for *international* sovereignty in the context of 'postcolonial' globalization can, and often does, feature a rush to institutional
conformity—which today includes expanded criminalization,
policing, and prisons. As a result, new or renovated state structures are often grounded in the exact same fatal power-difference
couplings (for example racism, sexism, homophobia) that radical
anti-colonial activists fought to expunge from the social order."[14]

This anticolonial protest tradition is being carried forward by
Indigenous activist groups like the Red Nation. Proclaiming "no
deportations on stolen land," the Red Nation's Beyond Borders

Caucus organized an occupation of the Tornillo Port of Entry in Texas (Rarámuri territory) to protest the detention of three thousand migrant children (2019). Their manifesto articulates the interconnected struggles of those caught up and crushed by prison imperialism: "We have an Indigenous-centered perspective of migrant justice and organizing that rejects the settler state's notions of citizenship and instead creates solidarity between Indigenous people and undocumented migrants. [. . .] We ask questions like, 'What would it look like if Native nations asserted their sovereignty to offer sanctuary to undocumented migrants and refugees?' And, 'What does solidarity look like between indigenous nations beyond colonial borders?'"[15] Working from this relational framework, they demand an end to family separation and an end to U.S. foreign policy that subverts democracy abroad. Following the first principle of their manifesto—that "migrant justice movements must be aligned with Indigenous and Black liberation"—they call for abolishing the prison industrial complex, Immigration and Customs Enforcement (ICE), the Border Patrol, and the school-to-prison/detention/deportation pipeline. Ultimately, at its most expansive, this means reimagining the nation-state itself: "We demand the abolition of all borders from Palestine to Turtle Island."[16]

These several streams of international movement building intensified during the global COVID-19 pandemic that began in January 2020. Organizations like the Black Alliance for Peace and the Alliance for Global Justice extended their call to restore the anti-imperialist and pro-peace agenda in social movement organizing in the United States, working to awaken people to the realities of imperialism in the face of massive denial, disavowal, and popular amnesia as even the mainstream left in the United States has not always kept foreign policy consistently in view. The Alliance for Global Justice calls for an end to the spread of U.S. international incarceration programs in over thirty-three countries and for the release of all "prisoners of empire."[17]

Responding to the local and global conditions made clearer by the pandemic, activists from around the world came together to promote international solidarity and global prison abolition. As the World Without Prisons coalition put it, "The COVID-19 pandemic has given new urgency to the need to abolish prisons, refugee camps, migrant detention centers and the inhuman capitalist carceral system." The inability to socially distance and properly protect oneself from the infectious disease made it clear that a sentence of any length could effectively become a death sentence.[18] The coalition is composed of individuals and organizations spanning the globe, including signatories from the United States, Brazil, South Africa, and the Middle East. The World Without Prisons coalition embraces a theoretical framework with deep roots in anti-carceral movement building, one that sees the connections between different forms of oppression on the local and global scale.[19] Together with pushing for the immediate release of prisoners, the World Without Prisons coalition is committed to developing alternatives, in terms of addressing harm on the interpersonal level and of transforming structures on the societal level.[20]

The Black Lives Matter (BLM) movement protestors who climbed the statue of Andrew Jackson in the nation's capital had their finger on the pulse of the groundswell of protest against racist state and vigilante violence. The equestrian statues of Jackson in Presidents Park in Washington, DC, and Jackson Square, New Orleans, were made by Clark Mills, the very same sculptor commissioned to take life casts of the Fort Marion prisoners. Statues of the avowed "Indian killer" and fellow slave-owning presidents like Thomas Jefferson and James Monroe venerate the early engineers of prison imperialism. Capturing and categorizing those forcibly held against their will, purgatory's ghosts—the life casts and human remains buried on school and prison grounds or stored in universities and cultural institutions—continue to haunt theories of governing the prison and attempts at governing the world. Life casts were used to form the basis of racist theories that have structured social hierarchies domestically and globally, past and present.[21] Removing statues and repatriating remains is not a cosmetic fix, as the international movement to Take 'Em Down makes clear, they are attached to systems of inequality that more and more people are tracing to their source.[22]

*   *   *

When members of the Northern Arapaho traveled to the Carlisle Indian Industrial School cemetery in Pennsylvania to meet with U.S. Army representatives to arrange for the return of Little Chief, Horse, and Little Plume, three children buried there, it marked the first official repatriation from federal Indian boarding schools in U.S. history (2016). At first, Little Plume could not be found—his grave contained the bones of two other children. Over the ensuing years, members of the Blackfeet Nation, Oglala Lakota, Standing Rock, Oneida Nation, Iowa Nation, Mondoc Nation, Omaha Nation, Unangax̂ (Aleut), and Rosebud Sioux came for their child ancestors.[23] So began the continuing process of returning the nearly two hundred children buried at the Carlisle Indian Industrial School alone. Among them, perhaps, are children transferred from the St. Augustine School for Apache Children at Fort Marion who were forcibly separated from their imprisoned parents and transferred to Carlisle after Henry Richard Pratt implemented the scheme.[24]

U.S. Department of the Interior secretary Deb Haaland (Pueblo of Laguna) launched the first federal investigation with the Federal Indian Boarding School Initiative in 2021, although official efforts to identify and return human remains began with the passage of the Native American Graves Protection Act (NAGPRA) in 1990.[25] Native American studies scholar Roxanne Dunbar-Ortiz estimates there are two million Indigenous people held in "storage" in the Smithsonian and other museums and by universities, state historical societies, National Park Service offices, warehouses, and curio shops.[26] Even as NAGPRA charges government and cultural institutions to identify and return American Indian, Native Alaskan, and Hawaiian Native peoples, similar initiatives have been undertaken by Indigenous people worldwide and are sanctioned under the UN Declaration on the Rights of Indigenous Peoples provisions on the rights of Indigenous communities to the repatriation of their human remains (2007). This global geography of marked and unmarked graves raises the question of what responsibility people within the United States have to the history of Indigenous people who were eliminated in prisons and reform schools in other sites of American empire, such as Puerto Rico, Panama, and the Philippines.

Responding to Harvard University's announcement about the human remains contained in the Peabody Museum, the National Native American Boarding School Healing Coalition asked that the seven hundred Native children's boarding school hair cuttings be returned to families and Tribal Nations.[27] As Native American studies scholar Philip Deloria (Dakota Nation) put it in the university's report: "There are obvious questions that stem from the history," such as who has the right to the bodies of the dead, for what purposes, and under what conditions? There are other, more existential questions, like "What wrongs come down to us? With what obligations for repair?" Human remains "have a gravity and meaning of their own," he explains, which pose "a spiritual challenge" to our communities: "I have now seen enough repatriation—including the psychic challenges to those working in the trenches and the transcendent power of moments of physical return—to have a felt understanding of the spiritual dimensions of these labors."[28]

The nineteen people listed as enslaved or likely to have been enslaved in Harvard's Steering Committee on Human Remains report were brought to Boston from places like St. Louis, Missouri, Marksville, Louisiana, and a Delaware peat bog.[29] Four came from the Caribbean and Brazil, including from Cuba, Martinique, and Rio de Janeiro. Among them are the cranial remains of "an unidentified African man from the Nago tribe who was injured during the Malê uprising in Bahia, Brazil."[30] He joins those who were executed, incarcerated, or transported and forcibly separated from their families by being "sold down river" and banished beyond U.S. borders for fighting for freedom in Gabriel Prosser's, Denmark Vesey's, and Nat Turner's revolts.

They, in turn, are joined by the millions of souls caught up and crushed in hundreds of black sites dotted across America's prison empire. The report recommends repatriating or returning the human remains to lineal descendants or descendant communities. As steering committee chair Evelyn Hammonds writes, "I hope our ancestors whose remains are in our care will see that we have begun our journey along the path that leads toward justice."[31]

What will it mean to begin to acknowledge and repair the harm done to those whose lives have been cut short, who have died in prison or soon after their release? If there is a way out of America's purgatory created by the ever-expanding prison system, it is animated by prison protests, solidarity strikes, and mass defense campaigns as well as by the movement to repatriate the human remains of people interned in federal and private institutions that spawned the entangled theories of penology and foreign policy to their ancestral burial grounds. Even as racism and colonialism still seek to dominate the world, structuring inequality globally, there are alternative paths beyond the fate of perpetual abjection and toward a celebration of life, solidarity, visions of freedom, and practices of liberation. This is the promise of a new age of internationalism. Decolonization is an historic process, Frantz Fanon reminds us, guided above all by a place-based, anti-capitalist, local and global theory of justice.

"Prison is a second-by-second assault on the soul," Mumia Abu-Jamal writes in *Live from Death Row*. While a person is "locked away in the netherworld," children grow into adulthood, and loving relationships "wither into yesterday's dust." Indeed, "The mind-numbing, soul-killing savage sameness that makes each day an echo of the day before . . . makes prison the abode of spirit death."[32] If the prison has been the epicenter of spirit death, following Abu-Jamal's formulation, then perhaps excavating the past to summon the significance of Chief Osceola, Felipe Salvador, Lester Greaves, Claudia Jones, Blanca Canales, Lolita Lebrón, Richard Oakes, Assata Shakur, and Jalil Muntaqim, may help settle purgatory's ghosts by amplifying their framework for challenging prison imperialism. As people in the prison movement have understood, the liberation of Black and Indigenous people within the United States was, and continues to be, intimately connected to the liberation of people in Africa, Latin America, Asia, and every part of the formerly enslaved and colonized world. Repatriating remains is not the end, but the beginning of reckoning with this history.

Acknowledgments

This book could not have been written without the insight and expertise of archivists and special collections librarians in the United States, Philippines, Panama, Puerto Rico, and Cuba. My sincerest appreciation.

I am most grateful to those who read and gave valuable feedback on all or parts of the manuscript at various stages: Walter Johnson, Vincent Brown, Evelyn Brooks Higginbotham, David Armitrage, Elizabeth Hinton, Kirsten Weld, Dylan Rodríguez, Dan Berger, Clint Smith, V.P. Franklin, Kyrah Malika Daniels, Clare Anderson, Christian DeVito, Franco Barchiesi, Shona N. Jackson, Keisha N. Blain, Quito Swan, Vicente Rafael, Moon Ho Jung, and Erin Gray. Special thanks to William Chiriguayo, master wordsmith, for dreaming up the title *American Purgatory* on the back of a napkin in New York City. My editor Marc Favreau and his team at The New Press are as talented as they are committed. Thank you to my agent Roz Foster, then at Sandra Dijkstra and now at Goldin Literary Agency, for her keen eye and belief in the project.

The cover art and portraits are by the brilliant artist Ayo Y. Scott. His father's artwork graces the cover of my best friend's late father's book, whose work inspired me to go in search of root causes in the first place. The maps are made by master cartographer Lynn Carlson, at Compass Cartographic, with whom I've collaborated for about a decade.

I am thankful for the community I have found among colleagues, students, staff, and friends at UC Davis: Moradewun Adejunmobi, Bettina Ng'weno, Milmon Harrison, Elisa Joy White, Kimberly Nettles-Barcelon, Shingirai Taodzera, Mark Jerng, Katherine Ampaw-Matthei, Anna Juline, Daniel Cordova, Erin Gray, Ofelia Cuevas, Justin Leroy, Bruce Haynes, Robyn Magalit Rodriguez, Keith Watenpaugh, Verónica Morales, Rana Jaleel, Beenash Jafree, Michael Singh, Orly Clergé, Darnel Degand, Erica Kohl-Arenas, Greg Downs, Chuck Walker, Rachel St. John, Génesis Lara, Marlené Mercado, Mia Dawson, Michaela Anang, Aaliayah McKnight Corcran, Vivienne Muller, Kirin Rajagopalan, London Legree, and Sade Johnson.

I have benefited from institutional support from the Andrew W. Mellon Foundation, American Council of Learned Societies, University of California Hellman Faculty Fellowship, UC Davis Humanities Institute, UC Davis Center for the Advancement of Multicultural Perspectives on the Social Sciences, Art, and Humanities, Brown University's Watson Institute for International and Public Affairs, Harvard University's Warren Center, and Harvard's Hutchins Center for African and African American Research.

I have deepest admiration and respect for the activists who challenge the prison system. Learning from and lifting up their stories in hopes of contributing in some way to the growing shift in consciousness provides solace from the feelings of inadequacy that come with writing anything that seeks to chip away at the giant edifice of the carceral state. I am particularly inspired by the tireless work of activists in New Orleans and the Bay Area, and have been sustained by working in community with friends and comrades like Michelle Ramos and the art-activists at Alternate ROOTS, who taught me the importance of placemaking, Pam Fadem and Rachel Klein, at the California Coalition for Women Prisoners, and each of the members of our writing group in California prisons. This book is for my students, who have taught me so much and who are busy building a better future.

Family makes all things possible. All my love and gratitude to the Weber family, the Rycroft family, the Alexander family, and Kraus sisters' clan. Thank you especially to my mother, brother, and stepmother for their support, to my sister and my aunt for their inspiration growing up, and to my dad for being endlessly interested in reading and discussing this stuff. Above all to my wife Veronica, my rock in all things, and our children, Elijah and Tallulah.

Notes

Preface: Purgatory's Ghosts

1. Claudia Jones, *West Indian Gazette* (1958), quoted in Carole Boyce Davies, *Left of Karl Marx: The Political Life of Black Communist Claudia Jones* (Durham, NC: Duke University Press, 2008), 87.

2. Benjamin D. Weber, "Fugitive Justice: The Possible Futures of Prison Records from U.S. Colonial Rule in the Philippines," *Archive Journal* (2017).

3. On policing the Philippines and the rise of the American surveillance state, see Alfred W. McCoy, *Policing America's Empire: The United States, the Philippines, and the Rise of the Surveillance State* (Madison: University of Wisconsin Press, 2009). The earlier origins of the surveillance state are rooted in the antiblack logics of racial slavery. See Simone Browne, *Dark Matters: On the Surveillance of Blackness* (Durham: Duke University Press, 2015).

4. Alliance for Global Justice, "Prison Imperialism," afgj.org/category /prison-imperialism.

5. Chalmers Johnson, *Blowback: The Costs and Consequences of American Empire* (New York: Henry Holt, 2000; 2004). On the impact of

racism and colonialism on the U.S. prison system, see Angela Y. Davis, *Are Prisons Obsolete?* (New York: Seven Stories, 2003); Khalil Gibran Muhammad, *The Condemnation of Blackness: Race, Crime, and the Making of Modern Urban America* (Cambridge, MA: Harvard University Press, 2010); Sarah Haley, *No Mercy Here: Gender, Punishment, and the Making of Jim Crow Modernity* (Chapel Hill: University of North Carolina Press, 2016); Dennis Childs, *Slaves of the State: Black Incarceration from the Chain Gang to the Penitentiary* (Minneapolis: University of Minnesota Press, 2015); Kali N. Gross, *Colored Amazons: Crime, Violence, and Black Women in the City of Brotherly Love, 1880–1910* (Durham: Duke University Press, 2006); Dan Berger, *Captive Nation: Black Prison Organizing in the Civil Rights Era* (Chapel Hill: University of North Carolina Press, 2014); Elizabeth Hinton, *From the War on Poverty to the War on Crime: The Making of Mass Incarceration in America* (Cambridge, MA: Harvard University Press, 2016); Heather Ann Thompson, *Blood in the Water: The Attica Prison Uprising of 1971 and Its Legacy* (New York: Pantheon, 2016); Jordan T. Camp, *Incarcerating the Crisis: Freedom Struggles and the Rise of the Neoliberal State* (Oakland: University of California Press, 2016); Dylan Rodríguez, *Forced Passages: Imprisoned Radical Intellectuals and the U.S. Prison Regime* (Minneapolis: University of Minnesota Press, 2006); Luana Ross, *Inventing the Savage: The Social Construction of Native American Criminality* (Austin: University of Texas Press, 1998); Kelly Lytle Hernández, *City of Inmates: Conquest, Rebellion, and the Rise of Human Caging in Los Angeles, 1771–1965* (Chapel Hill: University of North Carolina Press, 2017); Rebecca McLennan, *The Crisis of Imprisonment: Protest, Politics, and the Making of the American Penal State, 1776–1941* (Cambridge University Press, 2008); David Oshinsky, *Worse Than Slavery: Parchman Farm and the Ordeal of Jim Crow Justice* (New York: Free Press, 1996); Alex Lichtenstein, *Twice the Work of Free Labor: The Political Economy of Convict Labor in the New South* (Verso, 1996); Douglass Blackmon, *Slavery by Another Name: The Re-Enslavement of Black Americans from the Civil War to World War II* (Doubleday, 2008); Robert Chase, *We Are Not Slaves: State Violence, Coerced Labor, and Prisoners' Rights in Postwar America* (UNC Press, 2020); Robert Perkinson, *Texas Tough: The Rise of America's Prison Empire* (Picador, 2010). On global dimensions of the U.S. prison system, see Angela Y. Davis,

Freedom Is a Constant Struggle (Chicago: Haymarket Books, 2016); Angela Y. Davis, *Abolition Democracy* (New York: Seven Stories, 2005); Joy James, ed., *Warfare in the American Homeland: Policing and Prison in a Penal Democracy* (Durham, NC: Duke University Press, 2007); Ruth Wilson Gilmore, *Golden Gulag: Prisons, Surplus, Crisis, and Opposition in Globalizing California* (Oakland: University of California Press, 2007); Julia Chinyere Oparah, ed., *Global Lockdown: Race, Gender, and the Prison-Industrial Complex* (New York: Routledge, 2005); Jenna Loyd, Matt Mitchelson, and Andrew Burridge eds., *Beyond Walls and Cages: Prisons, Borders, and Global Crisis* (Athens, GA: University of Georgia Press, 2012); Dylan Rodríguez, *Suspended Apocalypse: White Supremacy, Genocide, and the Filipino Condition* (Minneapolis: University of Minnesota Press, 2009); A. Naomi Paik, *Rightlessness: Testimony and Redress in U.S. Prison Camps Since World War II* (Chapel Hill: University of North Carolina Press, 2015); Marisol Lebrón, *Policing Life and Death: Race, Violence, and Resistance in Puerto Rico* (Oakland: University of California Press, 2019); Stuart Schrader, *Badges Without Borders: How Global Counterinsurgency Transformed American Policing* (Oakland: University of California Press, 2019); Micol Seigel, *Violence Work: State Power and the Limits of Police* (Durham: Duke University Press, 2018).

1. Prisons and Placemaking

1. Frantz Fanon, *The Wretched of the Earth* (New York: Grove, 1963), 36.

2. National Park Service, "Castillo de San Marcos National Monument," www.nps.gov/casa/index.htm.

3. Mandy Izadi, *The Seminole South: A Hidden History of Water, Land, and Power* (New Haven, CT: Yale University Press, forthcoming).

4. Walter Johnson, "The Racial Origins of U.S. Sovereignty," *Raritan* 31, no. 3 (Winter 2012): 50–59.

5. Matthew J. Clavin, *The Battle of Negro Fort: The Rise and Fall of a Fugitive Slave Community* (New York: New York University Press, 2019); Nathaniel Millett, *The Maroons of Prospect Bluff and Their Quest for Freedom in the Atlantic World* (Gainesville: University of Florida Press, 2013).

Nathaniel Millett, "Defining Freedom in the Atlantic Borderlands of the Revolutionary Southeast," *Early American Studies* 5, no. 2 (Fall 2007): 367–94; Jane Landers, *Black Society in Spanish Florida* (Urbana: University of Illinois Press, 1999).

6. My discussion of the Black Fort is inspired by Walter Johnson's introductory lecture, "Slavery, Capitalism, Imperialism" (Harvard University, Cambridge, MA, Fall, 2011).

7. Clavin, *Battle of Negro Fort*, 93–4.

8. Clavin, *Battle of Negro Fort*, 81–93. See also Jane Landers, *Black Society in Spanish Florida* (Urbana: University of Illinois Press, 1999); Michael Gomez, *Exchanging Our Country Marks: The Transformation of African Identities in the Colonial and Antebellum South* (Chapel Hill: University of North Carolina Press, 1998); John K. Thornton, *African and Africans in the Making of the Atlantic World 1400–1800*, 2nd ed. (New York: Cambridge University Press, 2017).

9. On enslaved news networks, see Julius Scott, *The Common Wind: Afro-American Currents in the Age of the Haitian Revolution* (New York: Verso, 2020); Steven Hahn, *A Nation Under Our Feet: Black Political Struggles in the Rural South from Slavery to the Great Migration* (Cambridge, MA: Belknap, 2005).

10. Clavin, *Battle of Negro Fort*, 71–2, 100–101, 105–7. See also Deborah Rosen, *Border Law: The First Seminole War and American Nationhood* (Cambridge, MA: Harvard University Press, 2015); James Monroe to Anthony St. John Baker, July 10, 1815, *British and Foreign State Papers: 1818–1819* (London: James Ridgeway, 1835), 367–68.

11. Arthur Ashe Institute, "Massacre Unveiled: Remembering the Negro Fort," *UCLA* (2016), arthurashe.ucla.edu/2016/07/27/massacre-unveiled-remembering-the-negro-fort.

12. C.L.R. James, *Black Jacobins: Toussaint L'Ouverture and the San Domingo Revolution* (New York: Vintage Books, 1963; 1989); Laurent Dubois, *Avengers of the New World: The Story of the Haitian Revolution* (Cambridge, MA: The Belknap Press of Harvard University Press, 2004); Vincent Brown, *Tacky's Revolt: The Story of an Atlantic Slave War* (Cambridge, MA: The Belknap Press of Harvard University Press, 2022). On the idea of a racialized "spatial imaginary," see Clyde Adrian Woods, *Development Arrested: The Blues and Plantation Power in the Mississippi*

Delta (London: Verso, 1998); George Lipsitz, *The Possessive Investment in Whiteness: How White People Profit from Identity Politics* (Philadelphia: Temple University Press, 1998).

13. "Letter from the Secretary of the Navy, Transmitting, in Ordinance to a Resolution of the House of Representatives, Documents Relating to the Destruction of the Negro Fort in East Florida in the Month of July, 1816" (Washington: E. De Kraft, 1819).

14. Rosen, *Border Law.*

15. Arthur Ashe Institute, "Massacre Unveiled." See also National Park Service, "Aboard the Underground Railroad: British Fort," www.nps.gov /nr/travel/underground/fl1.htm.

16. Arthur Ashe Institute, "Massacre Unveiled."

17. M. Seymour, "Fort Marion, at St. Augustine—It's History and Romance," *Frank Leslie's Popular Monthly* Vol. 19 (Frank Leslie Publishing House, 1885); *St. Augustine Under Three Flags: Tourist Guide and History* (W.J. Harris Company, 1918), 17–21.

18. Quoted in John T. Sprague, *The Origins, Progress, and Conclusion of the Florida War* (New York: D. Appleton, 1848): "Coacoochee (Wild Cat) tells how he escaped from the prison at Ft. Marion (Castillo de San Marcos) in St. Augustine after being taken captive while negotiating under a flag of truce," November 29, 1837 (Sprague, 325). See also Kirk Munroe, "In the Dungeon of the Ancient Fortress" and "A Daring Escape," *Through Swamp and Glade: A Tale of the Seminole War* (New York: Charles Scribner's Sons, 1896; 1916), 245–54, 255–63; Rogers W. Young, "Fort Marion During the Seminole War, 1835–1842," *Florida Historical Society Quarterly* 13, no. 4 (1935): 193–223; Caroline Mays Brevard and Henry Eastman Bennett, "The Capture of Osceola and Coacoochee," *A History of Florida* (New York: American Book, 1904), 137–40.

19. National Park Service, "Escape of the Seminoles," www.nps.gov /parkhistory/online_books/source/sb3/sb3m.htm. See also Kirk Munroe, "In the Dungeon of the Ancient Fortress," and "A Daring Escape," *Through the Swamp and Glade*, 245–54; 255–63.

20. Richard Henry Pratt, "The Florida Indian Prisoners of 1875–1878," *Richard Henry Pratt Papers MS*, Box 19 (Yale University, Beinecke Library

Archive); "Prisoner List," *Pratt Papers MS*, Box 22; Richard Henry Pratt, *Battlefield to Classroom*, 92. See also Brad D. Lookingbill, *War Dance at Fort Marion: Plains Indian War Prisoners* (Norman, OK: University of Oklahoma Press, 2006), 37–41.

21. Nelson A. Miles and Marion P. Maus, *Personal Recollections and Observations of General Nelson A. Miles* (Chicago: Werner, 1896), 139. See also Stan Hoig, *The Sand Creek Massacre* (Norman, OK: University of Oklahoma Press, 1974); Ari Kelman, *A Misplaced Massacre: Struggling over the Memory of Sand Creek* (Cambridge, MA: Harvard University Press, 2013).

22. Lookingbill, *War Dance at Fort Marion*; Veronica Pasfield, "The Head, the Heart, and the Hands: Hampton, Carlisle, and the Hilo in/as Circuits of Transpacific Empire, 1819–1887" (PhD Dissertation, University of Michigan, Ann Arbor, 2013).

23. Pratt, "The Florida Indian Prisoners of 1875–1878," *Pratt Papers MS*, Box 19; "Letterbook of Florida Prisoners," *Pratt Papers MS*, Box 14.

24. *St. Louis Republican*, May 5, (1875), quoted in Lookingbill, *War Dance at Fort Marion*, 46.

25. Ah-Kah letter quoted in Lizzie Chapman, "The Indians at San Marcos," *The Independent* (1878). See also Pratt, "Letterbook of Florida Prisoners," *Pratt Papers MS*, Box 14.

26. Lizzie Chapman, "The Indians at San Marcos," *The Independent* (1878), quoted in Lookingbill, *War Dance at Fort Marion*, 85.

27. Ibid.

28. John L. Sipes, "Medicine Water. Mi-huh-heu-i-mup. Cheyenne Ft. Marion POW," John Sipes Cheyenne Family Oral Histories (2003), home.epix.net/~landis/medicinewater.html.

29. U.S. Department of Interior, Federal Indian Boarding Schools Initiative Investigative Report (2022), www.bia.gov/sites/default/files/dup/inlinefiles/bsi_investigative_report_may_2022_508.pdf.

30. Pratt, "The Fathers of the Republic on Indian Transformation and Redemption," Before the Society of American Indians (1913), 2–8, in *Pratt Papers, MS*, Box 19.

31. Richard Henry Pratt, "The Advantages of Mingling Indians with Whites," *Pratt Papers, MS*, Box 19, 761.

32. Luana Ross, *Inventing the Savage: The Social Construction of Native American Criminality* (Austin, TX: University of Texas Press, 1998). See also, Ward Churchill, *Kill the Indian, Save the Man* (San Francisco: City Lights, 2005), 12–14.

33. For a full list, see U.S. Department of Interior Federal Indian Boarding Schools Initiative Investigative Report (2022), List of Federal Indian Boarding Schools, www.bia.gov/sites/default/files/dup/inline-files /bsi_investigative_report_may_2022_508.pdf.

34. Richard Henry Pratt, *The Indian Industrial School, Carlisle, Pennsylvania: Its Origin, Purposes, Progress, and Difficulties Surmounted* (Carlisle, PA: Hamilton Library Association, 1908), 8.

35. Richard Henry Pratt, "Re: Freedom and Responsibility," (Girls School, Denver, 1905) 3, in *Pratt Papers, MS*, Box 19, Series 3: Addresses, Diaries, Writings, and Notes, 1862–1953.

36. Richard Henry Pratt, "Re: The Negro and Slavery Before a Colored Audience" (Philadelphia Training School, 1911), 2–4, in *Pratt Papers, MS*, Box 19, Series 3.

37. Pratt, "Re: The Nego and Slavery before a Colored Audience," 4.

38. Pratt, *The Indian Industrial School, Carlisle, Pennsylvania*, 21.

39. Ibid., 43.

40. Ibid., 35.

41. Ibid., 32.

42. Ibid., 10–13.

43. Luther Standing Bear, *My People the Sioux* (New York: Arcadia, 1928; 2017).

44. Ibid., 65–68.

45. Ibid., 69.

46. Ibid., 80; 71.

47. Ibid., 89.

48. See Austin Reed, *The Life and the Adventures of a Haunted Convict:*

The Recently Discovered Memoir of African American Life and Incarceration in the Nineteenth Century, ed. Caleb Smith, David Blight, and Robert Stepto (New York: Random House, 2016).

49. See Churchill, *Kill the Indians*, 68.

50. Ross, *Inventing the Savage*. See also Lisa Ford, *Settler-Sovereignty: Jurisdiction and Indigenous Peoples in America and Australia, 1788–1836* (Cambridge, MA: Harvard University Press, 2010).

51. Committee on Indian Affairs, "Removal of the Apache Indian Prisoners" (Washington DC, February 15, 1890), "perfect knowledge of the country," 14; "every bolder a fortress," 18.

52. John R. Welch, "Multiple Places, Histories, and Memories at a Frontier Icon in Apache Country," in *Archaeologies of Placemaking: Monuments, Memories, and Engagement in Native North America*, ed. Patricia E. Rubertone (New York: Routledge, 2016), 101–34.

53. Pasfield, 273.

54. Herbert Welsh, *The Apache Prisoners in Fort Marion, St. Augustine, Florida* (Philadelphia: Office of the Indian Rights Association, 1887). See also National Park Service, "Apache Incarceration," Castillo de San Marcos National Monument.

55. Welsh, *Apache Prisoners in Fort Marion*, 16–17.

56. Southern Christian Leadership Conference, *St. Augustine: 400 Years of Bigotry and Hate Supported and Maintained by Northern Tourism Dollars* (Atlanta: Southern Christian Leadership Conference, 1965), Flagler College, Civil Rights Library of St. Augustine. See also *The Heroic Stories of the St. Augustine Foot Soldiers Whose Brave Struggle Helped Pass the Civil Rights Act of 1964* (St. Augustine, FL: St. Augustine Foot Soldiers Remembrance Project, 2014), 12. Flagler College, Civil Rights Library of St. Augustine. See also "Martin Luther King, Jr., and FBI Files on the 1964 St. Augustine Demonstrations," *ProQuest*, January 20, 2014, about .proquest.com/en/blog/2014/st-augustine-florida-demonstrations-1964.

57. Langston Highes, *Montage of a Dream Deferred* (New York: Henry Holt, 1951).

58. Joseph Mosnier, "Joint Interview of Audrey Nell Edwards Hamilton and Ms. JoAnn Anderson Ulmer Regarding the St. Augustine Move-

ment," *Civil Rights History Project*, September 13, 2011, www.crmvet.org /nars/staug.htm.

59. See Dan Berger, *Captive Nation: Black Prison Organizing in the Civil Rights Era* (Durham, NC: University of North Carolina, 2014); See also Dan Berger and Toussaint Loussier, *Rethinking the American Prison Movement* (New York: Routledge, 2020).

60. "Martin Luther King and 17 Others Jailed Trying to Integrate St. Augustine Restaurant," *New York Times*, June 12, 1964; "Arrested at Monson Motor Lodge. St. Johns County Sheriff Office," June 11, 1964, Flagler College, Civil Rights Library of St. Augustine. See also Martin Dubrow, "The Black Girl Who Defied Segregation, Inspiring MLK and Jackie Robinson," *Washington Post*, February 1, 2021.

61. Jewish Women's Archive, "*Why We Went: A Joint Letter from the Rabbis Arrested in St. Augustine*," June 19, 1964, jwa.org/media/why-we -went-joint-letter-from-rabbis-arrested-in-st-augustine. See also Mitzi Steiner, "Why They Went: The Forgotten Story of the St. Augustine 17," *Tablet Mag*, June 17, 2019.

62. "J.B. Stoner Leads Segregation Rally," June 13, 1964, Flagler College, Civil Rights Library of St. Augustine.

63. Martin Luther King Jr. quoted in David J. Garrow, *Bearing the Cross: Martin Luther King, Jr., and the Southern Christian Leadership Conference* (New York: William Morrow, 1986; 2004), 328–31; quote at 331.

64. See for example, Massachusetts Chapter of the SCLC, "Florida Spring Project SCM-SCLC," March 3, 1964, Flagler College, Civil Rights Library of St. Augustine.

65. "Letter from a Group of Irate Loyal True Americans to Mary Peabody and Judge Bryan Simpson," April 5, 1964, Flagler College, Civil Rights Library of St. Augustine.

66. Virgil Stuart, "Appendix 25: Report of the St. Augustine Chief of Police Virgil Stuart to the Florida Legislative Investigative Committee on the Racial Unrest in St. Augustine during 1963 and 1964," March 17, 1965, 144–45. Flagler College, Civil Rights Library of St. Augustine.

67. R.O. Mitchell et al., *Racial and Civil Disorders in St. Augustine:*

Report of the [Florida] Legislative Committee, February 1965, Flagler College, Civil Rights Library of St. Augustine.

68. Stuart, "Appendix 25," 144–45.

69. Southern Christian Leadership Conference, *400 Years of Bigotry and Hate*; Mitchell et al., *Racial and Civil Disorders in St. Augustine*.

70. Southern Christian Leadership Conference, *400 Years of Bigotry and Hate*; Mitchell et al., *Racial and Civil Disorders in St. Augustine*.

71. "Come, See, Hear the one and only Mr. Hosea Williams . . . at the Freedom Tree on the lawn of the Old Fort," Flyer, May 17, 1964; Southern Christian Leadership Conference, *400 Years of Bigotry and Hate*.

72. *The Heroic Stories of the St. Augustine Foot Soldiers Whose Brave Struggle Helped Pass the Civil Rights Act of 1964*, 2014, Flagler College, Civil Rights Library of St. Augustine.

73. Martin Luther King Jr., "Beyond Vietnam: A Time to Break Silence," Riverside Church, New York, April 4, 1967.

74. Joseph Mosnier, "Joint Interview of Audrey Nell Edwards Hamilton and Ms. JoAnn Anderson Ulmer Regarding the St. Augustine Movement," *Civil Rights History Project*, September 13, 2011, www.crmvet.org /nars/staug.htm.

75. See Erin H. Kimmerle, Richard W. Estabrook, E. Christian Wells, and Antoinette T. Jackson, *Documentation of the Boot Hill Cemetery (8JA1860), at the Former Arthur G. Dozier School for Boys, Marianna, Florida*, Interim Report, Division of Historical Resources Permit No 1112.032 (Tampa: University of South Florida, Department of Anthropology, 2012), usfweb.usf.edu/usf-news-archive/article/articlefiles/5042 -boot-hill-cemetery-interim-report-12-12.pdf. See also U.S. Department of Justice Civil Rights Division, *Investigation of the Arthur G. Dozier School for Boys, Marianna, Florida*, December 1, 2011, www.justice.gov /sites/default/files/crt/legacy/2011/12/02/dozier_findltr_12-1-11.pdf; Brian Feldman, "Researchers Exhume 55 Bodies at Notorious Reform School," *The Atlantic*, January 29, 2014, www.theatlantic.com/national /archive/2014/01/researchers-exhume-55-bodies-notorious-reform -school/357483. Lindsey Bever, "First of 55 Bodies Buried at Florida Reform School Identified," *Washington Post*, August 11, 2014. www .washingtonpost.com/news/morning-mix/wp/2014/08/11/first-of-55

-bodies-buried-at-florida-reform-school-identified; "Exhumed Remains Identified from Graves at Notorious Florida School," *The Guardian*, September 25, 2014, www.theguardian.com/world/2014/sep/25/florida-dozier-school-bodies-identified-sweat-box; Richard Luscombe, "'Rape Dungeon' Allegations Emerge in Abuse Report on Dozier School for Boys," *The Guardian*, February 6, 2015, www.theguardian.com/us-news/2015/feb/06/dozier-school-for-boys-abuse-florida-new-allegations; Colson Whitehead's *The Nickel Boys* (London: Fleet, 2019) is based on the findings of the excavation and resulting investigations.

76. Ruth Wilson Gilmore, "Abolitionist Geographies," in *Futures of Black Radicalism*, ed. Gaye Theresa Johnson and Alex Lubin (London: Verso, 2017); See also Ruth Wilson Gilmore, *Abolition Geography* (London: Verso, 2023); Nick Estes, "Freedom Is a Place: Long Traditions of Anti-colonial Resistance in Turtle Island," *Versopolis*, March 23, 2020; George Lipsitz, *How Racism Takes Place* (Philadelphia: Temple University Press, 2011).

2. The Jefferson-Monroe Penal Doctrine

1. Thomas Jefferson to James Monroe, Washington, 1801, quoted in John P. Foley, *The Jefferson Cyclopedia: A Comprehensive Collection of the Views of Thomas Jefferson Classified and Arranged in Alphabetical Order Under Nine Thousand Titles Relating to Government, Politics, Law, Education, Political Economy, Finance, Science, Art, Literature, Religious Freedom, Morals, [etc.]* (New York: Funk and Wagnalls, 1900), 155. See also, Thomas Jefferson to James Monroe, Washington, 1801, in Paul Leicester Ford, ed., *The Writings of Thomas Jefferson* (New York: G.P. Putnam's Sons, 1892–99), vol. IV, 420, and vol. VIII, 104; Thomas Jefferson to Rufus King, Washington, 1802, vol. IV, 442, and vol. VIII, 161–2.

2. John P. Foley, *The Jefferson Cyclopedia*, 155–56.

3. John P. Foley, "Banishment as Punishment for Crime," *Colorado Springs Gazette*, April 21, 1901; John P. Foley, "Banishment," *Augusta Chronicle*, May 3, 1901. See also Foley, *Jeffersonian Cyclopedia*. This appears to be the only editorial Foley published in the newspaper.

4. See for example, Adam Jay Hirsch, *The Rise of the Penitentiary: Prisons and Punishment in Early America* (New Haven, CT: Yale University

Press, 1992). See also Michel Foucault, *Discipline and Punish: The Birth of the Prison* (New York: Vintage Books, 1995); Douglas Hay, Peter Linebaugh, John G. Rule, E.P. Thompson, and Cal Winslow, *Albion's Fatal Tree: Crime and Society in Eighteenth-Century England* (New York: Verso, 1977; 1988). See for example, Paul W. Keeve, *Prisons and the American Conscience: A History of U.S. Federal Corrections* (Carbondale: Southern Illinois University Press, 1995).

5. Ted C. Hinkley, "Alaska as an American Botany Bay," *Pacific Historical Review* 42, no. 1 (1973): 1–19.

6. Thomas Jefferson to Rufus King, Washington, 1802, in Ford, *Writings of Thomas Jefferson*, iv, 442, viii, 161–62; quoted in Foley, *Jefferson Cyclopedia*, 155–56.

7. Thomas Jefferson to James Monroe, Washington, 1801, quoted in Foley, *Jefferson Cyclopedia*, 155.

8. Ibid.

9. See Thomas Jefferson to Jared Sparks, Monticello, 1824, vii, 333, in Ford, *Writings of Thomas Jefferson*, x, 291; quoted in Foley *Jefferson Cyclopedia*, 154–55. On Jefferson as the "founding father of colonization," see David Kazanjian, "Racial Governmentality: Thomas Jefferson and African Colonization in the United States Before 1816," *Alternation* 5, no. 1 (1998): 39–84; David Kazanjian, *The Colonizing Trick: National Culture and Imperial Citizenship in Early America* (Minneapolis: University of Minnesota Press, 2003). On Jeffersonian racial dreams and nightmares see Walter Johnson, *River of Dark Dreams: Slavery and Empire in the Cotton Kingdom* (Cambridge, MA: Belknap Press of Harvard University Press, 2013), 18–45.

10. Johnson, "Racial Origins of U.S. Sovereignty"; Johnson, *River of Dark Dreams*, 18–45.

11. See Michael A. Gomez, *Exchanging Our Country Marks: The Transformation of American Identities in the Colonial and Antebellum South* (Chapel Hill: University of North Carolina Press, 1998), 1. See also Dan Kanstroom, *Deportation Nation: Outsiders in American History* (Cambridge, MA: Harvard University Press, 2010), 77, where he argues that litigation over state laws barring entry to free people of color following rebellions was important to the development of Supremacy Clause jurisprudence in the nineteenth century, and federal control of immigration more generally.

12. Ariella J. Gross, *Double Character: Slavery and Mastery in the Antebellum Southern Courtroom* (Athens, GA: University of Georgia Press, 2006), 31.

13. Glenn McNair, *Criminal Injustice: Slaves and Free Blacks in Georgia's Criminal Justice System* (Charlottesville: University of Virginia Press, 2009), 144. Michael Tadman estimates that over 1 million enslaved people were transported from exporting states to importing states and territories between 1790 and 1860 via the interstate slave trade (see Michael Tadman, *Speculators and Slaves: Masters, Traders, and Slaves in the Old South* (Madison, WI: University of Wisconsin Press, 1989), 12. Walter Johnson suggests that this expansionist mode of punishment transformed "the character of the terror by which slaveholders governed their slaves, from the individual sort registered directly on their bodies to a more displaced, systematic sort of violence that was registered in the forcible redistribution of those bodies over space." See Johnson, ed., *The Chattel Principle: Internal Slave Trades in the Americas* (New Haven, CT: Yale University Press, 2004), 9. See also Robert Gudmestad, *A Troublesome Commerce: The Transformation of the Interstate Slave Trade* (Baton Rouge: Louisiana State University Press, 2003); David Lightner, *Slavery and the Commerce Power: How the Struggle Against the Interstate Slave Trade Led to the Civil War* (New Haven, CT: Yale University Press, 2006).

14. On slaveholders' visions of pro-slavery empire generally, see Mathew Karp, *This Vast Southern Empire: Slaveholders at the Helm of American Foreign Policy* (Cambridge, MA: Harvard University Press, 2016); Johnson, *River of Dark Dreams*.

15. Abraham Lincoln, "First Annual Message," December 3, 1861. See Eric Foner, "Abraham Lincoln, Colonization, and the Rights of Black Americans," in *Slavery's Ghost: The Problem of Freedom in the Age of Emancipation*, ed. Richard Follett (Baltimore, MD: Johns Hopkins University Press, 2011), 42. See also Charles H. Wesley, "Lincoln's Plan for Colonizing the Emancipated Negroes," *Journal of Negro History* IV (January 1919): 7–21.

16. Foner, "Abraham Lincoln, Colonization, and the Rights of Black Americans," 41–5. Foner writes that Lincoln authorized the secretary of the interior to agree to the contract with Chiriqui Improvement Company to aid the federal government and to "secure the removal of the negroes from this country."

17. Article XIII, Sec. 1, 38th Congress, 2nd Session, Approved Feb.1, 1865, in *United States Statutes at Large*, vol. 13, 567. For the Senate debate on the Thirteenth Amendment (S.J. Res. 16), see *Congressional Globe* March 31, 1864; April 4–8, 1864; June 14–15, 1864. For the House debate, see *Congressional Globe*, January 6–7, 1865; January 9–13, 1865; January 28, 1865; January 31, 1865.

18. See "Law Enacting Emancipation in the Federal Territories," Ch. CXI.—An Act to Secure Freedom to all Persons Within the Territories of the United States in *U.S., Statutes at Large, Treaties, and Proclamations of the United States of America*, vol. 12 (Boston: Little, Brown, 1863), 432. "That from and after the passage of this act there shall be neither slavery nor involuntary servitude in any Territory of the United States, otherwise than in punishment of crimes whereof the party shall have been duly convicted."

19. Jack M. Balkin and Sanford Levinson, "Thirteenth Amendment in Context: The Dangerous Thirteenth Amendment," *Columbia Law Review*, no. 112 (2012): 1492.

20. Seward, "Speech at Detroit, 4 September, 1860," quoted in Hinton Rowan Helper, *The Negroes in Negroland, the Negroes in America; and Negroes Generally* (New York: G.W. Carleton, 1868), 180.

21. "Use for Alaska," *New York Tribune*, February 14, 1874.

22. E.C. Wines, ed., *Report on the International Penitentiary Congress of London held July 3–13, 1872 . . . to Which Is Appended the Second Annual Report of the National Prison Association of the United States . . .* (Washington, DC: Government Printing Office, 1873), 154; Edwin Pears, *Prisons and Reformatories at Home and Abroad; Being the Transactions of the International Penitentiary Congress Held in London . . .* (London: Longman, Greens, 1873), 47; 405; 475.

23. Pears, *Prisons and Reformatories at Home and Abroad*, 19.

24. Ibid., 405.

25. Ibid., 47.

26. Wines, *Report on the International Penitentiary Congress of London Held July 3–13, 1872*, 154.

27. H.W. Bellows, *Report of the Executive Committee of the National Prison Association*, in Wines, *Report on the International Penitentiary Congress of London held July 3–13, 1872*, 321–331. For a study of the influence

of Maconochie and Crofton on the "indeterminacy movement" in U.S. penology, see also Fiona Doherty, "Indeterminate Sentencing Returns: The Invention of Supervised Release," *New York University Law Review* 88 (June 2013).

28. Bellows, *Report of the Executive Committee*, in Wines, *Report on the International Penitentiary Congress*, 322.

29. Ibid., 321.

30. See for example, *Commercial Advertiser*, May 20, 1873; *Annapolis Gazette*, May 20, 1873; *Cincinnati Daily Gazette*, May 20, 1873; *Cincinnati Daily Times*, May 20, 1873; *Portland Daily Press*, May 22, 1873; *Richmond Whig*, May 23, 1873; *Newport Mercury*, May 24, 1873; *Farmers Cabinet*, May 28, 1873; *West Jersey Press*, May 28, 1873; *Jewish Messenger*, May 30, 1873; *St. Albans Messenger*, May 28, 1873; *San Francisco Daily Evening Bulletin*, June 2, 1873; *Boston Journal*, June 12, 1873; *New York Evening Post*, June 20, 1873; *New York Tribune*, February 14, 1874; *Boston Traveler*, February 21, 1874.

31. Charles Nordhoff, "What Shall We Do with Scroggs?," *Harper's Magazine*, 1873, 44.

32. Alexander Saxton, "Problems of Class and Race in the Origins of the Mass Circulation Press," *American Quarterly* 36, no. 2 (1984): 223.

33. Khalil Muhammad, *The Condemnation of Blackness: Race, Crime, and the Making of Modern Urban America* (Cambridge, MA: Harvard University Press, 2010).

34. "Penal Colonies: Transportation as Punishment for Crime," *National Police Gazette*, July 17, 1847.

35. Ibid.

36. Thomas Holt, *The Problem of Freedom: Race, Labor, and Politics in Jamaica and Britain, 1832–1938* (Baltimore, MD: Johns Hopkins University Press, 1992); Diana Paton, *No Bond but the Law: Punishment, Race, and Gender in Jamaican State Formation, 1780–1870* (Durham, NC: Duke University Press, 2004).

37. Benjamin D. Weber, "Emancipation in the West Indies and the Freedom to Toil: Manual Labor and Moral Redemption in Transatlantic Antislavery Discourse," *Journal of the Oxford University History Society* 6, no. 1 (2009): 1–18.

38. *Cincinnati Daily Gazette*, May 5, 1869, reporting on the opposition expressed by the *Portland Oregonian*.

39. See for example, "Should Alaska Be Made a Penal Colony," *Cincinnati Daily Times*, May 20, 1873; *Cincinnati Daily Gazette*, May 20, 1873; *Richmond Whig*, May 23, 1873.

40. "Our Botany Bay," *New York World*, September 18, 1869.

41. "News," *New York World*, December 17, 1868.

42. W.E.B. Du Bois, *Black Reconstruction: An Essay Toward a History of the Part Which Black Folk Played in the Attempt to Reconstruct Democracy in America, 1860–1880* (New York: Harcourt, Brace, 1935); See also David Roediger, *The Wages of Whiteness: Race and the Making of the American Working Class*, rev. ed. (London: Verso, 1999).

43. "Jackson Knights of Labor," *Jackson Daily Citizen*, February 20, 1885; "Michigan Legislature," *Jackson Daily Citizen*, February 20, 1885; "News," *Kansas City Times*, February 20, 1885; "News/Opinions," *Jackson Daily Citizen*, February 24, 1885.

44. "Views in Washington: Popular Belief in the Suggestion to Transport Convicts," *New York Herald*, March 30, 1887.

45. "Freemen and Convicts: The Vexatious Prison Labor Problem and Its Solutions—Views from Many Men—Transportation to Alaska Favored by Knights," *New York Herald*, March 31, 1887.

46. "Convict Labor: Col. Trowbridge's Proposed Solution to the Problem—Alaska as a Penal Colony—States to Collect Their Criminals and Let Army Watch Them," *New York Herald*, February 26, 1879. On Trowbridge's resolution, see also "A New Scheme for the Benefit for the Benefit of Labor—Alaska as a Penal Colony," *San Francisco Bulletin*, February 26, 1879; "A Flood of Resolutions," *New York Tribune*, February 27, 1879; "Alaska," *Cincinnati Daily Gazette*, February 28, 1879; "A Penal Colony," *Salt Lake Tribune*, March 1, 1879; "Convict Labor—A Proposal to Make Alaska a Penal Colony," *Indianapolis Sentinel*, March 6, 1879; "Political Notes," *Irish American Weekly*, March 8, 1879.

47. "Contract Convict Labor," *New York Herald*, February 6, 1884. See also "Alaska as a Penal Colony," *Boston Daily Journal*, February 15, 1884; "Legislative Acts," *Trenton Evening Times*, March 8, 1885.

48. "Alaska as a Penal Colony," *San Francisco Bulletin*, January 26,

1874. On the California resolution, see also "Penal Colony," *Sacramento Daily Union*, January 26, 1874; "A Penal Colony in Alaska," *Weekly Alta California*, January 31, 1874; "State Prison Reform," *San Francisco Bulletin*, February 5, 1874; "Reports," *Sacramento Daily Union*, February 6, 1874; "Special Mention," *Oakland Daily Transcript*, February 11, 1874; "Alaska Penal Colony," *Oakland Daily Transcript*, February 12, 1874; "Alaska as a Penal Colony," *San Francisco Bulletin*, February 14, 1874.

49. "Legislative Acts," *Kansas City Star*, December 10, 1885; "Rhode Island Legislature," *New York Herald*, February 12, 1886.

50. "Legislative Acts," *Kansas City Star*, December 10, 1885; "Rhode Island Legislature," *New York Herald*, February 12, 1886.

51. Carroll D. Wright, *National Bureau of Labor Report* (Washington, DC: Government Printing Office, 1886), 383.

52. Muhammad, *Condemnation of Blackness*, 35.

53. On the relation between empire and race science, see Laura Briggs, *Reproducing Empire: Race, Sex, Science, and U.S. Imperialism in Puerto Rico* (Berkeley: University of California Press, 2002); Matthew Frey Jacobson, *Barbarian Virtues: The United States Encounters Foreign Peoples at Home and Abroad, 1876–1917* (New York: Hill and Wang, 2000).

54. "Man and Criminal," *New York Herald*, April 3, 1887.

55. "Man and Convict—Poverty Nurtures Crime—How State Prisons Create Habitual Criminals—Transportation as a Remedy," *New York Herald*, April 3, 1887.

56. "Alaska as a Penal Colony—Member of the Prison Reform Association to Make an Inspection," *Morning Oregonian*, May 13, 1887.

57. John D. Milliken, "Report of the Committee on Criminal Law Reform of the National Prison Association of the United States," *American Lawyer* 6, no. 1 (January 1898).

58. Ibid.

59. "Negro Schoolhouse Burned," *Dallas Daily Times Herald*, March 16, 1901.

60. "The Corner's Verdict," *Dallas Daily Times Herald*, March 13, 1901.

61. "The Corsicana Negro Burned at the Stake," *Dallas Daily Times Herald*, March 13, 1901. See also Hazel V. Carby, "'On the Threshold of

Woman's Era': Lynching, Empire, and Sexuality in Black Feminist Theory," *Critical Inquiry* 12, no. 1 (Autumn 1985): 262–77; Robyn Wiegman, "The Anatomy of a Lynching," *Journal of the History of Sexuality* (January 1993); Christopher Waldrep, *Lynching in America: A History in Documents* (New York: New York University Press, 2006).

62. "The New Code: The Remarkable Dream of a Retired Police Justice While Henderson Was Burning at the Stake," *Fort Worth Register*, March 24, 1901. Together they hoped to scatter the plan far and wide through the presses, until the "country cries out for the New Code and an intrepid President to administer it."

63. Ibid.

64. Ibid.

65. Ibid.

66. Ibid.

67. Foley, "Banishment."

68. My use of the term "Black Press" follows the self-description of organizations like the Afro-American Press Association at the time and subsequent scholarly commentary. See George P. Marks III, ed., *The Black Press Views American Imperialism, 1898–1900* (New York: Arno, 1971).

69. "Alaska," *Weekly Louisianan*, February 8, 1879.

70. See for example, *The Yeoman*, December 22, 1878.

71. George W. Cable, *The Silent South: Together with the Freedman's Case in Equity and the Convict Lease System* (New York: Charles Scribner's Sons, 1885).

72. "Southern Gleanings," *Huntsville Gazette*, November 3, 1888.

73. "Georgia's Disgrace," *New York Age*, February 14, 1891. See also "Georgia's Disgrace," *Leavenworth Advocate*, February 28, 1891.

74. *Indianapolis Recorder*, February 18, 1899; quoted in Marks, *Black Press*, 116.

75. *Iowa State Bystander*, April 28, 1899, quoted in Marks, *Black Press*, 125.

76. "Is America Any Better Than Spain?," *Cleveland Gazette*, May 21, 1898.

77. Charles Gano Baylor, quoted in Marks, *Black Press*, 80, 82.

78. *Coffeyville American*, quoted in Marks, *Black Press*, 115.

79. *Cleveland Gazette*, December 23, 1899, quoted in Marks, *Black Press*, 160–62.

80. *Cleveland Gazette*, June 17, 1899; *Washington Bee*, January 28, 1899; *Richmond Planet*, November 11, 1899; quoted in Marks, *Black Press*, 130, 157.

81. *Philadelphia Defender*, January 27, 1900, quoted in Marks, *Black Press*, 165–66.

82. *Iowa State Bystander*, April 28, 1899, quoted in Marks, *Black Press*, 125.

83. Marks, *Black Press*, 149.

84. *Cleveland Gazette*, January 7, 1899, quoted in Marks, *Black Press*, 109.

85. Ida B. Wells-Barnett, *Lynch Law in Georgia*, Chicago, 1899, quoted in *The Progress of a People: A Special Presentation of the Daniel A.P. Murray Pamphlet Collection*, Library of Congress, retrieved September 15, 2016, memory.loc.gov/ammem/aap/aapmob.html. On the connections between lynching and anti-imperialism in the writings of Ida B. Wells, Francis E. W. Harper, and Anna Julia Cooper, see Carby, "'On the Threshold of Woman's Era.'"

3. Geographies of Counterinsurgency

Originally published in a slightly different form in "Fearing the Flood: Transportation as Counterinsurgency in the U.S.–Occupied Philippines," *International Review of Social History* 63, no. S26 (2018): 191–210.

1. Reynaldo Clemeña Ileto, "Casunod nang buhay na Pinagdaan ng Ating manga Capatid," in *Pasyon and Revolution: Popular Movements in the Philippines, 1840–1910* (Quezon City: Ateneo de Manila University Press, 1979; 2003), appendix 4, 263.

2. Manuel Xerez Burgos to Aguinaldo, January 1899, quoted in Dean Worcester, *Philippines Past and Present* (New York: MacMillan, 1914),

135 (my italics). See also J.R.M. Taylor, "The Philippine Insurrection Against the United States: A Compilation of Documents with Notes," in NA RG 350, File 2291-38; J.R.M. Taylor et al., *Compilation of Philippine Insurgent Records—Telegraphic Correspondence of Emilio Aguinaldo* (Washington, DC: Bureau of Insular Affairs, 1903); J.R.M. Taylor et al., *Report on the Organization for the Administration of Civil Government Instituted by Emilio Aguinaldo* (Washington, DC: Bureau of Insular Affairs, 1903); and J.R.M. Taylor, *The Philippine Insurrection Against the United States: A Compilation of Documents with Notes and Introduction* (Pasay City, Philippines: Eugenio Lopez Foundation, 1971).

3. Worcester, *Philippines Past and Present*, 135–39. Limjap asked Sandiko to authorize a battalion of six hundred *sandatahan* to seize the American armaments, listing the commanding officers. Sandiko passed the list on to Aguinaldo, and they mustered their troops at Calcoocan Station, on the outskirts of Manila.

4. Worcester, 139; Philip P. Brower, "The U.S. Army's Seizure and Administration of Enemy Records up to World War II," *American Archivist*, 1961.

5. J.R.M. Taylor, quoted in Worcester, *Philippines Past and Present*, 140; J.R.M. Taylor et al., *Compilation of Philippine Insurgent Records*.

6. Ranajit Guha, "The Prose of Counter-Insurgency," in *Selected Subaltern Studies*, ed. Ranajit Guha and Gayatri Chakravorty Spivak (New York: Oxford University Press, 1988), 45–84.

7. Worcester, *Philippines Past and Present*, 151.

8. See for example, Apolinario Mabini, *La Revolucion Filipina con otras documentos de la* época (Manila: Bureau of Printing, 1931); Vicente Rafael, "The Afterlife of Empire: Sovereignty and Revolution in the Philippines," in *Colonial Crucible: Empire in the Making of the Modern American State*, ed. Alfred W. McCoy and Francisco A. Scarano (Madison: University of Wisconsin Press, 2009), 342–52; Honeste A. Villanueva, "Apolinario Mabini: His Exile to Guam," *Historical Bulletin* 8, no. 1 (1964).

9. Greg Bankoff, *Crime, Society, and the State in the Nineteenth-Century Philippines* (Quezon City: Ateno de Manila University Press, 1996).

10. Ileto, *Pasyon and Revolution*; Dylan Rodriguez, "'Not Classifi-

able as Orientals or Caucasians or Negroes': Filipino Racial Ontology and the Stalking Presence of the 'Insane Filipino Soldier,'" in *Filipino Studies: Palimpsests of Nation and Diaspora*, ed. Martin F. Manalansan and Augusto F. Espiritu (New York: New York University Press, 2016), 151–75.

11. The War Department's first survey map of the archipelago reveals how overlapping Spanish and U.S. imperial regimes produced forms of carceral innovation in their attempt to control rebellious terrain. The Mapa Ethnographico, as it was called, symbolized some sixty-nine different ethnic groups, lumped into three racial types, and plotted onto discrete areas of land: *territorio de los cristianos hispano-filipinos* (colored orange), *territorio de los cristianos nuevos y los infieles* (yellow), and *territorio de los moros* (green). The War Department's first survey map kept the Spanish tripartite division of the archipelago into degrees of religious conversion, even retaining the color green to represent the Moro, predominantly Muslim, provinces in the south. It also split the archipelago into north and south, shading some areas as controlled by "civil provincial government," and others as controlled by "Moro and other non-Christian tribes."; *Report of the First Philippine Commission Atlas* (Washington, DC: Government Printing Office, 1899), 3. See also *Report of the First Philippine Commission Atlas / Atlas de Filipinas: Colección de 30 Mapas. Trabajados por delineantes filipinos bajo la dirección del P. José Algue, S.J., director del observatorio de Manila* (Washington, DC: Government Printing Office, 1899); Joseph Prentiss Sanger, Henry Gannett, Victor H. Olmsted, *Census of the Philippine Islands: Taken Under the Direction of the Philippine Commission in the Year 1903*, 4 vols. (Washington, DC: Government Printing Office, 1905).

12. Vicente Rafael, *White Love and Other Events in Filipino History* (Durham, NC: Duke University Press, 2000), 19–51.

13. Daniel Folkmar, *Album of Philippine Types (Found in Bilibid Prison in 1903): Christians and Moros (Including a Few Non-Christians). Eighty Plates, Representing Thirty-Seven Provinces and Islands, Prepared and Published Under the Auspices of the Philippine Exposition Board* (Manila: Bureau of Printing, 1904), 3. See also *Annual Report of the Philippine Commission, 1900–1903* (Washington DC: Government Printing Office, 1904): Ethnological survey also using serves of anthropologist

Daniel Fokmar, preparing for the exhibit of the Louisiana Purchase exhibition in St. Louis in 1904. Folkmar had been continuously occupied with physical anthropometry in Bilibid Prison, measuring some eight hundred individuals, among whom were represented all of the christianized Filipino tribes, and taking four photographs of each of about four hundred individuals.

14. *Annual Report of the Philippine Commission, 1900–1903* (Washington DC: Government Printing Office, 1904), 609. By 1903, the Philippine Commission's Bureau of Non-Christian Tribes reported that their ethnological survey led by David. P. Barrows of the Igorrots of Bontoc, taken to be most representative of the mountain region, would prove of great importance to "governing these very primitive tribes."

15. Ignacio Villamor, *Criminality in the Philippine Islands, 1903–1908* (Manila: Bureau of Printing, 1909); Ignacio Villamor, "Propensity to Crime," *Journal of the American Institute of Criminal Law and Criminology* 6, no. 5 (January 1916), 729–45.

16. Luke E. Wright, "Report of the Secretary of Commerce and Police," in *Annual Report of the Philippine Commission, 1903* (Washington, DC: Government Printing Office, 1904), 611.

17. Wright, "Report of the Secretary of Commerce and Police," 613.

18. Wright, 616.

19. These laws, as Ileto puts it, made revolutionaries into "bad men" and "bandits" as if overnight. Ileto, *Payson and Revolution*, 172.

20. See for example, Victor Hurley, *Jungle Patrol: The Story of the Philippine Constabulary (1901–1936)* (Salem, OR: Cerberus Books, 2011), 125–27.

21. Hurley, *Jungle Patrol*, 127. Hurley notes that the Constabulary had made concerted efforts to eliminate these "messiahs."

22. Ileto, *Payson and Revolution*, 209–52; Hurley, *Jungle Patrol*, 121; Philippine Commission, *Fifth Annual Report of the Philippine Commission* (Washington, DC: Government Printing Office, 1905), 64.

23. Ileto, *Payson and Revolution*, 228; Or, as Vic Hurley put it, "even if he was captured, his followers believed that he would escape or that he would have a second life after death" (Hurley, *Jungle Patrol*, 121).

24. Ileto, *Payson and Revolution*, 215.

25. Ileto, 99–101; Euginio Damiana, *Philippine Folk Literature: The Legends* (Quezon City: University of the Philippines Press, 2002), 4–5. See also Teodoro A. Agoncillo, *The Revolt of the Masses: The Story of Andrés Bonificio and the Katipinan* (Quezon City: University of the Philippines Press, 1956).

26. Ileto, *Payson and Revolution*, 210, 222; Hurley, *Jungle Patrol*, 121; Henry J. Reilly, "Filipino Bandit Terror in Luzon: Career of Felipe Salvador Shows Danger of Such Uprisings in Islands," *Chicago Tribune*, August 2, 1914. See also Salvador's autobiographic writings *Tatlong Tulisan*, quoted in Ileto, *Payson and Revolution*, 225. See also "Narrative of the Feelings and Supplications of the Accused Major Felipe Salvador," quoted in Ileto, *Payson and Revolution*, 215.

27. Hurley, *Jungle Patrol*, 126.

28. *Fifth Annual Report of the Philippine Commission* (Washington, DC: Government Printing Office, 1905), 64.

29. Hurley, *Jungle Patrol*, 121.

30. *Philippine Commission Report*, 1904, part 1, 201. Trowbridge was referring to their fear of Artemio Ricarte, another revolutionary threat, who had just landed in Manila.

31. On the term "racial management," see David Roediger and Elizabeth Esch, *The Production of Difference: Race and the Management of Labor in U.S. History* (New York: Oxford University Press, 2012).

32. Lyman. W. Kennon, "Report of Officer in Charge of Construction of Benguet Road," in *Sixth Annual Report of the Philippine Commission 1905* (Washington, DC: Government Printing Office, 1906), 375; Kennon, 376, 379.

33. W. Cameron Forbes Papers, Journals, First Series, Vols. 1–5, MS Houghton Library, Harvard University.

34. Kennon, "Report of Officer," appendix H, part 3, 359.

35. Ibid., 379.

36. Forbes Papers, Journal Vol. 1, October 1904, 88, 94.

37. Forbes Papers, Journal Vol. 1, March 1905; September 1905, 322.

38. George N. Wolfe, "Report of the Warden of Bilibid Prison," in *Sixth Annual Report of the Philippine Commission, 1905* (Washington, DC:

Government Printing Office, 1906), appendix E, 305–6.

39. Forbes Papers, Journal Vol. 1, January 1905, 136.

40. Ileto, *Payson and Revolution.*

41. Vicente Rafael, "Afterlife of Empire: Sovereignty and Revolution in the Philippines," in *The Colonial Crucible: Empire in the Making of the Modern American State*, ed. Alfred McCoy and Francisco A. Scarano (Madison: University of Wisconsin Press, 2009), 349; See also Vicente Rafael, *White Love and Other Events in Filipino History* (Durham, NC: Duke University Press, 2000).

42. Rafael, "Afterlife of Empire," 352. As discussed earlier, Rafael elaborates Apolinario Mabini's theory of sovereignty as based in *kalayaan*, which is understood as constant caring. He sees in this a theory of sovereignty understood in terms of "life beyond necessity" (following philosopher George Bataille's usage of the phrase).

43. On the ongoing legacies and interpretative stakes of efforts to undo imperial criminalization, see Benjamin Weber, "Fugitive Justice: The Possible Futures of Prison Records from U.S. Colonial Rule in the Philippines," *Archive Journal*, August 2017.

4. The Strange Career of the Convict Clause

Originally published in a slightly different form in "The Strange Career of the Convict Clause: U.S. Prison Imperialism in the Panamá Canal Zone," *International Labor and Working-Class History* 96 (2019): 79–102.

1. Joaquín Beleño, *Los forzados de Gamboa / Gamboa Road Gang* (Panama City: Ministerio de Educación, Departamento de Bellas Artes y Publicaciones, 1960), 35–36. "*La carretera es el Cementerio. . . . Para unos, la carretera es la civilización y el progreso, para mí es el sepulcro donde claudica para siempre el hambre voraz de toda esta fauna que sale de las montañas para enfrentearse a la civilización moderna.*"

2. *Canal Record*, vol. 3, 91, 374.

3. *Canal Record*, vol. 4, no. 2, September 7, 1910. The 19.7-mile road from Panama to Gorgona was completed by the end of that fiscal year.

See *Annual Report of the Isthmian Canal Commission for 1910–1911* (Washington, DC: Government Printing Office, 1911), 421.

4. Aimé Césaire, *Discourse on Colonialism*, trans. Joan Pinkham [1955] (New York: Monthly Review Press, 1972; 2000), 42–3, 77.

5. W.E.B. Du Bois, "The Spawn of Slavery: The Convict-Lease System in the South," *Missionary Review of the World* 24, no. 10 (October 1901). See also W.E.B. Du Bois, "Black Toward Slavery," in *Black Reconstruction: An Essay Toward a History of the Part Which Black Folk Played in the Attempt to Reconstruct Democracy in America, 1860–1880* (New York: Harcourt, Brace, 1935), 670–710.

6. David Oshinsky, *Worse Than Slavery: Parchman Farm and the Ordeal of Jim Crow Justice* (New York: Free Press, 1996); Douglass A. Blackmon, *Slavery by Another Name: The Re-Enslavement of Black Americans from the Civil War to World War II* (New York: Random House, 2008). See also Angela Y. Davis, "From the Prison of Slavery to the Slavery of the Prison: Frederick Douglass and the Convict Lease System," in *The Angela Y. Davis Reader*, ed. Joy James (Malden, MA: Blackwell, 1998), 74–95.

7. U.S. Constitution, Amendment XIII, 1865. (My italics.)

8. Theodore Roosevelt, "Letter of the President Placing the Isthmian Canal Commission Under the Supervision and Direction of the Secretary of War, and Defining the Jurisdiction and Functions of the Commission," Washington, DC, May 9, 1904, in *Executive Orders Relating to the Panama Canal, March 8, 1904, to Dec. 31, 1921* (Mount Hope, Canal Zone: The Panama Canal Press, 1921), 23.

9. William Jackson, "The Administration of Justice in the Canal Zone," *Virginia Law Review* 4, no. 1 (October 1916): 1–20. See also Lawrence Ealy, "Development of the Anglo-American System of Law in the Panama Canal Zone," *American Journal of Legal History* 2, no. 4 (October 1958): 283–303.

10. See Velma Newton, *The Silver Men: West Indian Labour Migration to Panama, 1850–1914* (Kingston, Jamaica: Ian Randle, 2004); Aims McGuinness, *Path of Empire: Panama and the California Gold Rush* (Ithaca, NY: Cornell University Press, 2007).

11. See Thomas C. Holt, *The Problem of Freedom: Race, Labor, and*

Politics in Jamaica and Britain, 1832–1938 (Baltimore, MD: Johns Hopkins University Press, 1992); Frederick Cooper, Thomas Holt, and Rebecca Scott, *Beyond Slavery: Explorations of Race, Labor, and Citizenship in Postemancipation Societies* (Chapel Hill: University of North Carolina Press, 2000); Rebecca Scott, *Degrees of Freedom: Louisiana and Cuba After Slavery* (Cambridge, MA: Belknap Press of Harvard University Press, 2005); Amy Dru Stanley, *From Bondage to Contract: Wage Labor, Marriage, and the Market in the Age of Slave Emancipation* (Cambridge: Cambridge University Press, 1998); Moon Ho-Jung, *Coolies and Cane: Race, Labor and Sugar in the Age of Emancipation* (Baltimore, MD: Johns Hopkins University Press, 2006).

12. See David R. Roediger and Elizabeth D. Esch, *The Production of Difference: Race and the Management of Labor in U.S. History* (New York: Oxford University Press, 2012); Gerald Horn, *The Deepest South: The United States, Brazil, and the African Slave Trade* (New York: New York University Press, 2007); Gerald Horn, *The White Pacific: U.S. Imperialism and Black Slavery in the South Seas After the Civil War* (Honolulu: University of Hawai'i Press, 2007); Matthew Pratt Guterl, *American Mediterranean: Southern Slaveholders in the Age of Emancipation* (Cambridge, MA: Harvard University Press, 2008).

13. See Julie Greene, *The Canal Builders: Making America's Empire at the Panama Canal* (New York: Penguin, 2009), 267–302; Michael Conniff, *Black Labor on a White Canal: Panama 1904–1981* (Pittsburgh, PA: University of Pittsburgh Press, 1985); Michael E. Donoghue, *Borderland on the Isthmus: Race, Culture, and the Struggle for the Canal Zone* (Durham, NC: Duke University Press, 2014). Michael Conniff and Julie Greene both suggest that Southerners did not make up the majority of the U.S. population in the Zone and point out that the racism of Northern whites was just as prevalent.

14. Michael Conniff characterizes the situation of Silver Roll employees being made to pay taxes to support police, prisons, and schools as "institutions of social control paid for by the controlled" in *Black Labor*, 39–40.

15. "Prison Labor on the Roads," *Canal Record* 1, no. 42 (June 17, 1908): 334.

16. *Canal Record* 1 (March 16, 1908): 236.

17. Ibid., 242, 257. On Blackburn, see "Jos. C.S. Blackburn, Ex-Senator, Is Dead," *New York Times*, September 13, 1918; "Senator Blackburn's Gun," *Nashville American*, March 1, 1907, 9; Joseph C.S. Blackburn Papers MS, Filson Historical Society, Louisville, KY.

18. See the *Annual Report of the Isthmian Canal Commission* (Washington, DC: Government Printing Office, 1908–14).

19. *Canal Record* 1 (1908): 334. "In this expense is computed the cost of housing the prisoners, food, medical attendance, and guards."

20. Ibid. One month's salary for 152 policemen was $16,045.48, while one month's work of 156 prisoners was calculated to be $1,606.65 total.

21. *Canal Record* 2 (1909): 363. Payroll for the total police force was well over $20,000 per month.

22. *Canal Record* 7 (1914): 489; *Canal Record* 8 (1915): 174.

23. *Daily Star and Herald*, March 21, 1913.

24. *Canal Record* 1 (1908): 334, 379. For other references to portable camps, see *Canal Record* 3 (1909): 91; *Canal Record* 4 (1910): 346; *Canal Record* 5 (1911): 33–4; *Canal Record* 6 (1913): n.23. For descriptions of prisoners being forced to provide their own food and shelter, see *Canal Record* vol. 1, 257, 334, 379; vol. 3, 91; vol. 4, 346; vol. 5, 33–34.

25. "Thatched Roof Native Home—Temporary Convicts' Corral in the Background Near Old Panama, Canal Zone, 1913" (New York, NY; London, Eng.; Sydney, Aus.: Keystone View Company, 1913).

26. "Temporary Corral of Prisoners Employed in Road Work, Showing Mess Table, Near Old Panama, Canal Zone" (New York, NY; London, Eng.; Sydney, Aus.: Keystone View Company, 1913).

27. Ibid. Although some claimed the Panama roadbuilding project was the first time the federal government had used convict labor on this kind of public works project, it had done so in the Philippines and Puerto Rico directly after occupying the islands. On the Philippines, see Benjamin D. Weber, "Fearing the Flood: Transportation as Counterinsurgency in the U.S.-Occupied Philippines," *International Review of Social History* 63, no. S26 (August 2018): 13–15. See also for example, Kennon, "Report of Officer"; *Reports of the Auditor of Porto Rico, United States Congressional Serial Set No.4830*, House of Representatives, 58th Cong., 3rd Sess., Doc. No. 143, (Washington, DC: Government Printing Office, 1906),

77, 106, 183.

28. Between 1904 and 1918 there were 74,702 arrests and the conviction rate averaged about 80 percent. The highest conviction rates and majority of the prison population were of "Black West Indians," people from Barbados, Jamaica, and Martinique. See "Police and Wardens Report," in *Annual Report of the Governor of the Canal Zone* (Washington, DC: Government Printing Office, 1918), 276–85. Of the nearly 7,000 arrests in 1912, over half were of Barbadians, Jamaicans, Martinicans, and Afro-Panamanians (Conniff, *Black Labor*, 36). Of the arrests that year, 3,500 were of West Indians, compared with 500 of U.S. citizens (Greene, *Canal Builders*, 283, 298).

29. "Zone Highways," *Canal Record* 1 (April 15, 1908): 258. See also "Prison Labor on the Roads," *Canal Record* 1, no. 42 (June 17, 1908): 334.

30. *Daily Star and Herald*, November 16, 1908.

31. *Daily Star and Herald*, March 31, 1911.

32. George W. Goethals, *Government of the Canal Zone* (Princeton, NJ: Princeton University Press, 1915), 65. Conniff points out that Goethals believed it customary for white men in tropical countries to direct "negro work" and felt it was not compatible with white men's pride of race to do work "traditional for negroes to do" (Conniff, *Black Labor*, 43).

33. Goethals, *Government of the Canal Zone*, 64.

34. For more on the depopulation campaign, in which police evacuated and destroyed over 1,135 homes in 1915 alone, see William F. Kessler, *History of the Canal Zone Police* (Mount Hope, Canal Zone: Panama Canal Zone Press, 1982). For the path-breaking analysis of how certain categories of surplus (land, state capacity, capital, and labor) drove the prison expansion boom in California, see Ruth Wilson Gilmore, *Golden Gulag: Prisons, Surplus, Crisis, and Opposition in Globalizing California* (Berkeley: University of California Press, 2007).

35. "Police for Canal Strip," *New York Times*, July 4, 1904, 3.

36. "Porto Rico's Police Chief Visits Gov. Cox: Col. Shanton Tells How He Changed the System There, Former Rough Rider Had Cleaned Up the Canal Zone Previously," *Boston Globe*, April 2, 1922, 11.

37. William K. Jackson, "The Administration of Justice in the Canal

Zone," *Virginia Law Review* 4, no. 1 (October 1916): 1–20. Conniff writes that chief canal engineer John Stevens authorized the recruitment of some twenty thousand Barbadians and paid their passage to the Zone in 1904, and as many as two hundred thousand West Indians migrated there during the construction era, 1904–14 (Conniff, *Black Labor*, 25).

38. Jackson, "The Administration of Justice in the Canal Zone," 14.

39. Taft to ICC chairman Shonts, April 13, 1905, quoted in Conniff, *Black Labor*, 25. While William Taft officially registered his objection to "slavery by debt," rather than by criminal conviction, he considered other forms of dependent and coerced labor—of women, children, and colonial subjects—to be part of the natural order of things. See for example, William H. Taft, *The Philippines* (New York: Outlook, 1902). Conniff notes that Chinese exclusion laws that applied in the Canal Zone as well as the United States also inhibited Steven's plan. For a comparative view of Taft and other colonial administrators' views on the subject, see Michael Salman, *The Embarrassment of Slavery: Controversies over Bondage and Nationalism in the American Colonial Philippines* (Berkeley: University of California Press, 2003).

40. See W. E. B. DuBois, *Black Reconstruction in America*; Steven Hahn, *A Nation Under Our Feet: Black Political Struggles in the Rural South from Slavery to the Great Migration* (Cambridge, MA: Harvard University Press, 2003).

41. "Attempt to Revive Slavery in Texas," *Weekly Louisianan*, November 28, 1874.

42. Executive Office Record Bureau, Panama Canal Periodical Reference Form, *Canal Record*, October 28, 1914, in, NARA RG 185, Repatriation of Laborers, File 46-D-8, EA1 34B, B913.

43. Police Chief Mitchell to Mr. Copeland, April 1, 1917, in Panama Canal Zone Executive Office Memo, in NARA RG 185, Repatriation of Laborers, File 46-D-8, EA1 34B, B913, F-6.

44. Ibid. (My italics).

45. Robert Lamastus estimated that 90 percent of the police force were ex-Army men. See "Lamastus to His Family," Cristobal, September 26, 1909, Lamastus-Crabb Family Papers MS, The Filson Historical Society,

Louisville, KY; Harry A. Franck, *Zone Policeman 88: A Close Range Study of the Panama Canal and Its Workers* (New York: Century, 1913; London: Dodo, reprint edition, 2012), 16, 59.

46. "Under the Stars and Bars," *New York Times*, January 8, 1893, 17; "Charges Against Marshall," *Washington Post*, November 11, 1907, 2. See also Kessler, *History of the Canal Zone Police.* Guy Johannes was the first civilian police chief, and he took office in 1917.

47. Robert Lamastus to his brother, Fort Flagler, Alaska, March 11, 1904.

48. Lamastus to his family, Culebra, Panama Canal Zone, March 15, 1910.

49. Lamastus to his family, Culebra, January 1, 1911.

50. L.S. Rowe, "The Larger Significance of the Pan American Highway," *BPAU* 64 (1930): 222.

51. Alex Lichtenstein, "The Private and the Public in Penal History," *Punishment and Society* 3, no. 1 (2001): 189–96; Alex Lichtenstein, "Good Roads and Chain Gangs in the Progressive South: 'The Negro Convict Is a Slave,'" *Journal of Southern History* 59, no. 1, (February 1993): 85–110. Lichtenstein notes that the felony convict labor force was not fully mobilized on chain gangs in Georgia until the convict lease was abolished in 1908.

52. Lichtenstein, "Penal History"; Lichtenstein, "Good Roads"; E. Stagg Whitin, "The Spirit of Convict Road-Building," *Southern Good Roads* 6 (December 1912): 13. Justice J. Christian defines the term "slave of the state" in reference to the Thirteenth Amendment's convict clause in *Ruffin v. Commonwealth*, 62 VA 790 (1871). See also Dennis Childs, *Slaves of the State: Black Incarceration from the Chain Gang to the Penitentiary* (Minneapolis: University of Minnesota Press, 2015).

53. E.W. James, "Plans for the Pan American Highway Project," *BPAU* 69 (1935): 383; "The Pan American Highway," *BPAU* 75 (1941): 393.

54. James, "Plans for the Pan American Highway," 385. See also E.W. James, "More Highways for the Americas—The Fourth Pan American Highway Congress," *BPAU* 75: 677; and E.W. James, "A Quarter Century of Road Building in the Americas," *BPAU* 79 (1945): 609–18.

55. James, "A Quarter Century," 616. Others included A.F. Tschiffely's

expedition from Buenos Aires to New York City in 1925–26, a 1935 road trip by the Automobile Club of Southern California from Texas to San Salvador, and brothers Joe and Arthur Lyons's trip from Nevada to Managua.

56. See "The Road and Street Exhibit at the Panama-Pacific International Exposition," September 4, 1915; "The Pan-American Road Congress and the Organization Under the Auspices of Which It Was Held," September 4, 1915, in *Good Roads: Devoted to the Construction and Maintenance of Roads and Streets* 10 (July–December 1915): 147. See also Henry Welles Durham, "Road and Street Work in the City of Panama," *Good Roads* 10 (July–December 1915): 144.

57. James, "A Quarter Century," 609. The South American portion of the Pan American Highway included some 4,147 miles of paved road, 1,646 miles of dry weather road, and 289 miles of trails.

58. George Shanton to Commercial Club of Mobile, quoted in Greene, *Canal Builders*, 284.

59. Samuel Fox, "Convict Labor for the Panama Canal," July 19, 1905, quoted in Greene, *Canal Builders*, 437–38. The ICC ultimately rejected his proposal.

60. Blake McKelvey, "Penology in the Westward Movement," *Pacific Historical Review* 2, no. 4 (December 1933): 418–28, 420. See also McKelvey, "The Prison Labor Problem: 1875–1900," *Journal of Criminal Law and Criminology* 25, no. 2 (July–August 1934): 254–70.

61. McKelvey, "Penology in the Westward Movement," 428. See also J.L. Gillin's *Taming the Criminal* (New York: Macmillan, 1931).

62. McKelvey, "Penology in the Westward Movement," 434.

63. Ibid., 418.

64. Thomas J. Tynan, "Prison Labor on Public Roads," *Annals of the American Academy of Political and Social Science* 46, no. 1 (1913): 58.

65. See for example, Newton, *Silver Men*; Michael E. Donoghue, *Borderland on the Isthmus: Race, Culture, and the Struggle for the Canal Zone* (Durham, NC: Duke University Press, 2014); Roediger and Esch, *Production of Difference*; and Carla Burnett, "'Unity Is Strength': Labor, Race, Garveyism and the Panama Canal Strike," *Global South* 6, no. 2 (Fall 2012): 39–64; Burnett, "'Unity Is Strength'"; Greene, *Canal Build-*

ers, 369–70.

66. Burnett, "'Unity Is Strength,'" 49–50.

67. Stoute to Garvey, July 8, 1919, quoted in Burnett, 49.

68. Keisha N. Blain, *Set the World on Fire: Black Nationalist Women and the Global Struggle for Freedom* (Philadelphia: University of Pennsylvania Press, 2018), 14. She later took the name Amy Ashwood Garvey, after agreeing to marry Marcus Garvey.

69. Marcus Garvey, "Conditions in Panamá," *Negro World*, June 28, 1919, in *The Marcus Garvey and UNIA Papers, Volume XI: The Caribbean Diaspora, 1910–1920*, ed. Robert A. Hill (Durham, NC: Duke University Press, 2011), 224–27.

70. Convict ships also invoked the ghost of slave ships. On the Middle Passage as carceral model for the U.S. prison regime, see Dylan Rodríguez, *Forced Passages: Imprisoned Radical Intellectuals and the U.S. Prison Regime* (Minneapolis: University of Minnesota Press, 2006).

71. Donoghue, *Borderland on the Isthmus*, 116. For a discussion of Lester Greaves's case, see Donoghue 50–1, 61, 86, 104, 111, 116–19, 136, and 230. On Joaquín Beleño's writing more generally, see Sonja Stephenson Watson, *The Politics of Race in Panama: Afro-Hispanic and West Indian Literary Discourses of Contention* (Gainesville: University of Florida Press, 2014), 42–68; Antonio D. Tillis, ed., *Critical Perspectives on Afro-Latin American Literature* (New York: Routledge, 2012).

72. *"Son of a bitch . . . Halt . . . Ei, You! Los gringos levantaron sus rifles, apuntando. No se moviieron. No tienen otra casa que hacer sino cumplir el reglamento. Pero ya Atá está ganando el camino de oro. Lentamente, como el gato perezoso que cruza la carretera. Nadie lo podrá detener. Nada lo detendrá . . . Los rifles siguen apuntándolo. [. . .] Y, orta vez, de la soleada villa de los brujos vino la voz del guardia . . . HALTTT . . . !!! Atá no se ha detenide. Sigue caminando. Está en medio del trillo y el camino cuando se oyen tres detonaciones. Sus piernas se estremecen . . . entra por aquel trillo. Los guardias se pegan de Nuevo los rifles a sus hombros [214] y vuelven a disparar. Ahora, Atá se estremece todo. Su camisa se va impregnando de sangre. No cae al suelo. Da tumbos. Abre los brazos, y trastabillea lentamente por el camino, moribundo."* Beleño, *Los forzados de Gamboa / Gamboa Road Gang*, 214–15.

73. *"La sangre le asoma en la boca. Y su voz está llena de sangre cuando dice.—At last . . . I am safe! Safe! Safe! Y cayó para siempre sobre su camino de oro. ¡Adiós Atá! ¡Al fin eres libre! ¡Estás a salvo!"* Ibid., 215.

74. Ronald Judy, "Provisional Note on Formations of Planetary Violence," *Boundary 2* 33, no. 3 (2006): 141. For a discussion of race, labor, and disposability more generally, see Ann Laura Stoler, "In Carceral Motion: Disposals of Life and Labour," in Clare Anderson, ed., *A Global History of Convicts and Penal Colonies* (London, UK: Bloomsbury, 2018); Cindy Hahamovitch, *No Man's Land: Jamaican Guestworkers in America and the Global History of Deportable Labor* (Princeton, NJ: Princeton University Press, 2011). Gabrielle E. Clark, "From the Panama Canal to Post-Fordism: Producing Temporary Migrants Within and Beyond Agriculture in the United States, 1904–2013," *Antipode* 49, no. 4 (September 2017): 997–1014.

75. Beleño, *los forzados de Gamboa / Gamboa Road Gang*, 36.

76. Aimé Césaire, *Discourse on Colonialism*, 42.

77. Ibid.

78. Davis, "From the Prison of Slavery," 74–95. See also Davis, "Racialized Punishment and Prison Abolition" in *The Angela Y. Davis Reader.*

79. The phrase "whites only welfare-state" is from Robin D.G. Kelley's lecture on racial capitalism. See Kelly, "What Is Racial Capitalism and Why Does It Matter?" (lecture, University of Washington Simpson Center for the Humanities, Seattle, WA, November 7, 2017), www.youtube.com/watch?v=--gim7W_jQQ. See also Walter Johnson, "To Remake the World: Slavery, Racial Capitalism, and Justice," *Boston Review* 20 (February 2018).

80. On prison imperialism spreading U.S.-style structural racism around the world today see, Alliance for Global Justice (AFGJ), "prison imperialism," https://afgj.org/prison-imperialism.

81. On this definition of colonialism and commonalities between modes of governance, see Jane Burbank and Frederick Cooper, *Empires in World History: Power and the Politics of Difference* (Princeton, NJ: Princeton University Press, 2010).

5. The Prison Without Walls

1. Blake McKelvey, "Penology in the Westward Movement," *Pacific Historical Review* 2, no. 4 (December 1933): 428. For the complete version of Rudyard Kipling's famously racist formulation, see Kipling, "The White Man's Burden: The United States and the Philippine Islands" (1899).

2. On "emancipatory internationalism," see Paul Ortiz, *An African American and Latinx History of the United States* (Boston: Beacon, 2018), 143–62.

3. Eight of the first ten people imprisoned at McNeil, and the overwhelming majority of those sent there over the first few decades (1875–1900) of the prison's operation, were convicted of selling liquor to Indians (*McNeil Island Registers, 1875–1953*, MS NARA Sea, RG 129). On Indian Prohibition Laws, see Jill E. Martin, "'The Greatest Evil': Interpretations of Indian Prohibition Laws, 1832–1953," *Great Plains Quarterly* (2003); Malcolm Holmes and Judith Antell, "The Social Construction of American Indian Drinking," *Sociological Quarterly* (2001); Luana Ross, *Inventing the Savage: The Social Construction of Native American Criminality* (Austin: University of Texas Press, 1998).

4. The Colville Indian Reservation was established by President Grant's 1872 Executive Order. The eleven "Confederated Tribes of the Colville Reservation" that were designated and removed from their lands along the Columbia and Okanogan Rivers and Methow and Colville Valleys were: the Colville, Nespelem, San Poil, Lakes Sinixt, Palus, Wenatchi, Chelan, Entiat, Methow, southern Okanogan, and the Moses Columbia.

5. Beth Lew-Williams, *The Chinese Must Go: Violence, Exclusion, and the Making of the Alien in America* (Cambridge: Harvard University Press, 2018), 95–111, 124. "The Anti-Chinese Riot at Seattle," *Harpers Weekly*, March 6, 1886.

6. McNeil Island *Daily Journals*, 1885–1890 (MS, NARA Sea RG 129, Box 1-2).

7. McNeil Island *Daily Journal*, August 16, 1888.

8. McNeil Island *Daily Journal*, November 16, 1888; April 3, 1889; March 16, 1890. See also Paul Keve, *The McNeil Century: The Life and*

Times of an Island Prison (Chicago: Nelson-Hall, 1984), 107–9. Individual acts of resistance inside prison were accompanied by subterfuge, collective protest, and organized campaigns on the outside. To resist and evade the exclusion apparatus of registration, identification, and surveillance, Chinese people devised an ingenious "paper sons" industry, paying off immigration officials in places like Angel Island. They even managed to push arch-imperialist Teddy Roosevelt's cabinet to roll back some of the most offensive and degrading elements of the new system. They protested police brutality when the Chinese ambassador was assaulted by the SFPD, organized a transpacific boycott, and engaged in sustained political struggle against mob violence, injustice, and indignity that, Christian Parenti argues, successfully checked the growth of federal surveillance regime. See Christian Parenti, *The Soft Cage: Surveillance in America from Slavery to the War on Terror* (New York: Basic Books, 2003), 61–76.

9. Elliot Young, "Caging Immigrants at McNeil Island Federal Prison, 1880–1940," *Pacific Historical Review* 88, no. 1 (2019): 48–85. Young calls McNeil the western birthplace of the federal immigration detention system that now holds 350,000 immigrants in 637 detention facilities around the country and expels an average of 380,000 immigrants each year. See also Juliet Stumpf, "The Crimmigration Crisis: Immigrants, Crime and Sovereign Power," *American University Law Review* (2006); Robert T. Chase, ed., *Caging Borders and Carceral States: Incarcerations, Immigrant Detentions, and Resistance* (Chapel Hill: University of North Carolina, 2019).

10. Elliot Young, "Caging Immigrants," 63.

11. Kelly Lytle Hernández, *City of Inmates: Conquest, Rebellion, and the Rise of Human Caging in Los Angeles* (Chapel Hill: University of North Carolina, 2017), 89, 144; Young, "Caging Immigrants," 59.

12. Lew-Williams, *Chinese Must Go*, 193.

13. Ibid., 209. The "afterlives" of exclusion can be traced through the Magnuson Act (1943), which repealed Chinese exclusion but allowed for quotas, the Luce-Celler Act (1946), which extended naturalization privileges to Asians, Indians, and Filipinos, and the McCarran-Walter Act, or Immigration and Nationality Act (1952), which ended racial prerequisites for naturalization but kept quotas by racial ancestry for Asians

while extending quotes by national origin to the rest of the world. The plenary power still allows the federal government to restrict migration on the basis of nationality and class, which can easily map onto categories of racial or religious difference (Lew-Williams, 232–34).

14. Hernández, *City of Inmates*, 93.

15. "La Junta para McNeil Island," *Regeneración* 4, no. 131, Los Angeles, California, March 8, 1913.

16. Hernández, *City of Inmates*, 129.

17. Christina Heatherton, "University of Radicalism: Ricardo Flores Magon and Leavenworth Penitentiary," *American Quarterly* (2014): 559.

18. Ibid., 577.

19. Ibid., 566; See also Gerald Horne, *Black and Brown: African Americans and the Mexican Revolution, 1910–1920* (New York: New York University Press, 2005); Paul Ortiz, *An African American and Latinx History of the US* (Boston: Beacon, 2018).

20. Heatherton, "University of Radicalism," 577; See also International Workers of the World, *An Open Letter to President Harding from 52 Members of the IWW in Leavenworth Penitentiary Who Refuse to Apply for Individual Clemency* (Chicago: General Defense Committee, 1922).

21. "Special to *The Call*," *New York Call*, September 25, 1919.

22. McNeil Island, Washington, U.S. Penitentiary, Photos and Records of Prisoners Received, 1887–1951, NARA Sea, Microfilm series M1619, roll 2.

23. "Special to *The Call*," *New York Call*, September 25, 1919.

24. Harvey O'Connor, *Revolution in Seattle: A Memoir* (New York: Monthly Review Press, 1964), 14.

25. Philip Grosser, *Uncle Sam's Devil's Island: Experiences of a Conscientious Objector in America During the First World War* (Boston, MA: Excelsior, 1933; Berkeley: Kate Sharpley Library, 2007), 16. His book refers to his confinement on Alcatraz, but McNeil was also likened to Devil's Island. See also Peter Brock, ed., *These Strange Criminals: An Anthology of Prison Memoirs by Conscientious Objectors from the Great War to the Cold War* (Toronto: University of Toronto Press, 2004); Dawn Collective, ed., *Under the Yoke of the State: Selected Anarchist Responses to*

Prison and Crime, Vol. I, 1886–1929 (Kate Sharpley Library); William Preston, *Aliens and Dissenters: Federal Suppression of Radicals, 1903–1933* (New York: Harper and Row, 1973).

26. Charles F.A. Man, "Model Prison Housing One Thousand Has No Wall," *Christian Science Monitor*, April 29, 1930. Reprinted in the *Island Lantern*.

27. Finch R. Archer, *The History of the Island Lantern Press, United States Penitentiary, McNeil Island, Washington* (McNeil Island, WA: Island Lantern Press, 1927), 39–44.

28. McKelvey, "Penology," 428; John Lewis Gillin, *Taming the Criminal: Adventures in Penology* (New York: Macmillan, 1931). For the complete version of Rudyard Kipling's famously racist formulation, see Kipling, "The White Man's Burden: The United States and the Philippine Island" (1899).

29. See John R. White, *Report to the Director of Prisons, 1907–1908* (in John R. White Papers, University of Oregon). See also *Report of the Phil. Commission 1905*, Vol. 3 (Washington, DC: Government Printing Office, 1906).

30. White, *Report to the Director of Prisons, 1907–1908*.

31. Ibid. See also W. Cameron Forbes, "General Plan for Iwahig," September 8, 1906, in W. Cameron Forbes, *Confidential Letter File*, Houghton Library, Harvard University, MS Am. 1366.1, V. 3, p. 221.

32. W. Cameron Forbes, "General Plan for Iwahig," 43.

33. Ibid.

34. Gillin, "From Bilibid to Iwahig," in *Taming the Criminal*, 35–65, 36.

35. Gillin, *Taming the Criminal*, 294.

36. Michael Salman, "The Prison That Makes Men Free: Iwahig Penal Colony and the Simulcara of the American State in the Philippines," in *Colonial Crucible: Empire in the Making of the Modern American State*, ed. Alfred W. McCoy and Francisco A. Scrano (Madison: University of Wisconsin, 2009): 116–28, 116.

37. See for example, Charles H.Z. Meyer, "A Half Century of Federal Probation and Parole," *Journal of Criminal Law Criminology and Police*

Science 42 (1952): 707–28; L.C. White, "The Federal Parole Law," *American Bar Association Journal* 12, no. 1 (1926): 51–53.

38. *Rules and Regulations for the Government and Discipline of the United States Penitentiary, McNeil Island, Washington* (Washington, DC: Government Printing Office, 1911), 8.

39. Ibid. Any federal officer authorized to serve criminal process (i.e., marshals) is required to execute such warrant by taking such prisoner and returning him to the prison "within the time specified in said warrant," 8.

40. *Weekly Island Lantern*, March 24, 1932, 3. Ostensibly run by prisoners, the *Island Lantern* primarily featured articles by prison administrators over the first two decades of its operation.

41. Robert F. Stroud, *Looking Outward: A Voice from the Grave* (1943–1962; 2013), 13. Stroud also believed parole was the brainchild of police chiefs, who wanted a larger pool of criminalized individuals for a longer period of time so they could pin unsolved crimes on them.

42. See *Island Lantern*, 1925–1945; Island Lantern Press, *The Story of the Island Lantern Press McNeil Island Washington* (McNeil Island Wash: Island Lantern Press, 1931).

43. *Island Lantern*, March 1, 1928, 12.

44. Ibid. This was just one among the "modern penological devises for individualizing punishment," the article continued, as offenders should be treated on the basis of "individual traits" not "the nature of their offense" (13). The history of parole covered in the *Island Lantern* was an explicitly imperial story. It had begun in England as a "ticket-of-leave" for Australia, explained one article. Another article evaluated the results of "convict colonization" in Devil's Island, Guiana, and other parts of the French empire (*Island Lantern* 6, no. 5 [January 1930]).

45. *Island Lantern* 4, no. 4 (July 1, 1927): 2.

46. *The Island Lantern: Special Prison Congress Number* 1 (September 1927): 10. Dr. Hart condemned the "diabolical cage system" of imprisoning men like wild beasts (10).

47. See "Honor Farm: A Record Achievement," *Island Lantern* 4, no. 4 (July 1927): 10–14; *Island Lantern: Special Prison Congress Number* 5, no. 4 (August 1, 1927); "The Prison Without Walls, 1870–1927," *Island Lantern* (October 1, 1927): 7–11, 13–14.

48. "Philippine Penal Colony," *Island Lantern* 2, no. 7 (October 1, 1925): 9.

49. Ibid. The next article in that issue similarly expressed progressive penology in terms of colonialism. "Model Prison"—federal prison for women in Alderson, West Virginia. "Will be the most enlightened penal institution in the world." No walls, instead prisoners will be housed in *"a colony of cottages"* with thirty women per cottage, governed by a "housekeeper"—outside work on five-hundred-acre farm for mental disorders and drug addicts (open-air treatment)—"self-government system" will be used.

50. Samuel J. Barrows, *The Indeterminate Sentence and the Parole Law: Reports Prepared for the International Prison Commission* (Washington, DC: Government Printing Office, 1899). (My italics.)

51. See Alexander W. Pisciotta, *Benevolent Repression: Control and the American Reformatory-Prison Movement* (New York: New York University Press, 1994). See also Z.R. Brockway, *Fifty Years of Prison Service: An Autobiography* (New York: Charities Publication Committee, 1912).

52. Barrows, "Indeterminate Sentence and the Parole Law," 9, 13.

53. Ibid., 14–15; 18.

54. Citizen's Inquiry on Parole and Criminal Justice, Inc., *Prison Without Walls: Report on New York Parole* (New York: Praeger, 1975). New York State, *Attica: The Official Report of the New York State Special Commission on Attica* (New York: Praeger, 1972). "Inmates are confused and angered by sentencing disparity and the arbitrary nature of parole board decisions. Parole is especially important since it is a way out of prison, but uncertainties about the process produce a sense of injustice and an air of hostility that make rehabilitative efforts futile and actually provide an example of lawlessness for offenders." On Attica, see Heather Ann Thompson, *Blood in the Water: The Attica Prison Uprising of 1971 and Its Legacy* (New York: Pantheon Books, 2016).

55. See for example, Graeme Wood, "Prison Without Walls," *The Atlantic*, September 2010. For earlier references, see "The Prison Without Walls, 1870–1927," [McNeil] *Island Lantern* (October 1, 1927); *Island Lantern: Special Prison Congress Number* (June 1930); Charles Mann, "Model Prison Housing One Thousand Has No Wall," *Christian Science Monitor*, April 29, 1930; Gillin, "From Bilibid to Iwahig," in *Taming the Criminal*, 36–65. Fred E. Hayes, "The Prison of Tomorrow," *The*

American Prison System (New York: McGraw Hill, 1939); John C. Burle, "Prison Without Walls," *Prison World*, 1939.

56. Graeme Wood, "Prison Without Walls," *The Atlantic*, September 2010.

57. Maya Schenwar and Victoria Law, *Prison by Any Other Name* (New York: New Press, 2021).

58. Angela Y. Davis, *Freedom Is a Constant Struggle: Ferguson, Palestine, and the Foundations of a Movement* (Chicago: Haymarket Books, 2016); James Kilgore, *Understanding E-Carceration: Electronic Monitoring, the Surveillance State, and the Future of Mass Incarceration* (New York: New Press, 2022); James Kilgore, *Challenging E-Carceration*, www.challengingecarceration.org. Kilgore credits Malkia Devich-Cyril with initially theorizing the term "e-carceration."

59. See Kilgore, *Understanding E-Carceration*; James Kilgore and Ruth Wilson Gilmore, "Understanding E-Carceration: A Book Launch," Event sponsored by The New Press and Haymarket Books, streamed live on January 18, 2022, Haymarket Books channel, www.youtube.com /watch?v=fc2JaRJWcFM.

60. James Kilgore and Ruth Wilson Gilmore, "Understanding E-Carceration: A Book Launch."

61. Todd Miller, *Empire of Borders: The Expansion of the U.S. Border Around the World* (New York: Verso Books, 2019)

62. Caitlin Dickerson, "'We Need to Take Away Children': The Secret History of the U.S. Government's Family Separation Policy," *The Atlantic*, September 2022.

63. Michelle Alexander, "The Newest Jim Crow: Recent Criminal Justice Reforms Contain the Seeds of a Frightening System of E-Carceration," *New York Times*, November 8, 2018.

6. The Imperial Boomerang

1. Benjamin Davis, *Communist Councilman from Harlem: Autobiographical Notes Written in a Federal Penitentiary* (New York: International Publishers, 1969), 206.

2. Erik S. McDuffie, *Sojourning for Freedom: Black Women, American*

Communism, and the Making of Black Left Feminism (Durham, NC: Duke University Press, 2011), 74–6. See also: Margaret Stevens, *Red International and Black Caribbean: Communists in New York City, Mexico and the West Indies, 1919–1939* (London: Pluto, 2017). John Munro, *The Anticolonial Front: The African American Freedom Struggle for Global Decolonization, 1945–1960* (Cambridge: Cambridge University Press, 2017). Winston James, *Holding Aloft the Banner of Ethiopia: Caribbean Radicalism in Early Twentieth-Century America* (London: Verso Books, 1999).

3. See Connor Woodman, "Chickens Come Home to Roost: the U.S. Empire, the Surveillance State and the Imperial Boomerang," *Verso* (blog), June 20, 2020. See also Alfred McCoy and Francisco A. Scarano, eds., *Colonial Crucible: Empire and the Making of the Modern American State* (Madison: University of Wisconsin Press, 2009); Marisol LeBrón, "Puerto Rico, Colonialism, and the U.S. Carceral State," *Modern American History*, 2019. Brady T. Heiner, "Foucault and the Black Panthers," *City: Analysis of Urban Change, Theory, Action* 11, no. 3 (2007): 313–56.

4. Alfred McCoy, *Policing America's Empire: The United States, the Philippines, and the Rise of the Surveillance State* (Madison: University of Wisconsin Press, 2009).

5. Johanna Fernández, *The Young Lords: A Radical History* (Chapel Hill: University of North Carolina Press, 2020), 214–15.

6. Ibid., 166.

7. Angelo Herndon, *Let Me Live* (New York: Random House, 1937): 324.

8. Ibid. See also Robin D.G. Kelley, "The Great Depression," in *Four Hundred Souls: A Community History of African America*, ed. Ibram X. Kendi and Keisha N. Blain (New York: One World, 2021), 292–96.

9. Herndon, *Let Me Live*. See also Kelley, "The Great Depression," 292–96.

10. Angelo Herndon, *The Scottsboro Boys: Four Freed! Five to Go!* (New York: Workers Library Publishers, 1937); See also Herndon, *Let Me Live* (1937).

11. Herndon, *Let Me Live* (1937).

12. Davis, *Communist Councilman*, 20.

13. Benjamin Davis to Claudia Jones, September 2, 1957, in Carole

Boyce Davies, *Left of Karl Marx: The Political Life of Black Communist Claudia Jones* (Durham, NC: Duke University Press, 2007), 231–32.

14. Davis, *Communist Councilman*, 206.

15. FBI Headquarters File 100-HQ-72390: NY File 100-18676, 85–113. vault.fbi.gov/Claudia%20Jones%20.

16. Davies, *Left of Karl Marx*, 231. See also Carole Boyce Davies, "Claudia Jones: Anti-Imperialist, Black Feminist Politics," in *Decolonizing the Academy: African Diaspora Studies*, ed. Carole Boyce Davies (Trenton, NJ: Africa World, 2003), 45–60.

17. McDuffie, *Sojourning for Freedom*, 82.

18. Ibid. See also Davies, *Left of Karl Marx*; Carole Boyce Davies, ed., *Claudia Jones Beyond Containment: Autobiographical Reflections, Essays, and Poems* (London: Ayebia Clarke, 2011); Charisse Burden-Stely, "Claudia Jones, the Long Duree of McCarthyism, and the Threat of U.S. Fascism," *Journal of Intersectionality* 3, no. 1 (Summer 2019): 44–66; Charisse Burden-Stelly, "Claudia Jones: Foremother of World Revolution," *Journal of Intersectionality* 3, no. 1 (Summer 2019): 1–3; Charisse Burden-Stelly, *Black Scare/Red Scare: Antiblackness, Anticommunism, and the Rise of Capitalism in the United States* (Chicago: University of Chicago Press, forthcoming, 2023); Charisse Burden-Stelly and Jodi Dean, eds., *Organize, Fight, Win: Black Communist Women's Political Writing* (London: Verso, 2022)

19. Mariame Kaba, *No Selves to Defend: A Legacy of Criminalizing Women of Color for Self-Defense* (Chicago: Chicago Alliance to Free Marissa Alexander, 2013), 18.

20. Claudia Jones, "Ben Davis: Freedom Fighter" (1954), in *Claudia Jones: Beyond Containment*, ed. Carole Boyce Davies (Banbury: Ayebia Clarke, 2010), 128–29. See also Gerald Horne, *Black Liberation/Red Scare: Ben Davis and the Communist Party* (Newark: University of Delaware Press, 1994).

21. Jones, "Ben Davis: Freedom Fighter," 136, 149.

22. Ibid., 149, 151.

23. Davies, *Claudia Jones: Beyond Containment*.

24. Davies, *Left of Karl Marx*, 110–11.

25. Claudia Jones, "For Consuela—Anti-Fascista," in Davies, *Left of Karl Marx*, 110–111. Poem also reprinted in Davies, *Claudia Jones: Beyond Containment*, 189.

26. Ibid.

27. Elizabeth Gurley Flynn, *The Alderson Story: My Life as a Political Prisoner* (New York: International Publishers, 1963; 1972), 140.

28. Ibid., 140–141.

29. Fernández, *Young Lords*, 214–15.

30. Flynn, *Alderson Story*, 143.

31. Fernández, *Young Lords*, 215.

32. Lolita Lebrón, "The Puerto Rican Struggle Continues," *Black Panther* 14, no. 28 (March 27, 1976): 5–6. "THE BLACK PANTHER presents Part 1 of an eloquent and moving statement by Lolita Lebron excerpted from a recent interview conducted at the federal penitentiary in Alderson West Virginia and reprinted from the Guardian newspaper. Ms. Lebron and four other Puerto Rican nationalists are the longest held political prisoners in the U. S."

33. Lolita Lebrón, 1920–(1976), in *Black Panther* 14, no. 28 (March 27, 1976):1–28, *Black Panther* 14, no. 28 (March 27, 1976):1–28 (San Francisco: Black Panther Party, Black Panther Productions, 1976), 5–6; Lolita Lebrón, 1920–(1976); in *Black Panther* 14, no. 28 (March 27, 1976):1–28, *Black Panther*, 14, no. 28 (March 27, 1976):1–28 (San Francisco: Black Panther Party, Black Panther Productions, 1976), 5–6.

34. Assata Shakur, *Assata: An Autobiography* (Chicago: Chicago Review Press, 2020), 253.

35. Ibid., 255.

36. Ibid., 168.

37. Ibid., 191.

38. Ibid., 192.

39. Safiya Bukhari, *The War Before: The True Life Story of Becoming a Black Panther, Keeping the Faith in Prison, and Fighting for Those Left Behind* (New York: Feminist Press at the City University of New York, 2010), 170.

40. Shakur, *Assata: An Autobiography*, 203.

41. Ibid., 267.

42. Ibid., 258.

43. Ibid., 259.

44. On abolishing racism all over the world. Shakur, 272.

45. Assata Shakur, "U.N. Human Rights Campaign Statement from Assata Shakur," *Freedom Archives* (November 5, 1979), freedomarchives.org/Documents/Finder/DOC513_scans/Assata_Shakur/513.StatementfromAssata.Nov.5.1979.pdf. See also Stephen Dillon, *Fugitive Live: The Queer Politics of the Prison State* (Durham: University of North Carolina Press, 2018).

46. Ramón Gutiérrez, "Internal Colonialism: An American Theory of Race," *Du Bois Review: Social Science Research on Race* 1, no. 2 (2004): 281–95.

47. Ibid., 281–82.

48. Ibid., 287. See also Harold Cruse, "Revolutionary Nationalism and the Afro-American," in *Rebellion of Revolution* (Minneapolis: University of Minnesota Press, 1968). Robert Blauner, "Internal Colonialism and Ghetto Revolt," *Social Problems* 16, no. 4 (1969): 393–408.

49. See Davis, *Abolition Democracy*. See also Erica R. Edwards, Roderick A. Ferguson, and Jeffrey O.G. Ogbar, eds., *Keywords for African American Studies* (New York: New York University Press, 2018).

50. Robert F. Williams, "Every Freedom Movement in the USA Is Labeled 'Communist,'" in U.S. Senate, Ninety-First Congress, Second Session, *Testimony of Robert F. Williams: Hearings Before the Subcommittee to Investigate the Administration of the Internal Security Act and Other Internal Security Laws of the Committee on the Judiciary* (Washington, DC: GPO, 1971), 150.

51. Frantz Fanon, *The Wretched of the Earth* (New York: Grove, 1963), 36.

7. Protesting Prison Imperialism

1. Quoted in Kent Blansett, *A Journey to Freedom: Richard Oakes, Alcatraz, and the Red Power Movement* (New Haven, CT: Yale University Press, 2018), 140.

2. Assata Shakur, "U.N. Human Rights Campaign Statement from Assata Shakur," *Freedom Archives* (November 5, 1979), freedomar chives.org/Documents/Finder/DOC513_scans/Assata_Shakur/513 .StatementfromAssata.Nov.5.1979.pdf.

3. Assata Shakur, *Assata: An Autobiography* (Chicago: Chicago Review Press, 2020), 198–199.

4. See LaNada War Jack, *Native Resistance: An Intergenerational Fight for Survival and Life* (Brookfield, MO: Donning, 2014); Blansett, *A Journey to Freedom*. See also Troy R. Johnson, *The Occupation of Alcatraz Island: Indian Self-Determination and the Rise of Indian Activism* (Urbana: University of Illinois, 1996); Paul Chaat Smith and Robert Allen Warrior, *Like a Hurricane: The Indian Movement from Alcatraz to Wounded Knee* (New York: New Press, 1997).

5. Alcatraz Proclamation. Quoted in Blansett, *A Journey to Freedom*, 132.

6. Richard Oakes delivering the Alcatraz Proclamation (November 9, 1969), Kron 4 News coverage from San Francisco University's *The Bay Area TV Archive*, diva.sfsu.edu/collections/sfbatv/bundles/209390.

7. Richard Oakes, "Alcatraz Scenes, Relief Fund, Richard Oakes Interview," November 24, 1969, *Bay Area Television Archive*, diva.sfsu .edu/collections/sfbatv/bundles/187780.

8. John Trudell, "Radio Free Alcatraz," Pacifica Radio Archive, www .pacificaradioarchives.org/recording/bb545701-bb545738.

9. Ibid.

10. "Radio Free Alcatraz 1969-12-30; Radio Free Alcatraz," December 30, 1969 (Boston, MA and Washington, DC: Pacifica Radio Archives, American Archive of Public Broadcasting [GBH and the Library of Congress]), americanarchive.org/catalog/cpb-aacip-28 -5717m0482m.

11. Quoted in Blansett, *A Journey to Freedom*, 140.

12. Blansett, *A Journey to Freedom*, 156.

13. Ibid.

14. Federal Bureau of Investigation, "Russell Means" (FBI file, 1972–2008), 265. vault.fbi.gov/russellmeans%201/Russell%20Means% 20Part%2039%20of%2040/view.

15. Occupation of Wounded Knee: Hearings Before the Subcommittee on Indian Affairs of the Committee on Interior and Insular Affairs, United States Senate, Ninety-Third Congress, First Session . . . June 16, 1973, Pine Ridge, South Dakota, June 17, 1973, Kyle, South Dakota. (Washington, DC: Government Printing Office, 1974). See also, Roxanne Dunbar Ortiz, *An Indigenous Peoples' History of the United States* (Boston: Beacon Press, 2014).

16. Leonard Peltier and Harvey Arden. *Prison Writings: My Life Is My Sun Dance*, 1st St. Martin's Griffin ed. (New York: St. Martin's Griffin, 2000).

17. Leonard Peltier, statement (June 1, 1977), quoted in Jim Messerschmidt and William M. Kunstler, *The Trial of Leonard Peltier* (Boston: South End, 1983), 114–15.

18. Deena Rymhs, "Discursive Delinquency in Leonard Peltier's Prison Writings," *Genre* (2002), 565.

19. Ruth Wilson Gilmore, *Golden Gulag: Prisons, Surplus, Crisis, and Opposition in Globalizing California* (Berkeley: University of California Press, 2007).

20. Quoted in Kent Blansett, *Journey to Freedom*, 140.

21. See Matt Meyer, ed., *Let Freedom Ring: A Collection of Documents from the Movements to Free U.S. Political Prisoners* (Oakland: PM Press, 2008), 125–213; Dan Berger, *Captive Nation: Black Prison Organizing in the Civil Rights Era* (Chapel Hill: University of North Carolina Press, 2014), 246.

22. Shakur, "Statement to the UN Human Rights Campaign."

23. "Let the People Speak to the United Nations," *Black Panther*, May 2, 1970. See also "Take Black Genocide Issue to the UN," *Black Panther*, March 21, 1970; "Why We Petition the UN to End Genocide," *Black Panther*, November 14, 1970.

24. Imari Obadele, "War in America: The Malcolm X Doctrine" (1966); Malcolm X, "Not an American but a World Problem" (1965); Malcolm X, "Oppressed Masses of the World Cry Out for Action Against a Common Oppressor," *Malcolm X Talks to Young People* (1965): 53–76; Malcolm X, "Appeal to African Heads of State" (1965); William Patterson / Civil Rights Corps, *We Charge Genocide* (1950); David Walker, *Appeal*

to the Colored Citizens of the World (1828). In the "Free Claudia Jones Now!" campaign, Jones's family, friends, and allies appealed to the UN for support. See Denise Lynn, "Claudia Jones and the Price of Anticommunism," *Black Perspectives* (September 2020).

25. Obadele, "War in America." See also Dan Berger, "'The Malcolm X Doctrine': The Republic of New Afrika and National Liberation on US Soil," in *New World Coming: The Sixties and the Shaping of Global Consciousness*, ed. Karen Dubinsky (Toronto: Between the Lines, 2009), 46–55. On the imprisoned Black radical tradition, see Garret Felber, Stephen Wilson, Dylan Rodrígues, Joy James, et al., "The Roots of the 'Imprisoned Black Radical Tradition,'" African American Intellectual History Society (AAIHS), *Black Perspectives*, August 24, 2020, www.aaihs.org/the-roots-of-the-imprisoned-black-radical-tradition.

26. Malcolm X, "The Ballot or the Bullet," April 3, 1964, in "In Honor of Malcolm X [El-Hajj Malik El-Shabazz]: Quotations from Last Major Speeches and Interviews," *Black Panther* (1975): 15. See also Malcolm X, "Not an American but a World Problem" (1965); Malcolm X, "Oppressed Masses of the World Cry Out for Action Against a Common Oppressor" (1965); Malcolm X, "Whatever Is Necessary to Protect Ourselves" (1964).

27. Malcolm X, "See for Yourself" (1965), 57; Malcolm X, "Appeal to African Heads of State" (1965); Malcolm X, "At the Audubon" (1965). See also Manning Marable, "Malcolm, Martin, and the Mandates of Justice" (New York, 1995), 136. See also Manning Marable and Vanessa Agard-Jones, eds., *Transnational Blackness: Navigating the Global Color Line* (New York: Palgrave Macmillan, 2008); Darryl C. Thomas, "Cedric J. Robinson's Meditation on Malcolm X's Black Internationalism and the Future of the Black Radical Tradition," in *Futures of Black Radicalism*, ed. Gaye Theresa Johnson and Alex Lubin (London: Verso, 2017).

28. Malcolm X, "The Black Revolution" (1964), 52.

29. Imari Obadele, "Open Letter to U.S. President Jimmy Carter from RNA President Imari Abubakari Obadele," *Black Scholar* (October 1978); See also Dan Berger, *Captive Nation*, 229–46; Akinyele O. Umoja, "Settler-Colonialism and the New Afrikan Liberation Struggle," in *Palgrave Encyclopedia of Imperialism and Anti-Imperialism*, ed. Immanuel Ness and Zak Cope (Cham: Palgrave Macmillan, 2021); Edward Onaci,

Free the Land: Republic of New Afrika and the Pursuit of a Black Nation State (Chapel Hill: University of North Carolina Press, 2020).

30. Berger, *Captive Nation*, 245; New Afrikan Prisoner Organization, "We Still Charge Genocide," 1977, brothermalcolm.net /TRANSFORMED/PDF/13.pdf; Obadele, "War in America." See also Dan Berger, "'Malcolm X Doctrine,'" 46–55.

31. Mariame Kaba and Ashley Farmer, eds., *A Call to Negro Women: A (Little-Known) Black Feminist Manifesto* (United States: Mariame Kaba 1951, 2019), tinyurl.com/call2negrowomen.

32. Ibid. See also Ashley Farmer, "Black Women March on Washington: The Sojourners for Truth and Justice and Black Women's Lives Matter, *Black Perspectives* (April 2015); Erik S. McDuffie, "A New Freedom Movement for Negro Women: The Sojourners for Truth and Justice and Human Rights in the Cold War Era," *Radical History Review* (Spring 2008): 81–106.

33. Dr. Mutulu Shakur, *We Want Our Freedom Anyway! On Political Prisoners, Human Rights, Genocide, the Crime Bill, and Control Units* (Paterson, NJ: Anarchist Black Cross Federation (ABCF), 1997), 10–24. See also Dr. Mutulu Shakur et al., "A Scientific Form of Genocide," (1990), in *Let Freedom Ring: A Collection of Documents from the Movements to Free U.S. Political Prisoners*, ed. Matt Meyer (Oakland: PM Press, 2008), 68–88.

34. Shakur, *We Want Our Freedom*, 13; 24.

35. See "International Tribunal on Political Prisoners/Prisoners of War in the USA," in Meyer, *Let Freedom Ring*, 125–236. See also Sundiata Acoli, "Unique Problems Associated with the Legal Defense of Political Prisoners and Prisoners of War," *Southern University Law Review* 24, no. 1 (Fall 1996).

36. J. Soffiya Elijah, "New Afrikan/Black Political Prisoners and Prisoners of War: Conditions of Confinement," in Meyer, *Let Freedom Ring*, 191–200.

37. Carol Anderson, *Eyes off the Prize: The United States and the African American Struggle for Human Rights, 1945–1955* (Cambridge: Cambridge University Press, 2003), 2, 5; see also Penny Von Eschen, *Race Against Empire: Black Americans and Anticolonialism, 1937–1957* (Ithaca,

NY: Cornell University Press, 1997); Brenda Gayle Plummer, *Rising Wind: Black Americans and U.S. Foreign Affairs, 1935–1961* (Chapel Hill: University of North Carolina Press, 1996); Gerald Horne, *Black and Red: W.E.B. Du Bois and the Afro-American Response to the Cold War, 1944–1963* (Albany: State University of New York Press, 1986); Robert Vitalis, *White World Order, Black Power Politics: The Birth of American International Relations* (Ithaca, NY: Cornell University Press, 2015).

38. Samuel Moyn, *The Last Utopia: Human Rights in History* (Cambridge: Belknap Press of Harvard University Press, 2010), 86, 12: see also Samuel Moyn, *Not Enough: Human Rights in an Unequal World* (Cambridge: Belknap Press of Harvard University Press, 2018); Walter Johnson, Robin D. G. Kelley et al., "Race, Capitalism, Justice," *Boston Review Forum* (Winter 2017).

39. Much in the way political theorist Adom Getachew shows how movements for anticolonial self-determination opened a transformative process that was broader than the single end point of nationalism. Adom Getachew, *Worldmaking After Empire: The Rise and Fall of Self-Determination* (Princeton, NJ: Princeton University Press, 2019). On international law in the unequal world system, see Anthony Anghie, *Imperialism, Sovereignty and the Making of International Law* (Cambridge: Cambridge University Press, 2005); Robert Vitalis, *White World Order, Black Power Politics: The Birth of American International Relations* (Ithaca, NY: Cornell University Press, 2015); Mark Ledwidge, *Race and US Foreign Policy: The African American Foreign Affairs Network* (New York: Routledge, 2012).

40. Stephen Wilson, Garrett Felber, et al., "Imprisoned Black Radical Tradition," Black Perspectives online forum, *African American Intellectual History Society* (AAIHS), 2020.

41. The Jericho Movement, cofounded by Jalil Muntaqim and Safiya Bukhari (1998), www.thejerichomovement.com. Spirit of Mandela Campaign. See also, Spirit of Mandela, spiritofmandela.org. On international movements to free political prisoners, see also Meyer, *Let Freedom Ring*.

42. *The Red Nation* podcast, hosted by Nick Estes, https://therednation.org/. See also the Red Nation, "10 Point Plan," therednation.org/10-point-program.

Epilogue: Out of Purgatory

1. Richard Wright, *The Color Curtain: A Report on the Bandung Conference* (New York: World, 1956), 65.

2. Spirit of Mandela campaign, spiritofmandela.org.

3. Herman Bell et al., "Joint Statement from the San Francisco 8," in *Let Freedom Ring*, ed. Matt Meyer (Oakland: PM Press, 2008), 736. The San Francisco 8 included Herman Bell, Ray Boudreaux, Richard Brown, Hank Jones, Richard O'Neal, Harold Taylor, Francisco Torres, and Jalil Muntaqim.

4. Laurence Ralph, *The Torture Letters: Reckoning with Police Violence* (Chicago: University of Chicago Press, 2020); Andrew S. Baer, *Beyond the Usual Beating: The Jon Burge Police Torture Scandal and Social Movements for Police Accountability in Chicago* (Chicago: University of Chicago Press, 2020). See also Chicago Torture Justice Memorials (CTJM), chicagotorture.org.

5. Free the Virgin Island 3 Campaign, https://vi3.org/; The Jericho Movement, www.jerichomovement.org; Alliance for Global Justice, "Political Prisoners in the USA," https://afgj.org/politicalprisonersusa.

6. We Charge Genocide, wechargegenocide.org/category/wcg-to-un. On this historic campaign, see Toussaint Losier, "A Human Right to Reparations: Black People Against Police Torture and the Roots of the 2015 Chicago Reparations Ordinance," *Souls* 20, no. 4 (2018).

7. Barbara Ransby, *Making All Black Lives Matter: Reimagining Freedom in the Twenty-First Century* (Oakland: University of California Press, 2018), 130–47; Losier, "A Human Right to Reparations"; Laurence Ralph, *The Torture Letters: Reckoning with Police Violence* (Chicago: University of Chicago Press, 2020); Allegra M. McLeod, "Envisioning Abolition Democracy," *Harvard Law Review* 132 (2018): 1613; Justin Hansford, "'The Whole Damn System Is Guilty as Hell': Interrupting a Legacy of Racist Police Culture Through a Human Rights Lens," *Harvard Journal of African American Public Policy* 13, no. 15 (2016).

8. Losier, "A Human Right to Reparations," 399–419. See also Chicago City Council, Reparations Ordinance, May 6, 2015, www

.chicago.gov/content/dam/city/depts/dol/supp_info/Burge-Reparations
-Information-Center/BurgeRESOLUTION.pdf; Chicago Torture
Justice Memorials, chicagotorture.org/about/; Black Youth Project
(BYP) 100, "Pay for Generational Oppression: Reparations Revisited,"
www.agendatobuildblackfutures.com/solutions.

9. United Nations Human Rights Council, "Statement on Protests
Against Systemic Racism in the United States," June 5, 2020, www
.ohchr.org/en/statements/2020/06/statemetn-protests-again-systemic
-racism-united-states.

10. My thinking on global abolitionism as the new human rights was
informed by conversations and correspondence with Dan Berger. On
human rights as "the last utopia," an international paradigm characterized by "the moral displacement of politics," see Samuel Moyn, *The Last
Utopia: Human Rights in History* (Cambridge, MA: Belknap Press of
Harvard University Press, 2010).

11. Angela Y. Davis, Gina Dent, Erica Meiners, and Beth Ritchie,
Abolition. Feminism. Now. (Chicago: Haymarket Books, 2022), 175, xii
(chart), 90, 142, 181.

12. As Angela Davis, Gina Dent, Erica Meiners, and Beth Ritchie
explain, the analysis is necessarily anti-capitalist, antiracist, and internationalist because structural relations of power are global as well
as national and local (Davis et al., *Abolition. Feminism. Now.*, 61). As
Davis reminds us, treating "mass incarceration" as a domestic problem
alone has led many to wrongly believe "that the problem of racialized
imprisonment will be solved by domestic civil rights activism—in other
words without necessarily disturbing larger, global frameworks of power
such as capitalism and heteropatriarchy (ibid., 61).

13. Ibid., 122.

14. Gilmore, *Abolition Geography*, 128.

15. Beyond Borders Caucus, *The Red Nation*, therednation.org/caucuses
/beyond-borders-caucus.

16. Beyond Border Caucus Manifesto, *The Red Nation*, therednation
.org/caucuses/beyond-borders-caucus.

17. Alliance for Global Justice, afgj.org/category/prison-imperialism.

And for the list, see afgj.org/politicalprisonersusa.

18. World Without Prisons, "Statement of Purpose," www
.worldwithoutprisons.org/31-2.

19. Ibid.

20. Ibid.

21. Cara J. Chang, "Harvard Holds the Remains of 19 Likely Enslaved
Individuals, Thousands of Native Americans, Draft Report Says," *Harvard Crimson*, June 1, 2022. See also Evelyn Hammonds et al., *Report of
the Harvard University Steering Committee on Human Remains in Harvard
Museum Collections* (Cambridge, MA: Harvard University, 2022), https:
//provost.harvard.edu/steering-committee-human-remains-university
-museum-collections.

22. Take 'Em Down NOLA, www.takeemdownnola.org.

23. The National Native American Boarding School Healing Coalition,
"Carlisle Repatriation," boardingschoolhealing.org/advocacy/carlisle
-repatriation.

24. U.S. Department of the Interior, Federal Indian Boarding
School Initiative, *Federal Indian Boarding School Initiative Investigative Report* (Washington, DC: Government Printing Office, May
2022), www.bia.gov/sites/default/files/dup/inline-files/bsi_investigative
_report_may_2022_508.pdf, Report appendix A-B, p. 332.

25. Ibid.; Native American Graves Protection Act, 1990, www.nps.gov
/subjects/nagpra/index.htm. See also U.S. Senate Report 101-473.

26. See Dunbar-Ortiz, *An Indigenous Peoples' History*, 231.

27. National Native American Boarding School Healing Coalition,
"Statement on Harvard University's Peabody Museum Announcement,"
November 10, 2022, boardingschoolhealing.org/statement-harvard-pea
body. See also Native American Rights Fund's Boarding School Healing
Project, narf.org/cases/boarding-school-healing.

28. Philip Deloria in Hammonds et al., *Report of the Harvard University
Steering Committee on Human Remains*, 15–16.

29. Hammonds et al., *Report of the Harvard University Steering Committee on Human Remains*.

30. Ibid., 10.

31. Ibid., 23.

32. Mumia Abu-Jamal, *Live from Death Row* (New York: Avon, 2022), 53–54.

Map data: Japan Aerospace Exploration Agency (2021). ALOS World 3D 30 meter DEM. V3.2, Jan 2021. Distributed by OpenTopography. https://doi.org/10.5069/G94M92HB.

Index

Caribbean islands (*continued*)
British colonies, 23, 51–52, 94;
French colonies, 2, 37; nineteenth-
century penal colonization
schemes, 44–45
Carlisle Indian Industrial School
(Pennsylvania), 16, 17–24, 25, 26,
202–3
Carmichael, Stokely, 170
Carpio, Bernardo, 75, 79–80
Carter, Jimmy, 186
Castillo de San Marcos (Florida),
1–2, 9, 26–27, 32–35;
construction (1695), 2, 26;
Freedom Tree, 32–33. *See also*
Fort Marion (St. Augustine,
Florida)
Cazadores (Filipino resistance
organization), 74
Census of the Philippine Islands, 72
Central Conference of American
Rabbis, 29
Central Intelligence Agency (CIA),
165, 189
Césaire, Aimé, 84, 103–4
chain gangs (road gangs): Black
convicts in the U.S. South, xi,
84–85, 98, 105; and convict
roadbuilding scheme in the
Panama Canal Zone, xi, 83–101,
102–3, 105–6
Chapman, Lizzie, 15
Cheyenne Nation, x–xi, 1, 11–13,
16, 21, 35
Chicago Alliance Against Racist and
Political Repression, 197
Chicago City Council, 197
Chicago Reparations Ordinance
(2015), 197
Chicago Torture Justice Memorials,
197
Chicanx protest movement, 169
Childress, Alice, 188
Chinese Exclusion Act (1882), 111,
112–13, 239n39, 245n13
Chinese migrants: acts of resistance
and political struggle against
exclusion apparatus, 244n8;

convict roadbuilding in the
Panama Canal Zone, 93–94,
239n39; exclusion laws, 111,
112–13, 239n39, 245n13;
prisoners at McNeil Island,
111–12; and white vigilante
violence, 111–12
Chiricahua Apache, 24–26
Chiriquí (Panama), 45, 97, 223n16
Chivington, John, 12
Choctaw Nation, 3
La Chorrera (Panama), 91
Churchill, Ward, 23–24
Citizen's Inquiry on Parole and
Criminal Justice Commission,
128–29, 249n54
Civilization Fund, 21
Civil Rights Act (1964), 33–34
Civil Rights Congress, 158, 184
Civil Rights Movement: Florida
Spring Project, 30–31; human
rights framework, 190–91; St.
Augustine Movement, 27–34, 36
Civil War, 18–19, 40, 44–45, 85
Clark, Ramsay, 128–29
Cleveland Gazette, 62, 63
Clinton Correctional Facility for
Women, 167
Coacoochee (Wildcat), 9–11
Coffeyville American, 63
COINTELPRO, 186, 192, 196
Cold War, 147, 162, 190–91; anti-
communist legislation, 146, 147,
152–53, 154, 159, 162, 192
Collazo, Oscar, 164–65
Colorados (Filipino resistance
organization), 74
Colorums (Filipino resistance
organization), 74
Colville Confederated Tribes, 109,
110, 244n4
Comanche Nation, x–xi, 1, 21
commerce clause of the U.S.
Constitution, 39, 43
Commercial Club of Mobile,
Alabama, 99–100
Committee on Indian Affairs, 25
Committee on Territories (U.S.

27272

INDEX

Haaland, Deb, 203
Hadjo, Talmus, 10
Haiti, 2, 45, 87. *See also*
Saint-Domingue, French colony of
Hamilton, Charles V., 170
Hammonds, Evelyn, 205
Hampton Normal and Agricultural
Institute (Virginia), 17, 19–20
Hansberry, Lorraine, 188
Harding, Warren, 114
Harlem Committee To Free Ben
Davis, 158
Harper's Magazine, 49
Harrison, Carter, 56
Harvard University, x–xi; Peabody
Museum, x–xi, 204; Steering
Committee on Human Remains,
204–5
Haskins, James, 188
Hawaii, 58, 113
Hawkins, Benjamin, 5
Hay-Bunau-Varilla Treaty (1904), 86
Helper, Rowan Hinton, 46
Henderson, John, 57–58
Hermanos del Tercio Orden
(Filipino resistance organization),
74
Hernández, Kelly Lytle, 113
Herndon, Angelo, 145, 146, 147–52,
155, 157, 187; arrest and trial
under Georgia's insurrection
statute, 148–52; prison memoir,
150; theory of radical Black
activism, 150
Hinds, Lennox S., 189–90
Hizon, Maximo, 71
Hoffman, Frederick L., 55
Holcombe, J.G., 91
Holder, Mark, 166
Hoover, Herbert, 116
Hoover, J. Edgar, 154, 192
House of Refuge (New York), 23
House Un-American Activities
Committee (HUAC), 153
Hughes, Langston, 27
human remains, repatriation of, 36,
202–6
human rights frameworks: Civil

Rights Movement, 190–91;
imprisoned Black radical
tradition and expanded/global,
158, 182–83, 184–86, 187–93,
195–98; Malcolm X Doctrine,
184–85; *Universal Declaration of
Human Rights* (1948), 190
Hunton, Dorothy, 188
Huntsville Gazette (Alabama), 61
Hurley, Vic, 75–76

Ibarruri, Dolores (La Pasionaria),
161
Ih-Tedda (daughter of Geronomo),
25
Immigration and Customs
Enforcement (ICE), 81, 200,
234n45
Immigration and Nationality Act
(McCarran-Walter Act) (1952),
245n13
immigration detention system,
federal, 112, 130–31, 200, 245n9;
"crimmigration," 110–14, 130–32,
245n9; "e-carceration," 130–31;
family separation, 131; Trump
administration's "zero tolerance"
policy and "prevention by
deterrence" doctrine, 131
imperial boomerang of coercive
control, 144–71; Césaire's theory
of the colonialism's boomerang
effect, 103–4; Cold War-era
anti-communist legislation, 146,
147, 152–53, 154, 159, 162, 192;
internal colonialism, xiii, 60, 63,
155, 169–71, 186; Jones on "prison
Jim Crow," 145, 154, 157–58;
Red Scare, 113–14, 116, 145–46;
repression of movement for self-
determination in the Black Belt
South, 145–54, 170; repression
of Puerto Rican nationalist
movement for self-determination,
146–47, 161–64, 165–66, 169;
repressive insurrection statutes,
148–53; Shakur's understanding
of, 165–67

Party statement), 183
#Let Us Breathe Collective, 197
ley de la mordaza (1948 Gag Law),
  146
Limjap, Jacinto, 69, 70, 230n3
Lincoln, Abraham, 44–45, 223n16
Little Plume, 202
Live from Death Row (Abu-Jamal),
  205–6
Locke, John, 182
Long, Terry D., 188
Los Angeles County Jail, 113
Louisiana Territory, so-called, 2, 44
loyalty oaths, 146
Luce-Celler Act (1946), 245n13
Luther Standing Bear, 23. *See also*
  Ota Kte (Plenty Kill)
lynchings: Davis on Herndon's trial
  before an all-white jury, 149;
  racial terror lynchings and early-
  twentieth century imperialism,
  56–59, 62, 64–65, 157
Lynch Law in Georgia (Wells), 64

Mabini, Apolinario, 71, 234n42
Maconochie, Alexander, 48–49
Magee, Ruchell "Cinque," 196
Magnuson Act (1943), 245n13
magonista movement (Mexico),
  113–14
Major Crimes Act (1885), 18
Making Medicine, 14
Malcolm X Doctrine, 184–86
Malê uprising in Bahia, Brazil, 204
mandatory minimum sentences, 81,
  132, 234n44
Mandela, Nelson, 189, 195–96
Mandela Rules, 195–96
"manifest destiny," 39, 52–53. *See
  also* penal colonization proposals
  (nineteenth century)
Manucy, Halstead "Hoss," 30
Manufacturers' Protective
  Association, 53–54
Marble, Manton, 53
Mariana Islands, 71
Martinique, 84, 85, 87
Marxism, 109, 169, 170

Marxist-Leninism, 156
Matos, Adolfo, 188
Mayflower II takeover (1970), 180
McCarran Internal Security Act
  (1950), 146, 154, 158, 192
McCarran-Walter Act (Immigration
  and Nationality Act of 1952),
  245n13
McCarthyism, 147, 153, 159, 162
McKay Commission report on the
  Attica Prison uprising, 129
McKelvey, Blake, 100, 108
McKinley, William, 63
McNeil Island Federal Penitentiary
  (Puget Sound), 108–17; American
  Prison Association meeting
  (1927), 109, 117, 125–26; anti-
  imperialists and war dissenters at,
  109, 113–17; Chinese migrants
  at, 111–12; "crimmigration"
  at, 110–14, 132, 245n9; Honor
  Farm, 109, 125–26, 128; *Island
  Lantern* newspaper, 117, 123–26,
  248n44, 249n49; map, 107; as
  model of progressive "prison
  without walls," 108–9, 117, 121,
  125–26, 128; parole release rules
  and regulations, 123–26; and
  people selling liquor to Indians,
  110, 244n3
Means, Hank, 180
Means, LaNada. *See* War Jack,
  LaNada
Means, Russell, 180
Medicine Water (Cheyenne chief),
  12–13, 16
Meiners, Erica, 199, 261n12
Mexican Revolution, 113–14
Michigan state legislature, 54
Middle Passage, x
Miles, Nelson A., 12, 25
Milliken, John D., 56–57
Mills, Clark, 202
Mimimic, 14
Mindanao, 72, 78
Miranda, Rafael, 165–66
Mochi (Cheyenne warrior), 12–13,
  16

About the Author

Benjamin Weber is an assistant professor of African American and African Studies at the University of California, Davis. He has worked at the Vera Institute of Justice, Alternate ROOTS, the Marcus Garvey and UNIA Papers Project, and as a public high school teacher in East Los Angeles. He lives in Davis, California.

Publishing in the Public Interest

Thank you for reading this book published by The New Press; we hope you enjoyed it. New Press books and authors play a crucial role in sparking conversations about the key political and social issues of our day.

We hope that you will stay in touch with us. Here are a few ways to keep up to date with our books, events, and the issues we cover:

- Sign up at www.thenewpress.com/subscribe to receive updates on New Press authors and issues and to be notified about local events
- www.facebook.com/newpressbooks
- www.twitter.com/thenewpress
- www.instagram.com/thenewpress

Please consider buying New Press books not only for yourself, but also for friends and family and to donate to schools, libraries, community centers, prison libraries, and other organizations involved with the issues our authors write about.

The New Press is a 501(c)(3) nonprofit organization; if you wish to support our work with a tax-deductible gift please visit www.thenewpress.com/donate or use the QR code below.